Civil Aircraft of the World

JOHN W. R. TAYLOR
& GORDON SWANBOROUGH

Charles Scribner's Sons
NEW YORK

Contents

Photo Credits

AiReview, Tokyo: 168 (foot)
Air Portraits: 20, 22, 95 (foot), 112 (top), 116 (top), 116 (foot), 119 (foot), 121 (top), 122 (foot), 129 (top), 129 (foot), 132 (centre), 134 (top), 134 (centre), 135 (foot), 142 (top), 150 (top), 151 (foot), 156 (foot), 158 (foot), 159 (foot), 169 (centre)
M. J. Axe: 8, 21, 23, 94 (top)
Dr Alan Beaumont: 44, 90 (top), 111 (centre), 120 (foot), 148 (foot), 153 (centre), 170 (centre)
Peter J. Bish: 33, 66 (foot), 75 (top), 88 (top), 120 (top), 132 (foot), 138 (centre), 139 (foot), 146 (centre)
John Blake: 106 (centre)
Austin J. Brown: 12, 42, 43, 52, 69 (top), 114 (foot), 119 (top), 131 (centre), 133 (centre), 135 (centre), 137 (foot), 144 (centre), 145 (foot), 155 (top), 155 (centre)
Liam Byrne: 19, 31, 34, 46, 53, 58, 60, 118 (centre), 136 (foot)
Antonio Camarasa: 109 (foot), 162 (centre), 163 (top)
P. Clifton: 142 (foot)
R. Davis: 148 (top)
Nicholas Denbow: 152 (top)
Don Downie: 106 (top), 115 (centre)
Paul Duffy: 128 (centre)
Foto Hunter: 164 (centre)
Martin Fricke: 6, 142 (centre), 143 (centre), 164 (top), 167 (top), 171 (centre)
J. M. G. Gradidge: 11 (top), 105, 109 (top), 114 (centre), 116 (centre), 117 (foot), 130 (centre)
M. J. Hooks: 132 (top)
Denis Hughes: 81 (top), 139 (top)
R. Killen: 27, 88 (foot)

Bernard Leblay: 159 (top)
Howard Levy: 150 (foot)
Neil Macdougall: 123 (foot), 124 (centre), 156 (top)
Ian MacFarlane: 170 (top)
Peter R. March: 121 (centre), 125 (top)
T. Matsuzaki: 49
J. McNulty: 74 (top)
R. Moulton: 126 (centre)
Ronaldo S. Olive: 108 (foot)
Stephen P. Peltz: 160 (foot), 169 (top)
J. D. R. Rawlings: 102 (foot), 112 (foot)
S. G. Richards: 26, 77 (top), 82 (foot), 123 (top). 124 (foot), 134 (foot)
Norman B. Rivett: 111 (top), 145 (top), 148 (centre)
Jean Seele: 167 (centre)
Brian M. Service: 38, 55, 87 (foot), 90 (foot), 104 (top), 153 (top), 157 (top)
Erik Simonsen: 79 (foot), 81 (foot)
K. E. Sissons: 87 (top)
M. G. Sweet: 108 (top), 110 (foot), 121 (foot), 123 (centre), 128 (top), 154 (foot)
Xavier Taibo: 85 (foot), 147 (foot)
Tass: 9, 40, 65 (foot), 66 (top), 160 (centre), 169 (foot)
Norman E. Taylor: 67 (top)
John Wegg: 10, 28, 36, 102 (top), 127 (top), 157 (foot), 158 (centre)
M. D. West: 14, 63 (foot), 107 (centre), 107 (foot), 111 (foot), 112 (centre), 135 (top), 137 (top), 138 (top), 138 (foot), 139 (centre), 152 (centre)
Gordon S. Williams: 80 (foot)

Printed in Great Britain
Library of Congress Catalog Card Number 78-53004
ISBN 0-684-15224-X

Introduction

For more than a quarter-century after World War II it seemed as if familiar types of piston-engined aircraft would not only go on flying for ever but would always outnumber the jets that had been designed to replace them. No matter how many jet-age transports were sold, airports still handled thousands of DC-3s, DC-4s, DC-6s, Il-14s, Convairliners and Constellations. In places where people flew for fun in Europe, the summer skies remained vibrant with the sound of Gipsy, Renault and Cirrus engines, powering Tiger Moth and Stampe biplanes, Proctors, Messengers and Austers that seemed ageless in their agility.

Now, at last, anno domini and the airworthiness authorities are taking clear toll of the veterans, *and* some of their still-young jet successors which have fallen foul of fatigue and noise limitations—unknown to designers of the 'thirties and 'forties who blended wood with Wasp radials from Pratt & Whitney. The DC-3, grandaddy of them all, is numbered now in hundreds rather than thousands, and is used mainly for freight carrying; other old-timers have disappeared completely from among the airliners. Even greater change is evident in the business aircraft and lightplane sections of this book, where a host of excitingly-modern designs have replaced types now notable only as "rare birds".

Big news at the time the last edition was published was the crisis resulting from a huge increase in fuel prices, the effect of which was still unpredictable. It threatened such forced economies that the authors felt bound to comment, almost apologetically, that "the Concorde is still included" despite its fuel-thirsty engines. Since then, this technologically-brilliant Anglo-French airliner has become the first supersonic airliner to enter scheduled passenger service, pointing the way to the future as surely as did its luckless predecessor of the 'fifties, the Comet 1, first of the passenger jets.

The wide-bodied, turbofan-powered Boeing 747, DC-10, TriStar and A.300 Airbus have established themselves as the pacemakers at subsonic speeds, recording unprecedented standards of safety, quietness, cleanliness and economy. They have been joined by the new Il-86, first Soviet wide-bodied passenger jet. Like the TriStar and Boeing 747, the Il-86 may eventually attain high standards of performance through the installation of Rolls-Royce RB.211 engines. Could there be something significant in the fact that the finest airliners built in America and Russia will then share the same power plant, made in Europe? It is symbolic of aerospace industry collaboration and interdependence for peaceful progress, from which the politicians might learn much.

GS / JWRT

November 1977

Part One

Aero Spacelines Guppies

USA

Outsize cargo transport, in service.
Data for Guppy-201
Photo: Guppy-201
Silhouette: Guppy-201.

Accommodation: Crew of 3–4.
Powered by: Four 4,912eshp Allison 501-D22C turboprops.
Span: 156ft 3in (47.62m).
Length: 143ft 10in (43.84m).
Gross weight: 170,000lb (77,110kg).
Cruising speed: 253mph (407km/h).
Max payload: 54,000lb (24,494kg).
Range: 505 miles (813km) with max payload.

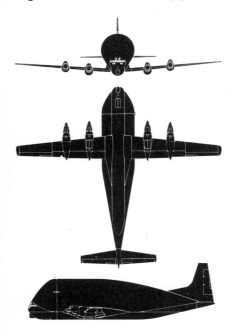

Development and Service:

Aero Spacelines Inc originated the scheme for transporting outsize items of space hardware in conversions of the Boeing 377 Stratocruiser with enlarged fuselages. The first conversion was based on a standard Stratocruiser, the fuselage of which was lengthened by 16ft 8in (5.08m) and modified to have a new upper lobe with an inside height of 20ft 4in (6.20m). This aircraft was known as the B-377PG Pregnant Guppy and first flew on September 19, 1962. The B-377SG Super Guppy was based on the C-97J with four 7,000ehp T34-P-7WA turboprops and had an even larger upper lobe to carry booster sections of up to 25ft (7.62m) diameter. The wing span was increased by 15ft (4.57m) and the fuselage lengthened by 30ft 10in (9.40m). First flight of the Super Guppy was made on August 31, 1965.

Of similar overall dimensions, the Guppy-201 is powered by Allison 501-D22C turboprops and is the 'production' version of the Super Guppy, although still based on components of existing Boeing 377/C-97 airframes; the first example flew on August 24, 1970. A further variant was the B-377MG Mini Guppy, the prototype of which flew on May 24, 1967, with R-4360-B6 piston-engines. The fuselage was longer and wider than that of the basic Boeing 377 on which it was based.

The Guppy-101 had a swing-nose and Allison 501-D22C engines; the sole example flew on March 13, 1970. Various of the Guppy versions were under contract to ferry components of the DC-10 and TriStar between the relevant production centres and assembly lines in the USA, but were retired in 1973. Two Guppy-201s purchased by Aérospatiale and operated by Aéromaritime, are used to support the Airbus A300B and Concorde programmes in Europe; and the Mini Guppy was still being operated in 1977 by American Jet Industries of Van Nuys, California.

Aérospatiale N.262, Frégate and Mohawk 298 France

Short-range airliner, in service.
Data: Mohawk 298.
Photo: Mohawk 298.
Silhouette: N.262.

Accommodation: Flight crew of 2 and up to 29 passengers.
Powered by: Two 1,120shp Pratt & Whitney PT6A-45 turboprops.
Span: 74ft 1¼in (22.60m).
Length: 63ft 3in (19.28m).
Gross weight: 23,370lb (10,610kg).
Max cruising speed: 246mph (396km/h).
Range: 633 miles (1,020km) with max payload (FAA reserves) at 254mph (408km/h).

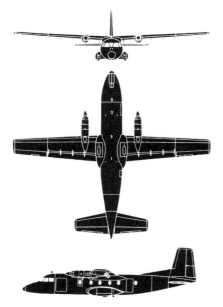

Development and Service:

The original prototype MH-250 Super Broussard, developed by Max Holste, had an unpressurised square-section fuselage and was powered by two Wasp piston engines. It flew on May 20, 1959, and was followed on July 29, 1960, by a second prototype, designated MH-260, with 986ehp Bastan IV turboprops and a longer fuselage. Ten pre-production 260s were built by Nord-Aviation and some of these were operated temporarily by Air Inter and Wideroe's Flyveselskap. Nord developed the 262 with a new circular-section pressurised fuselage and flew the prototype on December 24, 1962. The first four production aircraft (Series B) went into service with Air Inter in July 1964. These were followed by the generally similar Series A with 1,080ehp Bastan VIC engines. Principal users of this version, of which 67 were built, include Allegheny, Avna Aviation, Altair, Air Comores, Cimber Air, Ransome, Rousseau, STA (Algeria), Swift Air, Tunis Air and the French armed forces. During 1970, Aérospatiale introduced the Series C, with uprated Bastan VIIA engines and increased wing span. This version, and the military Series D, were named Frégate. Deliveries of the Frégate included one for the East African Community, two for Gabon Government and one for the French SFA, as well as 24 military Series Ds for the French Air Force. Production of the type ended in France early in 1975 with 110 built; but Allegheny in the USA inaugurated, with Aérospatiale help, a conversion programme to fit PT6A-45 engines, five-bladed propellers, air conditioning and new interiors. Known as the Mohawk 298, the first of these conversions flew on January 7, 1975, and FAA certification was obtained in October 1976; Allegheny put the first of a fleet of nine into service early in 1977.

Aérospatiale SE 210 Caravelle

France

Medium-range airliner, in service.
Photo: Caravelle 10R.
Data and silhouette: Caravelle VIR.

Accommodation: Flight crew of 2–4 and up to 99 passengers, single class.
Powered by: Two 12,600lb (5,725kg) st Rolls-Royce Avon 532R or 533R turbojets.
Span: 112ft 6in (34.30m).
Length: 105ft 0in (32.01m).
Gross weight: 110,230lb (50,000kg).
Max payload: 18,080lb (8,200kg).
Max cruising speed: 525mph (845km/h) at 25,000ft (7,620m).
Typical range: 1,430 miles (2,300km) with max payload (with reserves).

Development and Service:

The prototype Caravelle flew for the first time on May 27, 1955 and the first production aircraft three years later, on May 18, 1958.

The Caravelle I went into service with Air France and SAS in mid-May 1959. Caravelle Is (19 built) were delivered with Avon 522s and a gross weight of 95,900lb, but during 1961 they were converted (together with 13 Caravelle IAs with Avon 523s) to Caravelle III standard with Avon 527s and 101,400lb gross weight. Another 78 Caravelle IIIs were built as new aircraft. The Caravelle VIN (53 built) has Avon 531s and noise suppressors, but is otherwise similar to the III; the Caravelle VIR (56 built) has Avon 533s and thrust-reversers. The first major modification of the design produced the Caravelle Super B (also known as the Caravelle 10B or Super Caravelle). This had a 3ft 4in (1m) fuselage 'stretch', new wing leading-edge, improved flaps and other refinements, plus JT8D-1 turbofans. The first flight was made on March 3, 1964, and 22 were built. A version known as the Caravelle 10R (first of 20 flown on January 18, 1965) was similar to the VIR but has JT8D-7 turbofans. A further development of the 10R was the Caravelle 11R (6 built with longer fuselage and forward freight loading door, first flown on April 21, 1967. Biggest stretch of the basic design is represented by the final version, the Caravelle 12, first flown on October 29, 1970. This has JT8D-9 engines and 10ft (3.05m) longer fuselage than any previous version. Only customers were Sterling Airways, which ordered seven and received the first on March 12, 1971, and Air Inter, which leased five. Production of the Caravelle was completed at the end of 1972, a total of 282 being built, including three unsold prototypes.
The major Caravelle operators in 1977 included Aerotal Colombia, Aerovias del Cesar, Air Afrique, Air Burundi, Air Centrafrique, Air Charter International, Air France, Air Gabon, Air Inter, Alitalia, Aviaco, Catair, Euralair, FEAT, Finnair, IAC, JAT, LTU, Luxair, Minerve, Royal Air Maroc, Sabena, SAETA, SAN, SATA, Sobelair, Sterling, Syrian Arab, TAE, TransEurope and Tunis Air.

Airbus A300

International

Large-capacity short-haul transport in production and service.
Data for A300B-4.

Accommodation: Flight crew of 3. Up to 336 passengers (high-density layout).
Powered by: Two 51,000lb (23,130kg) st General Electric CF6-50C turbofans.
Span: 147ft 1$\frac{1}{4}$in (44.84m).
Length: 175ft 9in (53.57m).
Gross weight: 330,700lb (150,000kg) or 347,200lb (157,500kg).
Max payload: 74,555lb (33,820kg).
Max cruising speed: 567mph (911km/h) at 25,000ft (7,620m).
Range: 2,700 miles (4,300km) with max payload and typical reserves.

Development and Service:

Development of an 'airbus' transport as a collaborative venture was first discussed by British and French companies in June 1965. Subsequently, Germany joined a three-nation, consortium and a Memorandum of Under-

standing covering joint design studies was signed on September 26, 1967. Britain withdrew in March 1969 and the A300B continued subsequently as a Franco-German project, the principal partners being Aérospatiale in France and Deutsche Airbus in Germany (representing the German airframe companies MBB and VFW-Fokker). Hawker Siddeley is participating in the programme on a private commercial basis, and is responsible for design and production of the wing and general design and marketing assistance. Participation by the Dutch government was confirmed during 1970 and results in Fokker-VFW being responsible for the wing moving surfaces. Spain joined the project in 1971, and CASA is building portions of the tailplane. The initial production A300B has two General Electric CF6-50C turbofans and is produced in two variants. Two prototypes, flown on October 28, 1972 and February 5, 1973, were B-1s with fuselage length of 167ft 2$\frac{1}{4}$in (50.97m). One B-1 was refurbished for sale to TEA, but first production models are B-2s with dimensions as shown above. The first B-2 flew on June 28, 1973 and entered service in May 1974 with Air France, which acquired six. Lufthansa has seven, Air Inter has five and Indian Air Lines has three. South African Airways ordered four A300B-2Ks which have improved Krueger leading-edge flaps. The B-4 version has a gross weight of 330,700lb (150,000kg) and more fuel. First flown on December 26, 1974, it has been ordered by Air France (5), Lufthansa (2), Germanair (2), Korean Air Lines (6) and TEA (1). Four are being operated in 1977/78 on a trial basis by Eastern Air Lines (USA), which has a requirement for 50 aircraft in this category. A convertible freighter is available as the A300B-4 FC with a main deck cargo door and reinforced floor. A variant of the A300B-2/4 with 53,000lb (24,040kg) st Pratt & Whitney JT9D-59A engines is to be certificated and is likely to be the version used by SAS, which took an option on 12 in 1977.

Antonov An-12

USSR

Medium-range transport, in service.

Accommodation: Crew of five and passengers or freight.
Powered by: Four 4,000ehp Ivchenko AI-20K turboprops.
Span: 124ft 8in (38.0m).
Length: 108ft 7½in (33.1m).
Gross weight: 134,480lb (61,000kg).
Max payload: 44,090lb (20,000kg).
Max cruising speed: 373mph (600km/h).
Range: 2,110 miles (3,400km) at 342mph (550km/h) with 22,050lb (10,000kg) payload.

Development and Service:

This efficient but ageing freighter was closely related to the An-10 airliner, which first flew in March 1957 with 4,000hp Kuznetsov NK-4 engines. Production An-10s, with AI-20K engines, entered service with Aeroflot in July 1959 in an 84-seat version and were followed in February 1960 by the An-10A, which had some modifications to the arrangement and shape of the ventral fins, and was built in 100-, 120- and 130-passenger versions. No examples of the An-10 or An-10A were exported, and the type was withdrawn from Aeroflot service in 1973.

The An-12 was evolved from the same basic design, primarily as a military transport with rear-loading doors and a tail turret. Some examples, with the rear turret crudely faired in, were operated in civil markings by Aeroflot and one or two foreign airlines including Ghana and Cubana. They were followed by a definitive civil version, the An-12V, with the rear turret removed and a complete fairing in its place. The main cargo compartment is unpressurised, but there is a small pressurised compartment for 14 passengers just aft of the flight deck. Examples of the An-12 have been operated by LOT, Air Guinée, Bulair, Cubana and Aeroflot, and are seen frequently in Egyptian and Algerian civil markings, in addition to being operated by several air forces outside the Soviet Union. The An-10 was known by the NATO code-name "Cat"; the An-12 is "Cub".

Antonov An-22 Antheus

USSR

Heavy cargo transport, in service.

Accommodation: Flight crew of 5 or 6, 28–29 passengers and freight.
Powered by: Four 15,000shp Kuznetsov NK-12MA turboprops.
Span: 211ft 4in (64.40m).
Length: 189ft 7in (57.80m).
Gross weight: 551,160lb (250,000kg).
Max payload: 176,350lb (80,000kg).
Max level speed: 460mph (740km/h).
Max range: 6,800 miles (10,950km) with 99,200lb (45,000kg) payload.

Development and Service:

First flown on February 27, 1965, the An-22 is Russia's largest aircraft to date, and is a natural progression in the series of Antonov freighters which began with the twin-engined An-8 and includes the An-12, An-24, An-26 and An-32 (pages 8, 10 and 11). The basic aircraft is intended for use as a freighter and was produced in this role for Aeroflot (as well as for the Soviet military services). The rear fuselage incorporates a split door, the rearmost section hinging up into the hold, and the forward section hinging down to form a loading ramp. Rails on the underside of the rearmost door link, when the door is open, with similar fittings along the length of the cabin, and powered winches running on these rails facilitate loading and unloading. During 1967, an An-22 set up 14 records in payload-to-height categories, including a payload of 221,443lb (100,444.6kg) lifted to a height of 2,000m. Further record flights were made in 1972 and 1974, for speed over closed circuits with various payloads. The Antonov design bureau at one time projected a passenger version of the An-22 which was longer by 49ft 2½in (15m) and would accommodate up to 724 passengers on two decks; but this was never flown. The NATO code-name for the An-22 is "Cock"; Antheus is the name sometimes applied by Soviet sources to the type. About 30 to 50 were probably built before manufacture ended in 1974.

Antonov An-24, An-26 and An-30   USSR

Short-range airliner, in production and service.
Data: An-24V Srs II.
Photo: An-24T.
Silhouette: An-30.

Accommodation: Flight crew of 3–5 and up to 50 passengers.
Powered by: Two 2,550ehp Ivchenko AI-24A turboprops.
Span: 95ft 9½in (29.20m).
Length: 77ft 2½in (23.53m).
Gross weight: 46,300lb (21,000kg).
Max payload: 12,125lb (5,500kg).
Cruising speed: 280mph (450km/h) at 19,700ft (6,000m).
Range: 341–1,490 miles (550–2,400km) at 280mph (450km/h).

Development and Service:

Details of this feeder-liner were first given by Russian sources in mid-1960 and it entered service on Aeroflot's routes from Moscow to Saratov and Voronezh in September 1963. The production versions have longer engine nacelles than the prototypes, ventral fins and other changes. Refinements in the An-24V increased the number of seats to 50 and allowed operation at higher weights; the first production batch, Series I, had 2,550hp AI-24 engines while the current Series IIs have AI-24As with water injection. Two more versions announced in 1967 were the An-24RV, with a 1,985lb (900kg) st auxiliary turbojet in the rear of the starboard nacelle; and An-24T for mixed passenger/freight services, with ventral loading door and twin ventral fins. The An-24P is a version with special modifications for use in the fire-fighting role. A further variant, revealed in 1969, is the An-26, a more extensively modified, rear-loading transport, for military as well as civil use. This has a widened rear fuse-lage and 2,820ehp AI-24T engines. Another version in use in 1974 is the An-30, which differs from the An-24 primarily in having special equipment in the forward fuselage for aerial survey duties. About 800 An-24s (including An-26s and An-30s) have been built, and there are numerous foreign users, including Air Guinée (4), Air Mali (2), Air Mongol (5), Balkan Bulgarian Airlines (9), Cubana (10), EgyptAir (9), Interflug (7), Iraqi Airways (2), L.O.T. (17), and Tarom (20). All versions of the An-24 have the NATO code-name "Coke", while the An-26 is identified as "Curl" and the An-30 as "Clank".

Photo: An-30.

Antonov An-32 USSR

Short/medium-range transport, under development.

Accommodation: Flight crew of 5, and up to 13,225lb (6,000kg) of freight, 39 passengers, or 24 stretcher patients and a medical attendant.
Powered by: Two 5,110ehp Ivchenko AI-20M turboprop engines.
Span: 95ft 9½in (29.20m).
Length: 78ft 1in (23.80m).
Gross weight: 57,320lb (26,000kg).
Max payload: 13,225lb (6,000kg).
Normal cruising speed: 317mph (510km/h).
Range: 497–1,367 miles (800–2,200km).

Development and Service:

Displayed in public for the first time at the 1977 Paris Air Show, the An-32 is basically an An-26 with two uprated versions of the engines fitted to the Ilyushin Il-18. This big increase in power available for take-off is intended specifically to improve airfield performance, service ceiling and payload, notably during operations in 'hot or high' environments. The aircraft can, for example, operate from airfields 13,000 to 14,750ft (4,000–4,500m) above sea level in an ambient temperature of 25°C, and can carry three tons of freight for 680 miles (1,100km) with fuel reserves. Apart from the power plant, the most noticeable changes compared with the An-26 are the much enlarged ventral fins and slotted tailplane. Loading arrangements are the same as for the An-26, with a rear ramp which can slide forward under the cabin floor to facilitate direct loading of freight from a truck, or air-dropping of bulky items.

BAC One-Eleven

UK

Short-haul jet airliner, in production and service.
Data apply to Series 475.
Photo and silhouette: Series 500.

Accommodation: Flight crew of 2 and up to 89 passengers.
Powered by: Two 12,550lb (5,692kg) st Rolls-Royce Spey 512DW turbofans.
Span: 93ft 6in (28.50m).
Length: 93ft 6in (28.50m).
Gross weight: 92,000–98,500lb (41,730–44,678kg).
Max payload: 21,269lb (9,647kg).
Max cruising speed: 541mph (871km/h) at 21,000ft (6,400m).
Max range: 1,865 miles (3,000km) at 461mph (742km/h) with capacity payload and typical reserves.

Development and Service:

First flown on August 20, 1963, the One-Eleven was evolved by BAC from an earlier

project by Hunting Aircraft. The first production model flew on December 19, 1963 and airline services were started in April 1965 by BUA and later the same year by Braniff, Mohawk and Aer Lingus. The Series 200 aircraft for these customers had 10,330lb (4,686kg) st Spey 506 engines. On July 13, 1965, BAC flew a prototype of the Series 300/400, with 11,400lb (5,171kg) st Spey 511s and higher operating weights. The Series 400 was intended specifically for the US market, with American equipment. The same prototype was later modified to Series 500 standard, with longer fuselage, and first flew in this form on June 30, 1967. The Series 500 also has uprated Spey 512DWs, increased span and gross weight of up to 104,500lb (47,700kg); it entered airline service in 1968. During 1970, the Series 500 prototype was again modified, to Series 475 standard with the short fuselage of the original One-Eleven combined with the long-span wing and uprated engines. In this guise, it first flew on August 27, 1970. By mid-1973, orders for the One-Eleven totalled 210, all of which had been delivered; subsequently the Series 500 re-entered production to meet additional orders from Tarom for five and Cyprus Airways for two. In June 1977 an agreement was signed under which a very large number of Series 475 One-Elevens will be built in Romania for domestic use and for export sale in parallel with UK production. Principal users of the Series 200/300/400 are British Airways, Allegheny, British Caledonian, Dan-Air, Quebecair, Laker, Aer Lingus, Bavaria, Gulf Air, Tarom, TACA, Bahamasair and Austral. The 500 Series is used by Austral, Aviateca, Bavaria, British Airways, British Caledonian, Cyprus Airways, Dan-Air, Germanair, LACSA, Monarch, PAL and Transbrasil. The Series 475 has been purchased only by Faucett, Air Pacific, Air Malawi and the Oman Air Force.

BAC/Aérospatiale Concorde

International

Medium/long-range supersonic transport, in service.
Photo: Concorde 206.

Accommodation: Flight crew of 3 or 4, and up to 128 passengers.
Powered by: Four 38,050lb (17,260kg) st (with 17 per cent afterburning) Rolls-Royce Olympus 593 Mk 610 turbojets.
Span: 83ft 10in (25.56m).
Length: 203ft 9in (62.10m).
Gross weight: 408,000lb (185,070kg).
Max cruising speed: Mach 2.02 (1,354mph/2,179km/h) at 50,000ft (15,250m).
Range: 3,870 miles (6,230km) at Mach 2.02 with max payload.

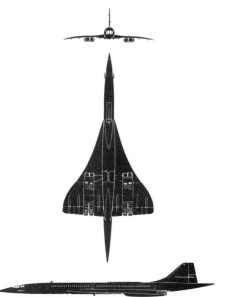

Development and Service:
Culminating several years of design effort in Britain, a joint design for a supersonic transport was evolved in 1962; on November 29 in that year the British and French Governments signed an agreement to initiate work as a joint venture. Overall, the project was divided equally between the two countries, as were its costs; Aérospatiale had design responsibility for the airframe, sharing its manufacture with BAC, and Rolls-Royce had design authority for the Olympus engines, with SNECMA contributing the exhaust system and afterburners. The first of two prototypes, known as Concorde 001 (F-WTSS), made its first flight at Toulouse on March 2, 1969, followed by 002 (G-BSST) at Bristol on April 9. Both prototypes reached Mach 2 for the first time during November 1970. First flown on December 17, 1971, was Concorde 01, the first of two pre-production models, with a longer fuselage, smaller windows, a revised windscreen with fixed step and a gross weight of 385,000lb. Concorde 02 first flew on January 10, 1973, and was externally similar to the production aircraft, with an extended rear fuselage fairing and revised wing leading-edge. The first of an initial batch of 16 production Concordes, identified now as Concorde 201, flew on December 6, 1973; by the end of 1976 nine more (202 to 210 inclusive) had flown. Following certification (in France on October 9 and in Britain on December 5, 1975) Concorde entered commercial service with Air France and British Airways on January 21, 1976, and both airlines inaugurated the first supersonic transatlantic services (to and from Washington) on May 24, 1976. They carried more than 45,000 revenue passengers during the first year of Concorde services, with an average 93% of available seats filled on British Airways' Washington services.

Boeing 707-120 and Boeing 720　　　　USA

Medium/long-range airliner, in service.
Photo: 707-138B.
Data: 720B.
Silhouette: 707-120B.

Accommodation: Flight crew of 3 and 90–167 passengers.
Powered by: Four 18,000lb (8,165kg) st Pratt & Whitney JT3D-3B turbofans.
Span: 130ft 10in (39.87m).
Length: 136ft 9in (41.68m).
Gross weight: 234,000lb (106,140kg).
Max payload: 41,065lb (18,626kg).
Max cruising speed: 611mph (983km/h) at 25,000ft (7,620m).
Range: 4,155 miles (6,690km) with full payload at 540mph (869km/h) (no reserves).

Development and Service:

First flown on December 20, 1957, the 707-120 (13,500lb P & W JT3C-6 engines) was tailored to the needs of US domestic operators, but it was used for a short time

on the North Atlantic route by Pan American, starting on October 26, 1958. Other original operators were TWA, Continental and American. The 707-120 is 144ft 6in (44.04m) long and has a gross weight of 257,000lb (116,575kg). A version of the -120 with a shorter fuselage was purchased only by Qantas, and a version with JT4A-3 engines, the 707-220, was sold only to Braniff, four being passed on to BWIA in 1971.
With aerodynamic refinements, the 707-120B differed from the -120 primarily in having JT3D-1 turbofan engines. American, Pan American and Qantas converted their earlier aircraft to this standard; in addition TWA bought 41 new 707-131Bs, American ordered 31 more 707-123Bs, and Qantas bought six 707-138Bs, with the same short fuselage as its earlier models. The Qantas aircraft were sold to Standard, PWA, Braniff, BWIA and Laker.
Smallest member of this Boeing family is the 720, with the same span of 130ft 10in (39.88m) but length of 136ft 2in (41.50m) and maximum weight of 229,000lb (103,875kg) with JT3C-7 or JT3C-12 engines. First flown on November 25, 1959, it was ordered by American (10); Braniff (5); Eastern (15); Aer Lingus (3); Pacific Northern (2) and United (29). A version with JT3D-1 or -3 turbofans has the same aerodynamic improvements as the 707-120B and is known as the 720B (data as quoted above). American Airlines' 720-023s were converted to this standard and 15 more were bought new. Other original customers for the 720B were Avianca (3); Continental (8); El Al (2); Ethiopian (3); Lufthansa (8); Northwest (17); PIA (4); Saudi Arabian (2) and Western (27). As a result of second-hand deals the Boeing 720 and 720B went into service with Pan American, MEA, Korean Airlines, Conair, Trans European, Monarch, Olympic, Air Rhodesia, Aero American, Voyager, Air Malta, Maersk Air, Aerocondor, Air Niugini, Alia, Yemen Airlines, Ariana Afghan Airlines and Somali.

Boeing 707-320, 707-420

USA

Long-range airliner, in production and service.
Photo and data: 707-320C.
Silhouette: 707-320C.

Accommodation: Flight crew of 3–5, and up to 202 passengers or 13 freight pallets.
Powered by: Four 18,000lb (8,165kg) st Pratt & Whitney JT3D-3B turbofans.
Span: 145ft 9in (44.42m).
Length: 152ft 11in (45.6m).
Gross weight: 333,600lb (151,454kg).
Max payload: 83,447lb (37,885kg).
Max cruising speed: 600mph (965km/h) at 25,000ft (7,620m).
Range: 3,925 miles (6,320km) with max payload at 532mph (856km/h) (typical reserves).

Development and Service:

The Intercontinental version of the Boeing 707 has a longer fuselage, larger wing and more power, plus longer range. The first of the larger models was the 707-320, first flown on January 11, 1959, with 15,800lb st JT4A-3 engines; later versions had up-rated -5, -11 or -12 engines. A contem-

porary was the 707-420, first flown on May 19, 1959, with R-R Conway 508 engines rated at 17,500lb (7,938kg) st. Following development of the 707-120B and the 720B with turbofan engines and aerodynamic improvements (see previous page), Boeing introduced the 707-320B with similar modifications. The first flight was made on January 31, 1962, and this version eventually succeeded the 707-320 in production. Similar to the -320B in most respects was the -320C, with a large freight-loading door in the forward fuselage side and able to carry mixed loads of freight and passengers. Airlines which have ordered a total of 588 Intercontinental 707s and the combined totals of their -320/320B/320/420 orders, are as follows: Air France (38), Air-India (11), Airlift International (3), Alia (2), American Airlines (47), Aerolineas Argentinas (6), Avianca (2), British Airways (30), Braniff (9), British Caledonian (2), Cameroon Air (1), China Air (2), CAAC (10), Continental (13), EgyptAir (10), El Al (8), Ethiopian (2), Executive Jet (2), Flying Tiger (4), Aer Lingus (4), Iran Air (3), Iraqi (3), Irish International (4), Korean (1), Kuwait (5), LAN-Chile (1), Libyan Arab (1), Lufthansa (23), MEA (4), Nigeria Airways (2), Northwest (36), Olympic (6), PIA (7), PAA (120), Pertamina (1), Qantas (21), Sabena (14), SAA (10), Saudi Arabian (6), Seaboard World (2), TAP (9), Tarom (3), TWA (67), Varig (9), Wardair (2), Western (5), and World Airways (9). Through secondhand deals and lease arrangements, many of these totals have changed, and other operators of the 707 in 1977 included Air Madagascar, AeroCondor, Air Manila, British Midland, BWIA, Britannia, Cathay Pacific, Condor, Dan-Air, DETA, East African, Gemini Air, International Caribbean, JAT, Jordanian World Airways, Luxair, MAS, Pacific Western, Perlita Air Service, Pioneer Airlines, Royal Air Maroc, Sabah Air, Sempati Air Transport, Transair, Transavia, Trek and Zambia.

Boeing 727

USA

Short/medium-range airliner, in production and service.
Photo: 727-81 (Series 100).
Data for Advanced -200.
Silhouette: Series 200.

Accommodation: Flight crew of 3 and 134–189 passengers.
Powered by: Three 16,000lb (7,257kg) st Pratt & Whitney JT8D-17 turbofans.
Span: 108ft 0in (32.92m).
Length: 153ft 2in (46.69m).
Normal gross weight: 209,500lb (95,026kg).
Max payload: 41,750lb (18,935kg).
Max cruising speed: 599mph (964km/h) at 24,700ft (7,530m).
Range: 2,940 miles (4,846km) with full payload (typical reserves) at 570mph (917km/h) at 30,000ft (9,145m).

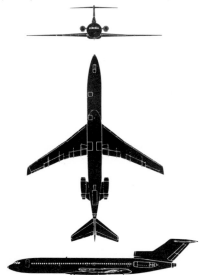

Development and Service:

Production of the Boeing 727 began at the end of 1960. The first basic 727-100 Series aircraft flew on February 9, 1963. Deliveries to United Air Lines began on October 29 that year and the first passenger service was flown by Eastern on February 1, 1964. Boeing also developed two variants with side-loading freight doors and fuselage fittings for mixed passenger/freight loads; these are the 727C convertible and 727QC 'quick-change' versions, the latter having passenger seats mounted on pallets for rapid installation. On July 27, 1967, Boeing flew the first 727-200, with a 10ft (3.05m) longer fuselage, 14,000lb (6,350kg) st JT8D-7 or 14,500lb (6,577kg) st JT8D-9 engines and other improvements. Subsequently, the uprated engines also became applicable to the 727-100 series, which have a maximum take-off weight of 169,000lb (76,657kg). The Advanced 727-200 appeared in 1972 with higher gross weights, quieter engines and other improvements. In 1977, the Advanced 727-200 was available with 14,500lb (6,577kg) st JT8D-9A or 15,500lb (7,030kg) st JT8D-15 or 16,000lb (7,257kg) st JT8D-17 or 17,400lb (7,892kg) st JT8D-17R engines (the last-mentioned with Boeing-developed automatic thrust reserve), and was certificated at weights up to 209,500lb (95,026kg) depending on configuration and fuel capacity. As the world's best-selling jet airliner, the Boeing 727 had amassed 1,461 orders from 84 operators by August 1977 and was still selling steadily. Deliveries by that time totalled 1,278.

Boeing 737

USA

Short-haul jet airliner, in production and service.
Photo, silhouette and data: Series 200.

Accommodation: Flight crew of 2, and up to 130 passengers.
Powered by: Two 16,000lb (7,257kg) st Pratt & Whitney JT8D-17 turbofans.
Span: 93ft 0in (28.35m).
Length: 100ft 0in (30.48m).
Max gross weight: 117,000lb (53,070kg).
Max payload: 35,100lb (15,920kg).
Max cruising speed: 576mph (927km/h) at 22,600ft (6,890m).
Max range: 1,580 miles (2,540km) with max payload (typical reserves) at Mach 0.78 at 30,000ft (9,145m).

Development and Service:

Deliveries of the basic Boeing 737 Series 100 began in December 1967, less than four years after design work was started. This was made possible by utilising many components and assemblies already in production for the Boeing 727. In particular, the basic body structure of the two types is similar, with identical doors, side panels, ceilings, seats and certain systems. The engines are basically the same, with identical thrust reversers, nose cowlings and starters. The Boeing 737 is in production at the company's complex of factories in the Seattle area, with final assembly in Plant No 2 at Boeing Field, where the first flight was made on April 9, 1967. The initial production version, for which Lufthansa was the first customer, is the Series 100, with 14,000lb (6,350kg) st JT8D-7 engines and up to 115 seats. Also in production are 'C' passenger/cargo convertible and 'QC' quick-change versions, the latter with palletized seats, and the Series 200 with a 6ft 4in (1.93m) longer fuselage, more seats and JT8D-9 or JT8D-15 engines. The first Series 200 flew on August 8, 1967, followed by the first passenger/cargo convertible model on September 18, 1968. Production of the -100 soon gave way to the longer-fuselage versions, only 30 of the initial model being built (for Avianca and MAS in addition to Lufthansa). The -200 has been further developed, with deliveries since May 1971 being of the Advanced -200 type. There have been progressive increases in engine thrust and certificated weight, with the JT8D-9A, -15, -17 and -17R available for installation (see details under Boeing 727 on previous page), and Boeing plans a further increase in gross weight to 129,500lb (58,740kg). Sales by August 1977 totalled 527, including the 30 -100s and the 19 -200s delivered to the USAF as T-43 navigation trainers. Deliveries totalled 494 at that time.

17

Boeing 747

USA

Long-range 'jumbo' transport in production and service.
Data: Model 747-200.
Photo: Model 747-200 (Rolls-Royce).
Silhouette: Series 200.

Accommodation: Flight crew of 3–4, and 363–500 passengers.
Powered by: Four 53,000lb (24,040kg) st Pratt & Whitney JT9D-70A turbofans.
Span: 195ft 8in (59.64m).
Length: 231ft 4in (70.51m).
Gross weight: 800,000lb (362,874kg).
Max payload: 155,429lb (70,500kg).
Max speed: 608mph (978km/h) at 30,000ft (9,150m).
Range: 4,600 miles (7,400km) with max payload.

Development and Service:

The Boeing Co announced details of the Boeing 747 in April 1966, with a preliminary commitment from Pan American for 25. Largest passenger transport yet put into production, the aircraft quickly became known as the 'Jumbo Jet'. It has one main cabin level, with capacity for a maximum of 500 seats arranged ten-abreast across the 20ft (6.10m) width. The basic layout provides for 306 economy class passengers and 57 first class, with a lounge on an upper level behind the flight deck seating eight or, in later models, up to 32 economy-class passengers. The first 747 (a company-owned prototype) flew for the first time on February 9, 1969. Pan American inaugurated services on the New York–London route on January 22, 1970. Early aircraft had 43,500lb (19,730kg) st JT9D-3D turbofans, and a gross weight of 710,000lb (322,050kg); but late in 1970 Boeing certificated the 747A at 733,000lb (332,480kg), with JT9D-3AW engines and the 46,950lb (21,296kg) st JT9D-7A or 48,570lb (22,030kg) st JT9D-7AW are also now available. On October 11, 1970, the Boeing 747B made its first flight, this being a further development with an initial gross weight of 775,000lb (351,535kg) and JT9D-7 or JT9D-7A engines; subsequent development of this -200 model (now the basic variant) has made available the 48,000lb (21,772kg) st JT9D-7F, the 50,000lb (22,679kg) st JT9D-7FW and, from 1976, the 53,000lb (24,040kg) st JT9D-70A, with gross weights eventually going up to 820,000lb (371,946kg). In addition, Boeing has certificated versions of the 747 powered by the General Electric CF6-50E of 52,500lb (23,814kg) st (first flown on June 26, 1973) and the Rolls-Royce RB.211-524B at 50,100lb (22,725kg) st (first flown September 3, 1976).
In September 1973 Boeing began delivery to Japan Air Lines of the 747SR, a special short-range, reduced-weight version; and in the same month announced an order from Pan American for the 747SP, which has a 48ft

Continued opposite

Bristol 175 Britannia

UK

Medium/long-range airliner, in service.
Photo: Britannia 307F.
Data and silhouette: Series 310.

Accommodation: Crew of 9, including cabin staff, and 82–133 passengers.
Powered by: Four 4,445ehp Bristol Siddeley Proteus 765 turboprops.
Span: 142ft 3½in (43.39m).
Length: 124ft 3in (37.89m).
Gross weight: 185,000lb (83,990kg).
Max payload: 34,900lb (15,845kg).
Max cruising speed: 402mph (647km/h) at 21,000ft (6,405m).
Range: 4,268miles (6,867km) with max payload at 357mph (574km/h).

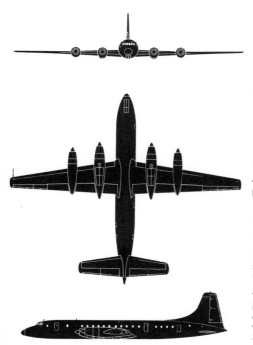

Development and Service:

The Britannia was designed to a 1947 BOAC requirement for a medium-range transport for Empire routes, and the prototype (Srs 100) with Proteus turboprops flew on August 16, 1952. BOAC ordered and put into service 15 Britannia 102s (3,900ehp Proteus 705) of the same size as the prototype. This version was followed by a family of long-fuselage Britannias evolved primarily to meet BOAC requirements for an Atlantic transport but including the Srs 300s which were similar to the Srs 100s in range performance. The fully developed version was the Britannia 310, individual customer variants in this series having model numbers up to 324. As well as the longer fuselage, extra fuel capacity and higher weights, these Britannias had uprated Proteus 755 or 765 engines. By mid-1977, almost all the original Britannias had been retired from commercial service, exceptions being two leased from Monarch by Aer Turas and one operated by Redcoat Air Cargo. During 1975, however, the RAF retired and offered for sale 22 Britannias that were generally similar to the Srs 310s. Several of these were acquired for commercial use, including eight by Young Cargo in Belgium, one by Gemini Air Transport, two by Air Faisel and four by Agence et Messageries Aeriennes du Zaïre.

Boeing 747 continued:

(14.6m) shorter fuselage and greater range. First flights of these versions were made on September 4, 1973, and July 4, 1975 respectively. For cargo-carrying, Boeing developed the 747F (first flown November 30, 1971), basically a -100 with upward-hinged nose for straight-in loading, and more recently the 747 Combi, with a side-loading cargo door for more flexible mixed passenger/cargo loads. The total of 342 747s sold by August 1977 includes 11 747Fs and six 747C nose-loading convertibles, 28 Combis and 14 -100s converted to have side-loading. Deliveries totalled 308 at that time.

Canadair 400 and CL-44 Forty Four
Canada

Long-range passenger/freighter, in service.
Photo: CL-44D4.
Silhouette and data: Canadair 400.

Accommodation: Flight crew of 4, and 63,272lb (28,725kg) freight or 214 passengers.
Powered by: Four 5,730hp Rolls-Royce Tyne 515/10 turboprops.
Span: 142ft 3½in (43.37m).
Length: 151ft 9¾in (46.28m).
Gross weight: 210,000lb (95,250kg).
Max payload: 63,272lb (28,725kg).
Max cruising speed: 386mph (621km/h) at 20,000ft (6,100m).
Range: 3,260 miles (5,245km) with max payload.

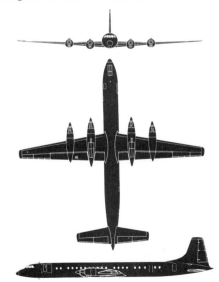

Development and Service:

The Canadair CL-44D is a long-range freighter based on the Bristol Britannia and its derivative, the Canadair Argus maritime reconnaissance aircraft. The first of 12 military CL-44Ds for the RCAF (designated CC-106 Yukon) flew on November 15, 1959. This version has normal side-loading through large freight doors. A commercial version was developed as the CL-44D4, in which the entire rear fuselage is hinged to swing sideways, so that vehicles and bulky freight can be loaded straight into the cabin from the rear. The first swing-tail CL-44D4 flew on November 16, 1960. The last of four CL-44s purchased by Loftleidir for low-fare transatlantic services was modified before delivery to CL-44J or Canadair 400 standard, with a 15ft (4.57m) longer fuselage and seats for up to 214 passengers. It first flew in this form on November 8, 1965; three other CL-44Ds were later converted to the same standard for Loftleidir and were used later by Cargolux. Users of the CL-44D4 in 1977 included Tradewinds, Transmeridian, TMAC (Hong Kong), Transvalair and Transporte Aereo Rioplatense. On November 26, 1969, the Conroy CL-44-O made its first flight, this being a modified CL-44D with an oversize or 'guppy'-type fuselage which has been operated on lease by Transmeridian. The CAF disposed of its Yukons in 1971/72 and several entered service, as CL-44-6s, with commercial operators such as ANDES of Ecuador, Aeronaves del Peru, Aerotransportes Entre Rios, Affretair, Société Genérale d'Alimentation and Transporte Aereo Rioplatense.

Convair-Liner 240, 340 and 440, and Convair 580 and 600/640

USA

Medium-range airliner, in service.
Data: Convair 640.
Photo: Convair 440.
Silhouette: Convair 580.

Accommodation: Flight crew of 3–4, and 44–56 passengers.
Powered by: Two 3,025ehp Rolls-Royce Dart 542-4 (RDa10) turboprops.
Span: 105ft 4in (32.12m).
Length: 81ft 6in (24.84m).
Gross weight: 55,000lb (24,950kg).
Max payload: 15,800lb (7,167kg).
Range: 1,900 miles (3,060km).

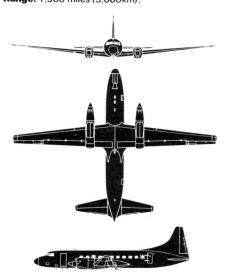

Development and Service:

The original Model 240 (first flight March 16, 1947) was built as a DC-3 replacement, with 2,400hp R-2800-CA18 engines, span of 91ft 9in (27.98m), gross weight of 42,500lb (22,544kg), and accommodation for 40 passengers. Very few remain in airline service, supplemented by improved 340s and 440 Metropolitans. The first 340 flew on October 5, 1951, featuring increased span, longer fuselage accommodating 44 passengers, new engines (R-2800-CB16 or CB17) and increased loaded weight of 47,000lb (21,318 kg). The prototype Model 440 Metropolitan flew on October 6, 1955, with redesigned engine nacelles and other detail changes to improve performance and reduce cabin noise. Turboprop versions were developed with Allison 501-D13 and Rolls-Royce Dart engines. The first Convair 600 (240 conversion) flew on May 20, 1965 and the first 640 (340/440 conversion) on August 20, 1965. Central Airlines was the first to take delivery of the Dart-engined version, on September 20, 1965. Allison-powered Convair 580s were acquired by Allegheny Airlines (42, including those originally operated by Lake Central), Avensa (7), Frontier Airlines (32), and North Central (34); Dart-engined Convair 600/640 conversions were operated by Air Algerie (4), Caribair (6), Hawaiian (8), Martinair (2), Pacific Western (3), SATA (1), and Texas International (25). By 1977, several of these airlines had withdrawn the turboprop Convairs, leading to their acquisition second-hand by other operators, including (Model 580) Aspen Airways, Great Lakes Airlines, Sierra Pacific and SAHSA; and (Model 600/ 640) Seulawah Mandala, Evergreen and Zantop.

Convair 880 and 990 Coronado

USA

Medium-to-long-range passenger transport, in service.
Photo, silhouette and data: CV-990A.

Accommodation: Flight crew of 3-5, and up to 106 passengers.
Powered by: Four 16,000lb (7,280kg) st General Electric CJ805-23B turbofans.
Span: 120ft 0in (36.58m).
Length: 139ft 2½in (42.43m).
Gross weight: 253,000lb (114,760kg).
Max payload: 26,440lb (11,992kg).
Max cruising speed: 615mph (990km/h) at 20,000ft (6,100m).
Range: 3,800 miles (6,115km).

Development and Service:

The Convair family of high-speed jet transports was first announced in April 1956, when TWA and Delta ordered 30 and 10 res-

pectively, under the projected names of Skylark 600 and Golden Arrow. The original version, which became known as the Convair 880, first flew on January 27, 1959, with 11,200lb (5,080kg) st CJ805-3 engines. Additional fuel capacity was offered in the Convair 880-M, which also introduced up-rated engines and higher operating weights. This version flew on October 3, 1960, and was specified by various foreign airlines ordering the type. Most operators had phased-out their Convair 880s by 1973, the last of the original users being Cathay Pacific, which had acquired several from JAL in addition to its own original fleet. This Hong Kong-based airline also had replaced its 880s by Boeing 707s by 1975, and in 1976 sold five 880-Ms to International Air Bahama.

Developed from the Convair 880 to meet the needs of American Airlines for a trans-continental trunk transport, the Convair 990 Coronado (known until the end of 1960 as the Convair 600) had a 10ft (3.05m) longer fuselage and turbofan engines. It was also distinguished by four 'area-rule' conical fairings aft of the wing trailing-edges. The first flight was made at San Diego on January 24, 1961. The 990 was certificated in December 1961 and during 1962 American Airlines began putting 20 CV-990As into service, the 'A' in the designation indicating a series of modifications, especially to the engine pod and pylon shape, to reduce drag. Swissair had seven, of which two were leased to Balair; two were operated by Garuda Indonesian Airways, two by Varig, and three were used by Aerolineas Peruanas (APSA) until this company ceased operations in 1971. By 1977, none of the original operators of the Convair 990 still had the type in service, but ex-American Airlines aircraft were used (primarily on IT flights) by Modern Air Transport (with three) and Spantax (with 12). Nomads Inc. operated one as a business transport.

Curtiss C-46 Commando

USA

Medium-range airliner, in service.

Accommodation: Flight crew of 2, and up to 62 passengers.
Powered by: Two 2,000hp Pratt & Whitney R-2800-51MI piston-engines.
Span: 108ft 0in (32.92m).
Length: 76ft 4in (23.27m).
Gross weight: 48,000lb (21,770kg) (as freighter).
Max payload: 17,600lb (7,983kg).
Max cruising speed: 187mph (301km/h) at 7,000ft (2,133m).
Typical range: Up to 1,170 miles (1,883km) with 5,700lb (2,585kg) payload.

Development and Service:

The Curtiss-Wright CW-20 was designed in 1938 as a pressurised airliner for US operators, and a prototype made its first flight on March 26, 1940. This particular aircraft eventually found its way into service with BOAC during the War, being known as the St. Louis. In unpressurised form, the CW-20 was adopted for production for the USAAF as the C-46.

Over 3,000 of these rugged and capacious transports were built, and hundreds survived the war to serve, primarily as freighters, with airlines in the early post-war years, particularly in South and Central America. In 1977, fewer than 100 survived, operating mostly in more remote areas and at airfields with minimum facilities.

Several different modification schemes have been introduced to improve the performance of the C-46 and so allow it to meet changing civil airworthiness requirements, leading to designations such as Super 46C and C-46R. One version, designated C-46F, had two Marboré auxiliary turbojets under its fuselage.

Dassault-Breguet Mercure

France

Short/medium-range large-capacity transport, in service.
Data for Mercure 100.

Accommodation: Flight crew of 2–4, and up to 162 passengers.
Powered by: Two 15,500lb (7,030kg) st Pratt & Whitney JT8D-15 turbofans.
Span: 100ft 3in (30,55m).
Length: 114ft 3½in (34,84m).
Gross weight: 124,560lb (56,500kg).
Max payload: 35,715lb (16,200kg).
Max cruising speed: 575mph (926km/h) at 20,000ft (6,100m).
Range: 690 miles (1,110km) with 150 passengers (with reserves).

Development and Service:

The Mercure programme was launched by Dassault as a private venture in 1968, in an attempt to provide a European alternative to established US short-haul "twins". The French Government agreed subsequently to provide 56 per cent of the launching costs, and Dassault concluded agreements with companies outside France in respect of a further 30 per cent shared between Italy, Belgium, Spain, Switzerland and Canada. The first prototype had 15,000lb (6,800kg) st JT8D-11 engines, with which it made its first flight on May 28, 1971. It was re-engined subsequently with JT8D-15s, in which form it flew again in September. A further series of modifications made in November included the introduction of dihedral on the tailplane. A second prototype, also with JT8D-15 engines, made its first flight on September 7, 1972, followed by the first production example on July 19, 1973. Air Inter, the French domestic airline, placed an order for 10 Mercures, of which the first was delivered on May 15, 1974 and entered service later that summer. Delivery of the fleet of 10 was completed in 1975, when Mercure production came to an end. Under the name of Super Mercure and more recently as Mercure 200, Dassault-Breguet projected an improved development of the basic design, and in 1976 this formed the basis of the ASMR (advanced short-to-medium range) transport proposal under study jointly by Dassault-Breguet and McDonnell Douglas Corporation, with CFM-56 turbofans and a stretched fuselage to seat about 180 passengers.

De Havilland DHC-7 Dash-7

Canada

Short-range STOL third-level and commuter airliner, in production and service.

Accommodation: Flight crew of two and 48–54 passengers.
Powered by: Four 1,474eshp Pratt & Whitney (Canada) PT6A-50 turboprops.
Span: 93ft 0in (28.35m).
Length: 80ft 4in (24.50m).
Gross weight: 43,000lb (19,522kg).
Max payload: 11,640lb (5,290kg).
Max cruising speed: 280mph (452km/h) at 7,500ft (2,286m).
Range: 520 miles (835km) with max payload and 1,380 miles (2,280km) with max fuel.

Development and Service:

De Havilland Canada is continuing its successful range of specialised STOL aircraft with the Dash-7, the largest aircraft built by the Ontario company to date. Earlier aircraft in the series were the Beaver, Otter, Twin Otter, Caribou and Buffalo. The Dash-7, which is designed and built with the financial backing of the Canadian Government, is a completely new design, utilising de Havilland's accumulated expertise in achieving short take-off and landing characteristics through aerodynamic lift systems—that is, the use of large double-slotted flaps operating in the slipstream from the four large-diameter, slow-turning propellers. During preliminary market studies for the DHC-7, several Canadian operators placed provisional letters of intent, but the first firm order, announced in December 1973, came from Wideroe's Flyveselskap A/S of Norway, for two Dash-7s; during 1976, difficulties experienced by this company placed that order in jeopardy also, and the options at the end of the year comprised a total of 21 for Air Alpes (4), Hughes Airwest (2), Eastern Provincial (3), Ethiopian Airlines (5), Greenlandair (2), Rocky Mountain (3) and Quebecair (2). The Dash-7 prototype first flew on March 27, 1975, and a second followed later in the year. Production of an initial series of 50 had been authorised by the end of 1976, with the first production Dash-7 to fly by mid-1977 and to enter service soon after. Initial confirmed orders came from Rocky Mountain and Wardair.

Douglas DC-3 (and Dakota, C-47)   USA

Medium-range passenger or freight transport, in service.
Photo: Dakota 6.
Data apply to Dakota 4.

Accommodation: Flight crew of 3, and up to 36 passengers.
Powered by: Two 1,200hp Pratt & Whitney R-1830-90C or -90D piston-engines.
Span: 95ft 0in (28.96m).
Length: 64ft 5in (19.66m).
Gross weight: 28,000lb (12,701kg).
Max payload: 6,620lb (3,000kg).
Normal cruising speed: 170mph (274km/h) at 6,000ft (1,828m).
Max range: 1,510 miles (2,420km).

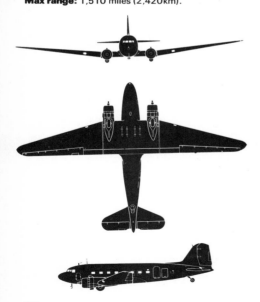

Development and Service:

Most widely-used air transport in history, this aircraft began life as the 14-passenger Douglas D S T (Douglas sleeper transport) and 21-passenger DC-3 of 1936. These, in turn, had been developed, by way of the DC-2, from the DC-1, which made its first flight on July 1, 1933. The DST was first flown at Santa Monica on December 22, 1935 and entered service in May 1936, with American Airlines. During the war, it became America's standard medium-range military transport, under such designations as C-47, C-53 and C-117, and many of the 10,225 then built were converted subsequently for civil use. In addition, 430 new DC-3s were produced, mostly before the war, with a few after 1945. In civil use, these aircraft are usually known as DC-3s or Dakotas, the latter being the RAF name for the military transport version during the war. Although the use of the DC-3s on scheduled passenger services is now dwindling, there are parts of the World where this aircraft's performance and low cost have for many years made it indispensable, and it is still quite widely used for charter, cargo and other flights. ICAO statistics indicated that 871 DC-3s were still in service as commercial transports in 1969, representing just over 12 per cent of the total number of transport aircraft then operating in the ICAO contracting states. This figure has subsequently declined, fewer than 500 being in active civil use by 1975, but the withdrawal of time-expired civil examples has been to some extent off-set by availability on the civil market of additional ex-military machines.

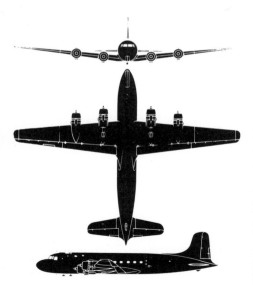

Douglas DC-4 (and Carvair)   USA

Medium-range passenger and freight transport, in service.
Photo: C-54E.
Data and silhouette: DC-4.

Accommodation: Flight crew of 2 or 3 and up to 85 passengers.
Powered by: Four 1,450hp Pratt & Whitney R-2000 piston-engines.
Span: 117ft 6in (35.82m).
Length: 93ft 5in. (28.47m).
Gross weight: 73,000lb (33,112kg).
Max cruising speed: 207 mph (333km/h).
Typical range: 1,150 miles (1,850km) with max payload.

Development and Service:

The prototype DC-4, which received its American C of A as a civil airliner in May 1939, was a triple-finned design with four 1,450hp P & W R-2180 Twin-Hornet engines and seats for 52 passengers; it was first flown on June 7, 1938. After service trials, the design was scaled down, refined and put into production. Before it could enter airline service, US wartime requirements led to its further modification into a military transport, and most of the aircraft of this type remaining in service today are ex-military C-54 Skymasters, although 79 commercial DC-4s were built post-war. The C-54 was first flown on February 14, 1942, and entered service during 1943; airline service began early in 1946. Few major airlines still use the DC-4, and less than 100 remain in service with independent operators and charter companies throughout the world, for freighting, with large loading doors and special floors.
Based on the Douglas DC-4 airframe, the Carvair is a specialised freighter, the design of which was originated by Aviation Traders Ltd. The primary requirement was the carriage of vehicles on cross-channel services to and from Britain, and for this purpose the front end of the DC-4 was extensively redesigned to permit straight-in loading of cars or freight. This called for relocation of the flight deck in a "hump" high above the normal fuselage top line; associated with this modification was an increase in vertical tail area, and internal changes included the re-routing of control runs. The prototype Carvair conversion (G-ANYB) made its first flight on June 21, 1961, and 21 were eventually converted. By the end of 1976, British Air Ferries, the last company flying cross-channel vehicle-ferry services, had phased its Carvairs out of service but a handful remained in service elsewhere.

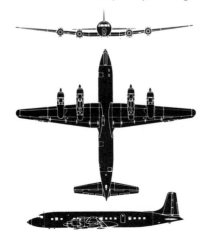

Douglas DC-6 and DC-7 Series   USA

Long-range airliner, in service.
Photo: DC-6B.
Data and silhouette: DC-7C.

Accommodation: Flight crew of 3–5, and 69–105 passengers.
Powered by: Four 3,400hp Wright R-3350-18EA-4 Turbo-Compound piston-engines.
Span: 127ft 6in (38.8m).
Length: 112ft 3in (34.23m).
Gross weight: 143,000lb (64,865kg).
Max payload: 21,500lb (9,752kg).
Cruising speed: 310mph (499km/h) at 20,000ft (6,100m).
Typical range: 4,100 miles (6,600km) at 274mph (440km/h) with 15,000lb (6,804kg) payload.

Development and Service:

The DC-6 was developed after the war as a larger, more powerful and pressurised successor to the DC-4, the prototype being built to a military order with the designation XC-112. The first flight was made on February 15, 1946. The initial airline version had 2,400hp R-2800-CA-15 engines and was 100ft 7in (30.66m) long. It was followed by the longer DC-6A Liftmaster freighter and the DC-6B passenger-carrying version. The DC-6A, built initially for Slick Airways, had a length of 105ft 7in (32.2m), while the DC-6B was further lengthened to 106ft 8in (32.51m) by installation of an optional nose radar. First flights were made, respectively, on September 29, 1949 and February 10, 1951. Including 167 military models of the DC-6A (USAF C-118A, USN R6D-1), Douglas built 704 aircraft of the DC-6 series, of which 175 were DC-6s, 77 DC-6As and 286 DC-6Bs. More than 100 DC-6s and DC-6Bs continue in use in various parts of the world, principally as freighters and for low-cost charter flights, including one or two modified to have swing-tail straight-in loading.

A further development of the DC-4/DC-6 line, the basic DC-7 differed mainly in having four 3,250hp R-3350-18DA1 engines, a length of 108ft 11in (33.24m), and a loaded weight of 123,200lb (55,429kg). The DC-7B was an intercontinental version with 3,350hp R-3350-18DA4 engines, increased fuel tankage and a loaded weight of 126,000lb (57,153 kg). Final development was the very-long-range DC-7C Seven Seas (data above). These three variants made their first flights on May 18, 1953 (DC-7), April 25, 1955 (DC-7B) and December 20, 1955 (DC-7C), and production totalled 336. The advent of jet transports rendered the DC-7s obsolete for service on the international trunk routes for which they had been designed, but many operators converted their aircraft to DC-7F standard as freighters and a handful of these remain in service in various parts of the world.

Fokker-VFW F.27 Friendship and Fairchild Hiller F-27/FH-227

Netherlands/USA

Short/medium-range airliner, in production and service.
Photo: Series 200.
Data and silhouette: Series 500.

Accommodation: Flight crew of 2–4, and 36–56 passengers.
Powered by: Two 2,255ehp Rolls-Royce Dart 532-7R turboprops.
Span: 95ft 2in (29.00m).
Length: 82ft 2½in (25.04m).
Gross weight: 45,000lb (20,410kg).
Max payload: 13,585lb (6,162kg).
Normal cruising speed: 298mph (480km/h) at 20,000ft (6,100m).
Typical range: 1,082 miles (1,741km) with 52 passengers.

Development and Service:

The first prototype of the Friendship (PH-NIV), which flew on November 24, 1955, was powered originally by Dart 507 turboprops and had seats for 28 passengers. The second prototype (PH-NVF), flown on January 31, 1957, was representative of production aircraft, which are still being built by Fokker-VFW in the Netherlands. The first Fokker-built production Friendship flew on March 23, 1958, and the first built under licence by Fairchild in the USA flew on April 15, 1958. Deliveries of the latter began in August of that year, and West Coast Airlines was the first to operate the F-27, on September 28, 1958. Deliveries of the Fokker-built F.27 also began in 1958, to Aer Lingus, which started operating this type in December. Fokker variants are identified as Mk.100 with Dart 514 engines; Mk. 200 with more powerful Dart 532-7s; Mk. 300, as 100 but with large cargo loading door and freight floor; Mk. 400, as 300 but with Dart 532-7s; Mk. 500 with 4ft 11in (1.5m) fuselage 'stretch' (first flown November 15, 1967); and Mk. 600, as Mk. 200 with added cargo door and QC features, but without the Mk. 400 freight floor. In 1976, Fokker flew a prototype of the F.27 Maritime, a radar-equipped variant for offshore patrol, based on the Mk. 600 airframe. Back in 1965, Fairchild had introduced two longer-fuselage versions, the FH-227 with 6ft (1.83m) stretch and FH-227B with further refinements to permit operation at higher weights. The FH-227C/D/E are modernised versions. Total orders by mid-1977 were for 656 aircraft, for 145 customers in 56 countries. The total includes 128 F-27s and 77 FH-227s by Fairchild. Over 150 of the total have been delivered for military or executive use; the remainder were for airlines.

Fokker-VFW F.28 Fellowship

Netherlands

Short-range jet airliner, in production and service.
Photo, data and silhouette: Mk. 4000.

Accommodation: Flight crew of 2, and up to 85 passengers.
Powered by: Two 9,850lb (4,468kg) st Rolls-Royce Spey 555-15H turbofans.
Span: 82ft 3¾in (25.09m).
Length: 97ft 1¾in (29.61m).
Gross weight: 70,990lb (32,200kg).
Max cruising speed: 523mph (843km/h) at 21,000ft (6,400m).
Range: 1,025 miles (1,650km) with max payload.

Development and Service:

Fokker announced first details of the F.28 in April 1962. Two German companies, MBB and VFW-Fokker, participate in the programme to the extent of some 35 per cent

(with the German Government contributing 60 per cent of the German share); Shorts have a 19 per cent share in the Fellowship programme, and are responsible for the detail design and construction of the outer wings and other, smaller components. First flight of the F.28 (with Spey 550 engines) was made on May 9, 1967, with the second and third aircraft following later in that year. The first order was placed by LTU of Germany; other orders brought total sales to 128 by mid-1977, the customers including Aerolineas Argentinas, Aero Peru, Air Gabon, Air Ivoire, Air Nauru, Ansett Airlines of Australia (for MacRobertson-Miller and Airlines of NSW), Aviaction, Burma Airways, Braathens, Garuda, Germanair, Ghana Airways, Iberia, Itavia, Linjeflyg, Martinair, Nigeria Airways, Perlita/Pertamina, Transair and THY, the governments of Argentina, Ivory Coast, Togo, Peru, Congo, The Netherlands, Malaysia, Nigeria and Colombia. The Fellowship Mk. 2000 has its fuselage lengthened by 7ft 3in (2.2m) to accommodate up to 79 passengers. The prototype F.28 converted to Mk. 2000 standard was flown for the first time on April 28, 1971. A further development programme was initiated in 1972 to provide the F.28 with leading-edge slats, permitting an increase in weight without penalising airfield performance. Other modifications included quietened and uprated Spey engines and extended wingtips. The new models were designated Mk. 5000 (short fuselage) and Mk. 6000 (long fuselage); the prototype Mk. 2000 was converted to a Mk. 6000 and flew in this form on September 27, 1973. More popular than these slatted models are the Mk. 3000 and Mk. 4000, with the extended-span wing and engine improvements but no slats; these, respectively, have Mk. 1000 and Mk. 2000 fuselage lengths. The Mk. 1000C and Mk. 3000C have a forward freight door and convertible interiors.

Handley Page H.P.R.7 Herald

UK

Short-range airliner, in service.
Photo and data apply to Series 200.

Accommodation: Flight crew of 3, and 38–56 passengers.
Powered by: Two 2,105ehp Rolls-Royce Dart 527 turboprops.
Span: 94ft 9½in (28.89m).
Length: 75ft 6in (23.01m).
Gross weight: 43,000lb (19,500kg).
Max cruising speed: 275mph (442km/h) at 15,000 ft (4,575m).
Max payload: 11,700lb (5,307kg).
Typical range: 700 miles (1,125km) with max payload at 275mph (442km/h) with reserves.

Development and Service:

Design of the original H.P.R.3 Herald, by the Reading subsidiary of Handley Page Ltd., was based on an extensive market survey conducted from 1950 onwards. As originally projected, the Herald had four Leonides Major piston-engines and two prototypes were flown in this form, but changing market conditions led to a reappraisal of the design and the substitution of two Darts for the four piston-engines. Both prototypes (G-AODE and G-AODF) were re-engined to this standard, the first flight with Darts being made on March 11, 1958. The first Series 100 production aircraft (G-APWA) flew in October 1959, and three went into service with BEA on Scottish routes. These aircraft were sold to Autair in 1966 and then to Lineas Aereas La Urraca in 1970.

A Herald Series 200 version, with 42-in longer fuselage, was announced in 1960, and British Island Airways had a fleet of 12 of this version operational in 1977. Other users of the Herald 200 at that time were British Air Ferries (8), Air Manila (1), Arkia (4) and Europe Aero Service (2). Also during 1977, eight military Herald Srs 400s originally supplied to the Royal Malaysian Air Force were re-acquired for civil use by UK operators.

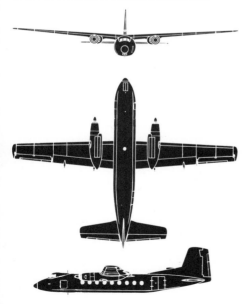

31

Hawker Siddeley (Avro) 748

UK

Short-range airliner, in production and service.
Photo: Series 2A.
Data apply to Series 2A.

Accommodation: Flight crew of 2–3, and 40–58 passengers.
Powered by: Two 2,280ehp Rolls-Royce Dart 532-2L or -2S turboprops.
Span: 98ft 6in (30.02m).
Length: 67ft 0in (20.42m).
Gross weight: 46,500lb (21,092kg).
Max payload: 12,500lb (5,670kg).
Economical cruising speed: 278mph (448km/h) at 17,000ft (5,180m).
Range: 530 miles (852km) with max payload at 259mph (417km/h), with reserves.

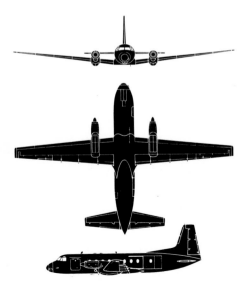

Development and Service:

The Hawker Siddeley Group decided to go ahead with the design and development of this twin-Dart feeder-liner in January 1959. The first prototype (G-APZV) flew for the first time on June 24, 1960, followed by the second (G-ARAY) on April 10, 1961, and the first Series 1 production aircraft (G-ARMV), with 1,880ehp Dart 514 engines, on August 30, 1961. Later in 1961, G-ARAY was fitted with 2,105ehp Dart R.Da.7 engines as the prototype Series 2. Skyways Coach Air (now part of Dan-Air) ordered three Series 1s and became the first company to operate the 748 in the Spring of 1962. Other orders for the Series 1 came from Aerolineas Argentinas, BKS Air Transport (now Northeast) and Smiths Aviation Division. Civil users of the Series 2 and more powerful Series 2A include Air Ceylon, Air Gabon, Air Illinois, Air Malawi, Air Pacific, Amoco Canada, Avianca, Board of Trade (CAFU), Botswana Airways, Bouraq Indonesian, British Airways, COPA (Panama), Dan-Air, Gateway Aviation, Ghana Airways, Korean Airlines, LAN-Chile, LIAT, LAV, Mandala Airways, Merpati, Midwest, Mount Cook Airlines, PAL, Polynesian, Quebecair, Rousseau, Royal Nepal Airlines, SAA, SAESA, SATA, SATENA, TACV, TAME, Thai Airways, Varig and Zambia Airways, in addition to several air forces and military agencies. Indian Airlines Corporation received 18 Series 2s from a production line set up in India by the Kanpur Division of Hindustan Aeronautics Ltd. Total production reached 310 by the beginning of 1977, and Hawker Siddeley flew for the first time in that year a maritime reconnaissance version of the design, known as the Coastguarder.

Hawker Siddeley (AW 650) Argosy   UK

Turboprop freighter, in service.
Photo: Argosy 660 (ex-RAF C Mk. 1).
Data and silhouette apply to Series 222.

Accommodation: Normally freight only. Can carry up to 89 passengers.
Powered by: Four 2,230ehp Rolls-Royce Dart 532-1 turboprops.
Span: 115ft 0in (33.05m).
Length: 86ft 9in (26.44m).
Gross weight: 93,000lb (42,185kg).
Max payload: 32,000lb (14,515kg).
Normal cruising speed: 280mph (451km/h) at 18,000ft (5,490m).
Range: 485 miles (780km) with max payload.

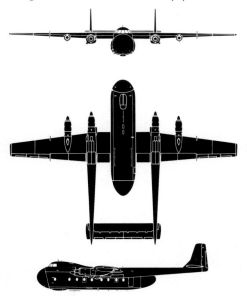

Development and Service:

The A.W.650 was designed by Armstrong Whitworth (when still operating as an independent company within the Hawker Siddeley Group) as a variant of the A.W.66 Eland-engined military freighter project. Production of an initial batch of 10 was initiated as a private venture and the first of these, named Argosy, made its first flight on January 8, 1959. The following year, American freight operator Riddle Airlines concluded a contract for seven Argosies, with deliveries starting in December 1960; the other three aircraft of the original batch went to BEA, in 1961, after modifications to meet that airline's specific requirements. Designated Argosy 101, four of these original aircraft were being operated by Air-Bridge Carriers in the UK in 1977, one of the quartet being on lease to Air Anglia; a fifth example is used by Rolls-Royce Ltd to carry engine components between its UK factories and its European partner companies. An improved version of the Argosy was developed as the Series 200, with a new wing structure, higher weights and other refinements. The first of these new models flew on March 11, 1964, and BEA subsequently placed an order for five, designated Argosy 222. These entered service in 1965 and a sixth was acquired later to replace one that had been destroyed, this completing production of the Argosy for the commercial market. Four of the Argosy 222s were sold by BEA in 1970 to Midwest, a division of Transair in Canada, and two of these remained in Canada in 1977, the other two then being in service with Safe Air, flying freight between the two main islands of New Zealand. Two ex-RAF Argosy C Mk 1s with different rear fuselage loading doors, went into service in 1977 with Via Nova International, flying supplies in Zaïre.

Hawker Siddeley (DH 106) Comet 4

UK

Medium–range airliner, in service.
Photo: Comet 4B.
Data and silhouette: Comet 4B.

Accommodation: 71–101 passengers.
Powered by: Four 10,500lb (4,760kg) st Rolls-Royce Avon 525 turbojets.
Span: 107ft 10in (32.87m).
Length: 118ft 0in (35.97m).
Gross weight: 158,000lb (71,665kg).
Max payload: 23,900lb (10,840kg).
Max cruising speed: 526mph (846km/h) at 23,500ft (7,160m).
Typical range: 3,120 miles (5,020km) with max payload at 462mph (743km/h).

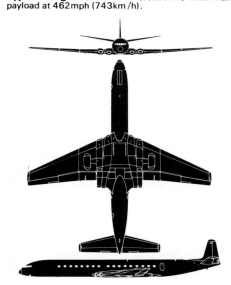

Development and Service:
The first Comet 4 (G-APDA), one of a batch of 19 ordered by BOAC, made its first flight at Hatfield on April 27, 1958, and the next two ('PDB and 'PDC) flew the first-ever jet services across the Atlantic on October 4, 1958. This was the initial version of a new family of Comets evolved from the world's first commercial jet transport. Its predecessors were the Comet 1 and 1A, with four de Havilland Ghost engines, used by BOAC and other operators; the Comet 2 with slightly longer fuselage and Avon 504 engines delivered to RAF Transport Command; and the Comet 3 with much longer fuselage and many other changes. The first production Comet 4B, with shorter wing and no tanks on the wings, flew on June 27, 1959, and this type entered service with BEA in April 1960. The Comet 4C combines the long fuselage of the 4B and the long span of the Comet 4; the first flew in October 1959. The only remaining commercial operator of the Comet is Dan-Air, which had built up a fleet of nine 4Bs and 11 4Cs by the beginning of 1977, having acquired the last three 4Cs from EgyptAir, the only other recent user of the type.

Photo: Trident Two.

Hawker Siddeley (DH 121) Trident   UK

Short/medium-range airliner, in production and service.
Photo: Trident Two.
Data apply to Trident 2E.
Silhouette: Trident Three.

Accommodation: Flight crew of 3 or 4, and 128–180 passengers.
Powered by: Three 11,960lb (5,425kg) st Rolls-Royce Spey Mk 512-5W turbofans.
Span: 98ft 0in (29.87m).
Length: 114ft 9in (35.0m).
Gross weight: 144,000lb (65,500kg).
Max payload: 29,600lb (13,426kg).
Max cruising speed: 596mph (960km/h) at 30,000 ft (9,150m).
Typical range: 2,464 miles (3,965km) with 21,378lb (9,679kg) payload and typical reserves.

Development and Service:

British European Airways (now British Airways) set down its general requirements for a short-haul jet transport in July 1956. To this specification, the DH. 121, Bristol 200 and Avro 740 were eventually offered and the DH. 121 was selected in 1958. A contract for 24 was confirmed on August 12, 1959. The first of the BEA Trident 1s (G-ARPA) made its first flight on January 9, 1962, with 9,850lb (4,468kg) st Spey 505 engines, up to 103 seats, and span of 89ft 10in (27.38m). The basic model was followed by 15 Trident 1Es with 11,400lb (5,170kg) st Spey 511-5 engines, up to 115 seats, 95ft (28.96m) wing span and improved high-lift devices, principally for other customers but some eventually serving with BEA/British Airways. By the beginning of 1977, few Trident 1s remained in service. In 1965, BEA ordered 15 Trident Twos (2Es) with higher operating weights and longer range. The first flight of this version was made on July 27, 1967, and it entered service in April 1968. Two were bought subsequently by Cyprus Airways, and China ordered 33 for CAAC, with deliveries continuing in 1977. This variant was followed by the Trident Three, which has a longer fuselage, more seats and a R-R RB. 162-86 jet in the rear fuselage to boost take-off performance. The first flight was made on December 11, 1969; and the first take-off using the RB.162 was made on March 22, 1970. BEA ordered 26 Trident Threes and put the type into service in April 1971. China placed an order for two Super Trident 3Bs, with 152 seats, increased fuel and gross weight of 158,000lb (71,667kg), delivery of these aircraft in 1975 completing production of the Trident Three series.

35

Ilyushin Il-14 and Avia 14

USSR

Short-range airliner, in service.
Photo: Il-14.

Accommodation: Flight crew of 3, and 18–28 passengers.
Powered by: Two 1,900hp ASh-82T piston-engines.
Span: 103ft 11in (31.67m).
Length: 69ft 9in (21.26m).
Gross weight: 38,000lb (17,235kg).
Max payload: 5,400lb (2,450kg).
Max cruising speed: 198mph (318km/h) at 9,500ft (2,900m).
Typical range: 920 miles (1,480km) with full payload at 161mph (260km/h).

Development and Service:
Ilyushin's Il-14, developed from the similar but lower-powered Il-12, was one of the most-produced post-war transports, having been built by the thousand for use by the Soviet Air Force, Aeroflot and the airlines of China and countries in eastern Europe. Two versions were built for civil use: the Il-14P, seating 18–26 passengers, and the Il-14M with a longer cabin to seat 24–28. The East German State Aircraft Factory built 80 examples of the Il-14P, and many more were produced at the Avia factory in Czechoslovakia. The Czech-built Avia-14 could be fitted with tip-tanks; the passenger version was known as the Avia-14 Salon, and a version with large loading doors and strengthened floor was built as a freighter. Many Il-14P and Il-14M airliners were later converted to Il-14T freighters and are still in service in Russia. A few others can be seen in service with airlines such as Cubana and Mongolian. CAAC of China is believed to have more than 50 still operational.

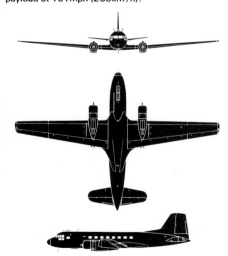

Ilyushin Il-18

Medium-range airliner, in service.
Data for Il-18D.

Accommodation: Flight crew of 4–5, and up to 122 passengers.
Powered by: Four 4,250ehp Ivchenko AI-20M turboprops.
Span: 122ft 8½in (37.40m).
Length: 117ft 9in (35.90m).
Gross weight: 141,100lb (64,000kg).
Max payload: 29,750lb (13,500kg).
Max cruising speed: 419mph (675km/h) at 30,000ft (9,150m).
Range: 2,300 miles (3,700km) with max payload (1-hour reserve) at 388mph (625km/h).

Development and Service:

The Il-18 is a contemporary of the American Electra, and is comparable in performance with the Electra and Vanguard. It was first flown in July 1957, and a batch of 20 was quickly produced for service trials and proving and development flights. These test aircraft were powered alternately with the AI-20 engine and the earlier Kuznetsov NK-4 of similar power. The former was standardised in the production Il-18. Scheduled freight services were operated by Il-18s in the early months of 1959, followed by the first passenger services, on routes from Moscow to Alma Ata and Adler, on April 20. The Il-18 was introduced on many new domestic and international routes by Aeroflot from 1960. It is the most successful Soviet airliner for export, deliveries having been made to Air Guinee (3), Air Mali (3), Air Mauritanie (1), Balkan Bulgarian Airlines (12), CAAC in China (at least 15), CSA (11), Cubana (5), EgyptAir (5), Ghana Airways (8, later returned to Russia), the East German Interflug (16), LOT (8), Malev (9), Royal Afghan Airlines (1), Tarom (14), and Yemen Arab Airlines (1), as well as to several foreign governments and air forces. The standard Aeroflot version is the 90/110-seat Il-18V, with 4,000ehp AI-20K engines. The Il-18E (more accurately rendered from the Soviet form as Il-18Ye) has more powerful AI-20M engines and revised internal layout, and the Il-18D is similar with increased fuel capacity, higher weights and other improvements. More than 800 Il-18s are believed to have been built, mostly for Aeroflot.

Ilyushin Il-62 and Il-62M

USSR

Long-range jet airliner, in production and service.
Photo: Il-62.
Data and silhouette: Il-62M.

Accommodation: Flight crew of 5, and up to 198 passengers.
Powered by: Four 25,350lb (11,500kg) st Soloviev D-30KU turbofans.
Span: 141ft 9in (43.20m).
Length: 174ft 3½in (53.12m).
Gross weight: 364,000lb (165,000kg).
Max payload: 50,700lb (23,000kg).
Normal cruising speed: 528–570mph (850–920km/h).
Range: 4,970 miles (8,000km) with max payload (1-hour fuel reserve).

Development and Service:

First details of the Il-62 were given in the Soviet press in September 1962, followed in January 1963 by the first flight of the prototype. In September 1963, it was reported that three Il-62s were being flight tested, with 16,535lb (7,500kg) st Lyulka AL-7 engines fitted temporarily. When the intended 20,150lb (10,500kg) st Kuznetsov NK-8-4 engines became available, considerable flight development was undertaken, including work necessary to overcome low-speed handling problems associated with the wing design. The Il-62 entered scheduled service with Aeroflot during 1967, replacing Tu-114s and Tu-104s on selected internal routes. In September 1967, Il-62s took over from Tu-114s on the service to Montreal, this being the first transatlantic jet service by Aeroflot. It was followed by inauguration of a Moscow-New York service in July 1968; and the Il-62 first appeared at London Airport on May 11, 1968, operated on lease by CSA. Subsequently, Aeroflot also introduced the Il-62 on its London route. CSA has seven Il-62s, Cubana two, the East German Interflug five, LOT six, Tarom three, CAAC five and EgyptAir took delivery of seven (although the last-mentioned were quickly returned to Russia). Aircraft of this type can be seen in joint Aeroflot/Japan Air Lines insignia when operated on the pooled services between Moscow and Tokyo. The re-engined Il-62M appeared in 1971 and entered service with Aeroflot in 1974. In addition to the more powerful and more economic engines, it has an extra fuel tank in the fin; high-density versions for 198 passengers have been studied, although normal seating capacity is 186.

Ilyushin Il-76

USSR

Medium/long-range freight transport, in production and service.

Accommodation: Basic flight crew of three.
Powered by: Four 26,455lb (12,000kg) st Soloviev D-30KP turbofans.
Span: 165ft 8in (50.50m).
Length: 152ft 10½in (46.59m).
Gross weight: 346,125lb (157,000kg).
Max payload: 88,185lb (40,000kg).
Normal cruising speed: 528mph (850km/h) at 42,650ft (13,000m).
Range: 3,100 miles (5,000km) with max payload.

Development and Service:

First flown on March 25, 1971, the prototype Il-76 was one of the most important new aircraft shown at the 1971 Paris Air Show. Its nominal task is to carry 40 tonnes of freight for a distance of 5,000km (3,100 miles) in under six hours. It can take off from comparatively short, unprepared airstrips and official statements said it would be used first in Siberia, the north of the Soviet Union and the Far East, where operation of other types of transport is difficult. It is also expected to be the subject of Soviet export efforts within the next two years. It was clear from the start that the Il-76 also had military potential, and it is already in service with the Soviet Air Force to replace the An-12 as a tactical transport (with a rear gun turret) and also possibly as a flight refuelling tanker. The entire accommodation is pressurised, and advanced mechanical handling systems are installed in the main cabin for loading and unloading containerised freight via the rear ramp-door. There is a large ground-mapping radar under the navigator's station in the glazed nose, and a computer is fitted for use with the automatic flight control and automatic landing approach systems. The main eight-wheel bogies of the undercarriage retract inward into large blister fairings under the fuselage; two more large blister fairings cover the actuating mechanism. During development the rear fuselage has been modified, to increase the depth of the aft clamshell loading doors. During a series of record flights in 1975, an Il-76 carried its design payload of 88,185lb (40,000kg) over a closed circuit of 3,100 miles (5,000km) at a speed of 507.019mph (815.968km/h), and lifted 154,590lb (70,121kg) to a height of 11,875m (38,960ft).

Ilyushin Il-86

USSR

Large-capacity medium-range transport, under development.

Accommodation: Flight crew of 3–4. Up to 350 passengers nine-abreast in a single-class layout; typical mixed-class layout for 206 eight-abreast and 28 six-abreast.
Powered by: Four 28,660lb (13,000kg) st Kuznetsov NK-86 turbofans.
Span: 157ft 8½in (48.06m).
Length: 195ft 4in (59.54m).
Gross weight: 454,150lb (206,000kg).
Max payload: 92,500lb (42,000kg).
Cruising speed: 560–590mph (900–950km/h) at 30,000ft (9,000m).
Range: 1,460 miles (2,350km) with full passenger payload.

Development and Service:

Evolution of an "airbus" type of aircraft to operate on Aeroflot trunk routes within the Soviet Union, where air traffic has been growing at a rapid pace in recent years, began in the late 'sixties, when design proposals were made by the Antonov, Ilyushin and Tupolev design bureaux. Of these proposals, that by Ilyushin (known as the Il-86) was selected for further development in 1972. The favoured configuration was then rear-engined, similar to that of the Il-62, with a much enlarged fuselage. Further design study, however, showed that the weight penalty of the rear-engined arrangement was unacceptable in an aircraft of this size, and by the end of 1972 work was concentrated on an aircraft with four wing pods, using, for the first time in a Soviet airliner, the classic configuration favoured on the US West Coast. A unique feature of the Il-86, from the earliest design stage, is the provision of vestibules at lower-deck level, beneath the main passenger floor, allowing passengers to board by way of airstairs in the vestibule doors, stow their carry-on baggage and then proceed up internal stairways to the main deck. Also beneath this deck are two cargo holds designed to accommodate standard LD3 containers. When first announced, it was expected that the Il-86 would fly in 1975, powered by Soloviev D-30KP turbofans; a delay of one year ensued when it was decided to make use of a more powerful and newer Kuznetsov engine that is reported to have undergone initial flight testing beneath the wing of an Il-76. The Il-86 made its first flight on December 22, 1976, and is expected to reach Aeroflot service by 1980.

Lockheed L-100 Hercules

USA

Commercial freighter, in production and service.
Photo: L-100-20.
Data and silhouette: L-100-30.

Accommodation: Crew of 3, plus freight.
Powered by: Four 4,508ehp Allison 501-D22A turboprops.
Span: 132ft 7in (40.41m).
Length: 112ft 8½in (34.35m).
Gross weight: 155,000lb (70,308kg).
Max payload: 52,550lb (23,836kg).
Max cruising speed: 377mph (607km/h) at 20,000ft (6,100m).
Range: 2,130 miles (3,425km) with max payload (45-min fuel reserve).

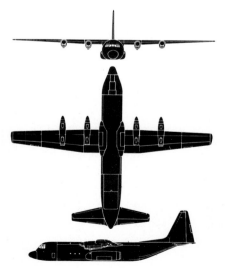

Development and Service:

By early 1977, Lockheed's Georgia company had sold more than 40 Hercules freighters for commercial use, in addition to over 1,400 in military guise. The first civil Hercules was a demonstrator based on the military C-130E and identified as Model 382; this was certificated in February 1965 and was subsequently modified to L-100-20 standard and sold. The first commercial variants were the Model 382B and L-100, similar to the C-130E, with differing standards of freight handling equipment and with 4,050ehp Allison 501-D22 engines. The Model 382E introduced a fuselage 'stretch' of 8ft 4in (2.54m) and is now known as the L-100-20, with uprated D22A engines. The first flight was made on April 19, 1968. A later development was the Model 382G, or L-100-30 (data above), with a further fuselage stretch of 6ft 8in (2.03m). This variant was developed primarily for Saturn Airways, which initially ordered three to provide a regular service between Britain and California carrying RB.211 engines for TriStars and now has 12 of this type in its fleet. The first L-100-30 flew for the first time on August 14, 1970. Several operators of the earlier Hercules versions ordered L-100-30s or had their aircraft converted to the new standard. Other users in 1977 included Safair, Alaska International and Pacific Western. In 1976, Lockheed announced forthcoming development of the L-100-50 Hercules, with a fuselage 20ft (6.1m) longer than that of the L-100-30 and with a gross weight of 170,000lb (77,180kg), primarily for short-range cargo flights, with a max payload of 60,000lb (27,240kg). A twin-turboprop L-400 version is also projected.

Lockheed L-188 Electra

USA

Medium-range airliner, in service.
Data apply to L-188C.

Accommodation: Flight crew of 3–4, and 66–99 passengers.
Powered by: Four 3,750ehp Allison 501-D13 turboprops.
Span: 99ft 0in (30.17m).
Length: 104ft 8in (31.90m).
Gross weight: 116,000lb (52,615kg).
Max payload: 26,400lb (11,975kg).
Max cruising speed: 405mph (652km/h) at 22,000ft (6,700m).
Typical range: 2,500 miles (4,020km) with 22,000lb (9,980kg) payload at 380mph (611km/h).

Development and Service:

Development of the Electra was begun to meet the specific needs of US domestic operators in 1956, and the first flight was made on December 6, 1957. Fourteen airlines ordered 165 Electras, and the last of these were delivered in May 1962. Eastern Air Lines was first to put the Electra into service, on January 12, 1959, followed by American Airlines on January 23 and other US operators during 1959. First overseas airlines to use the Electra were Cathay Pacific, Ansett-ANA, TAA, and Qantas, all in 1959. The first Electra operator in Europe (and the only European airline to order the Electra) was KLM, which operated the type from 1959 to 1968. Major US airlines which operated large fleets of Electras have replaced them with jet aircraft, but the type has seen service with many smaller airlines, mainly in North, Central and South America and Australasia, on passenger and freight services, and some of these operators still use it. Considerable numbers of Electras have been modified for freighting, by Lockheed Aircraft Services, with a large freight-loading door in the forward fuselage. About 100 Electras were reported in airline service in 1976.

Lockheed L-1011 TriStar

USA

Large-capacity medium/long-range transport, in production and service.
Data for L-1011-200.
Photo: L-1011-100.

Accommodation: Up to 400 passengers.
Powered by: Three 48,000lb (21,772kg) st Rolls-Royce RB.211-524 turbofans.
Span: 155ft 4in (47.34m).
Length: 177ft 8½in (54.2m).
Gross weight: 466,000lb (211,374kg).
Max payload: 72,800lb (33,022kg).
Cruising speed: 560mph (901km/h) at 35,000ft (10,670m).
Range: 4,450 miles (7,160km) with 273 passengers.

Development and Service:

The Lockheed company re-entered the commercial aircraft scene in June 1968 when it decided to go ahead with production of the Model 385 TriStar – its first airliner since the turboprop Electra. After early studies of a twin-engined design to meet an American Airlines outline specification of 1965, Lockheed elected to use a three-engined layout, with two underwing pods and the third engine in the rear fuselage. A broadly similar layout was chosen independently for the competitive DC-10. Initial orders for the TriStar came from Eastern Air Lines and Delta Air Lines. First flight was made at Palmdale on November 16, 1970, and four more TriStars had flown by December 1971; airline deliveries began in April 1972. The first TriStar passenger service was operated by Eastern on April 15, and scheduled services began eleven days later. Firm orders totalled 159 plus 50 options by the beginning of 1977, the customer airlines comprising Air Canada, All Nippon, British Airways, Cathay Pacific, Delta, Eastern, Gulf Air, LTU, Saudia and TWA. Most TriStars in this total are of the original L-1011-1 type, with 42,000lb (19,050kg) st RB.211-22B engines and 430,000lb (195,045kg) gross weight. Also in service are a few L-1011-100s with the same engines and 466,000lb (211,374kg) weight and including extra fuel for increased range, and L-1011-200s with this extra fuel and uprated engines. The L-1011-250 is on offer with RB.211-524B engines, still more fuel and 496,000lb (224,982kg) weight; British Airways has ordered the L-1011-500 with these engines and weights but with the fuselage shortened to 164ft 2½in (50.0m) for 6,000-mile (9,650-km)-plus ranges, to enter service in 1979.

McDonnell Douglas DC-8 Series 10 to 50   USA

Long-range airliner, in service.
Photo: DC-8 Series 54F.
Data and silhouette: DC-8 Series 50.

Accommodation: Flight crew of 3–5, and 116–179 passengers.
Powered by: Four 18,000lb (8,172kg) st Pratt & Whitney JT3D-3B turbofans.
Span: 142ft 5in (43.41m).
Length: 150ft 6in (45.87m).
Gross weight: 325,000lb (147,415kg).
Max payload: 34,360lb (15,585kg).
Max cruising speed: 580mph (933km/h) at 30,000ft (9,150m).
Range: 5,720 miles (9,205km) with max payload.

Development and Service:

The US domestic versions of the DC-8 were known as the Series 10 with 13,500lb (6,124 kg) st P&W JT3C-6 and Series 20 with 15,800lb (7,167kg) st P&W JT4A-3 engines, and weights of 273,000lb (123,830kg) and 276,000lb (125,190kg) respectively. Many Series 10s were converted to Series 50. Current operators of the Series 20 are Air Haiti, ONA and United.

Intercontinental models have increased fuel capacity and fly at weights up to 325,000lb. They comprise the Series 30 with 16,800lb (7,620kg) st JT4A-9 or 17,500lb (7,945kg) st JT4A-11 engines, and the Series 40 with 17,500lb (7,945kg) st Rolls-Royce Conway 509s. The Series 50 has 17,000lb (7,718kg) JT3D-1 or 18,000lb (8,172kg) st JT3D-3 or -3B turbofans and was available as a conversion of earlier models as well as a new aircraft. In 1961, Douglas announced the DC-8F Jet Trader, a variant of the Series 50 which incorporated a large cargo loading door in the fuselage side and could accommodate mixed loads of passengers and palletized freight.

Operators of the Series 30 in 1977 include African Safari, Air Afrique, Air Zaïre, Capitol, National, ONA, PAL, Spearair, Tabsa, TAE, Thai, United and Viasa. The Series 40 is operated by Air Canada, Alitalia and CP Air. Several of the airlines noted above added Series 50 DC-8s to their fleets; other users of the turbofan model include Aeromexico, Aero Peru, Affretair, Air Jamaica, Airlift, Air New Zealand, Balair, Braniff, CP Air, Delta, Garuda, IAS Cargo Airlines, Iberia, Kar Air and Scanair. Jet Traders are used by many operators of passenger DC-8s and by JAL, KLM, Martinair, Saturn, SATA and Seaboard. Production of all models up to and including the Series 50 ended in November 1968, with 294 built.

McDonnell Douglas DC-8 Super Sixty Series   USA

Long/very-long-range airliner, in service.
Photo and data: DC-8 Super 63.
Silhouette: DC-8 Super 63.

Accommodation: Flight crew of 3–5, and up to 259 passengers.
Powered by: Four 19,000lb (8,618kg) st Pratt & Whitney JT3D-7 turbofans.
Span: 148ft 5in (45.23m).
Length: 187ft 5in (57.12m).
Gross weight: 350,000lb (158,760kg).
Max payload: 67,735lb (30,719kg).
Max cruising speed: 600mph (965km/h) at 30,000ft (9,150m).
Range: 4,500 miles (7,240km) with max payload (normal reserves).

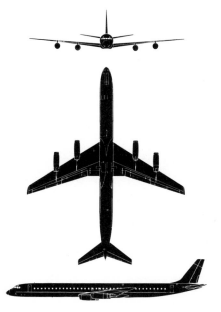

Development and Service:

For 10 years after starting work on the DC-8 programme, Douglas maintained the same overall dimensions for all variants of the design. In 1965, however, three new versions emerged, offering two alternative fuselage lengths and other changes to meet specific airline requirements. The three new models are known collectively as the Super Sixty Series. All have turbofan engines—either 18,000lb (8,172kg) st JT3D-3Bs or 19,000lb (8,618kg) st JT3D-7s—and comprise the Super 61, similar to the Series 50 with fuselage lengthened by 36ft 8in (11.18m) to accommodate up to 259 passengers; the Super 62 with fuselage lengthened only by 6ft 8in (2.03m) but with other modifications for maximum range including extended wingtips, more fuel and low-drag nacelles and pylons; and the Super 63 combining the long fuselage of the Super 61 with the aerodynamic refinements of the Super 62. All three models were available in all-passenger or Jet Trader configuration. The first Super 61 flew on March 14, 1966, the first Super 62 on August 29, 1966, and the first Super 63 on April 10, 1967.

A total of 262 Super Sixty Series DC-8s were built, and were operated by the following airlines in 1977: Super 61 and 61F, Air Canada, Air Gabon, Air Jamaica, Capitol, Delta, Eastern, JAL, Japan Asia Airways, National, ONA, Saturn, Spantax, Trans International and United; Super 62 and 62F, Aeromaritime, Air Jamaica, Alitalia, Balair, Braniff, Finnair, JAL, SAS, Scanair, Swissair, Thai Airways, UTA and United; Super 63 and 63F, Affretair, Air Afrique, Air Canada, Air Ceylon, Airlift International, Air Zaïre, Balair, Capitol, Cargolux, CP Air, Flying Tiger, Iberia, International Air Bahama, KLM, Loftleidir, ONA, SATA, SAS, Seaboard, Surinam Airways, Trans International, Transcarga, UTA, Viasa and World Airways.

McDonnell Douglas DC-9 Srs 10 and 20   USA

Short/medium-range jet airliner, in service.
Photo: Series 10 Model 11.
Data and silhouette: Series 10.

Accommodation: Flight crew of 2, and up to 90 passengers.
Powered by: Two 12,250lb (5,556kg) st Pratt & Whitney JT8D-5 (Model 11) or 14,000lb (6,350kg) st JT8D-1 (Model 15) turbofans.
Span: 89ft 5in (27.25m).
Length: 104ft 4¼in (31.82m).
Gross weight: 77,700lb (35,245kg) for Model 11, 90,700lb (41,140kg) for Model 15.
Max payload: 18,050lb (8,188kg) for Model 11, 21,381lb (9,698kg) for Model 15.
Max cruising speed: 561mph (903km/h) at 25,000ft (7,620m).
Max range (Model 11): 1,311 miles (2,110km) with 50 passengers, with reserves.

Development and Service:

Design studies for the DC-9 were started by Douglas soon after the DC-8 had been launched. After several configurations had been considered, the now-familiar rear-engined short/medium-range airliner was announced in April 1963. First flight of the prototype was made on February 25, 1965, followed by four more DC-9s in the initial Series 10 form by the middle of that year. Certification was completed in record time, to permit Delta Air Lines to fly the first commercial service only nine months after the DC-9's first flight, on November 29, 1965. The basic version, known as the Series 10 Model 11, was followed by the Model 15, with more powerful engines and increased fuel capacity. Freight versions were DC-9Fs, fitted with a large cargo-loading door in place of the normal passenger door at the front on the port side. The same door is installed on DC-9CF convertible passenger/cargo versions of the aircraft. Altogether, 113 DC-9 Series 10s were sold, plus 24 DC-9 Srs 10F/CFs; these variants are no longer in production. After the Series 30 had been developed as the first step in stretching the DC-9 (see next page), the company produced 10 Series 20s to a special SAS requirement, featuring the Series 10 fuselage with Series 30 wings for 'hot and high' airfield operation. The first Series 20 flew on September 18, 1968, with JT8D-9 engines.

McDonnell Douglas DC-9 Srs 30, 40 and 50   USA

Short/medium-range jet airliners, in production and service.
Photo and data: Series 50.
Silhouette: Series 50.

Accommodation: Flight crew of 2, and up to 139 passengers.
Powered by: Two 16,000lb (7,257kg) st Pratt & Whitney JT8D-17 turbofans.
Span: 93ft 5in (28.47m).
Length: 133ft 7in (40.7m).
Gross weight: 121,000lb (54,400kg).
Max payload: 33,000lb (14,950kg).
Max cruising speed: 565mph (909km/h) at 25,000ft (7,620m).
Max range: 1,547 miles (2,546km) with reserves.

Development and Service:

As a first step towards evolving a complete family of short-haul transports from the basic DC-9 Srs 10, Douglas developed the Srs 30 with more powerful engines, increased span, a 14ft 11in (4.6m) longer fuselage and new high-lift devices in the form of full-span wing leading-edge slats and double-slotted flaps. The first flight of a Series 30 was made on August 1, 1956, and Eastern Air Lines began scheduled services with this version on February 1, 1967. Successive Srs 30 variants have offered 14,000lb (6,350kg) st JT8D-7, 14,500lb (6,575kg) st JT8D-9, 15,000lb (6,804kg) st JT8D-11 and 15,500lb (7,031kg) JT8D-15 engines; and an extended-range version became available in 1976 with extra fuel, increased gross weights and JT8D-17 engines. Next came the Series 40, first flown on November 28, 1967, with JT8D-9s or JT8D-15s, more fuel and an increased length of 125ft $7\frac{1}{4}$in (38.28m), providing accommodation for 125 passengers; gross weight of this version, operated only by SAS and Toa Domestic, is 114,000lb (51,710kg). The Series 50 is lengthened by a further 12ft $7\frac{1}{4}$in (3.84m) compared with the Series 30, to seat up to 139 passengers, and has JT8D-15 or JT8D-17 engines. The first Srs 50 flew on 17 December 1974 and this variant entered service with Swissair on 24 August 1975. Like the Srs 10 (see previous page), the Srs 30 is available in convertible passenger/freight configuration with large side loading door, and some 35 of these had been sold in addition to more than 520 Srs 30s by early 1977 (excluding 38 for the US Services). The overall total of about 900 DC-9s sold or on option includes 59 Srs 40s and over 50 Srs 50s.

McDonnell Douglas DC-10

USA

Large-capacity medium / long-range transport, in production and service. Photo silhouette, and data: Series 30.

Accommodation: Flight crew of 5, and up to 345 passengers.
Powered by: Three 49,000lb (22,226kg) st General Electric CF6-50A or 51,000lb (23,133kg) st CF6-50C turbofans.
Span: 165ft 4in (50.39m).
Length: 181ft 7¼in (55.35m).
Gross weight: 555,000lb (251,744kg).
Max payload: 104,500lb (47,400kg).
Max cruising speed: 594mph (956km/h) at 31,000ft (9,450m).
Range: 4,433 miles (7,134km) with max payload (with reserves).

Development and Service:

Design of the DC-10 was crystallised during 1966, after American Airlines had circulated an outline requirement for a large-capacity transport capable of operating from smaller airports on its US domestic network and over short-to-medium ranges. Following initial studies of a twin-engined aeroplane, the company selected a three-engine layout and orders from American Airlines and United Air Lines early in 1968 signalled a go-ahead. The initial variant was the Series 10, intended primarily for US domestic service, powered by 41,000lb (18,597kg) st CF6-6D1 engines and with a gross weight of 440,000lb (199,580kg). The first Series 10 flew for the first time on August 29, 1970, and first airline services were flown in August 1971.

This version has been ordered by American (30), Continental (16), National (14), Laker (4), THY (3), United (37) and Western (10). For operation over very long ranges, the Series 30 (data above) has uprated CF6 engines, a 10ft (3.05m) increase in span and an additional, central main undercarriage leg. Orders have been placed by Aeromexico (2), Air Afrique (3), Air New Zealand (8), Air Siam (1), Air Zaire (2), Alitalia (8), British Caledonian (2), Finnair (2), Garuda (1), Iberia (6), JAT (2), KLM (7), Korean Airlines (5), Lufthansa (10), Martinair (4), National (4), Nigeria Airways (2), ONA (2), PAL (3), PIA (4), Sabena (3), SAS (7), Singapore International (3), Swissair (9), TIA (3), Thai (2), UTA (6), Varig (4) and Viasa (6), World Airways (3) and Wardair (2). The Series 40 is similiar to the 30 but has 48,500lb (22,000kg) st Pratt & Whitney JT9D-20 or 53,000lb (24,040kg) st JT9D-59A engines, the gross weight with the latter being 572,000lb (259,500kg). Purchasers are JAL (6) and Northwest (22). The Martinair, ONA, Sabena, TIA, World and eight of the Continental Srs 10 aircraft are convertible passenger/freighters.

NAMC YS-11

Japan

**Short/medium-range airliner, in service.
Photo shows aircraft equipped for
geological survey duty.
Data: YS-11A-200.
Silhouette: YS-11A-300.**

Accommodation: Flight crew of 2, and 52–60
passengers.
Powered by: Two 3,060ehp Rolls-Royce Dart
542-10K turboprops.
Span: 105ft 0in (32.00m).
Length: 86ft 3½in (26.30m).
Gross weight: 54,010lb (24,500kg).
Max payload: 14,508lb (6,581kg).
Max cruising speed: 291mph (469km/h) at
15,000ft (4,575m).
Range: 680–2,000 miles (1,090–3,215km) at
281mph (452km/h) at 20,000ft (6,100m).

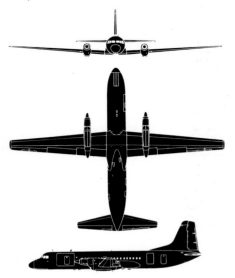

Development and Service:

First post-war Japanese transport of original
design, the YS-11 was developed by a consortium of the nation's manufacturers, primarily
to meet the requirements of Japanese civil
and military operators. The first of two prototypes flew on August 30, 1962, and the
first production model in the autumn of 1964.
Toa Airways (later merged with JDA to
become Toa Domestic) operated the first airline service with the YS-11 on April 1, 1965,
and All Nippon also began using the type
during that year.
In 1966, NAMC announced a new series of
YS-11s with higher operating weights, permitting an increase of up to 2,970lb
(1,347kg) in payload for a given range. These
new versions were the YS-11A-200 passenger model (first flown on November 27,
1967), YS-11A-300 mixed passenger/cargo
type (flown in 1968) and YS-11A-400
freighter (first flown on September 17, 1969);
the 300 and 400 have enlarged doors for
freight loading, the latter having been built
only for military use. During 1970, certification was obtained for the YS-11A-500 and
-600, similar respectively to the -200 and
-300 with 1,100lb (500kg) increase in gross
weights, but only a few examples of these
variants were sold by the time YS-11 production came to an end, in 1972. A total of 182
YS-11s had been built; operators in 1977
included Air Ivoire, All Nippon, Austral, Bouraq
Indonesian, China Airlines, Merpati Nusantara,
Olympic, PT Perlita Air Service, Piedmont,
Reeve Aleutian, SGA (Zaïre), Southwest
(Japan), Toa Domestic, Transair (Canada) and
VASP.

Shorts Belfast

UK

Turboprop freighter, in service.

Accommodation: Flight crew of two or three and up to 78,000lb (35,400kg) of freight, as individual items or on pallets.
Powered by: Four 5,730eshp Rolls-Royce Tyne RTy.12 turboprops.
Span: 158ft 9$\frac{1}{2}$in (48.82m).
Length: 136ft 5in (41.69m).
Max gross weight: 230,000lb (104,300kg).
Max cruising speed: 352mph (566km/h) at 24,000ft (7,300m).
Max range: 5,300 miles (8,530km) at 336mph (540km/h).

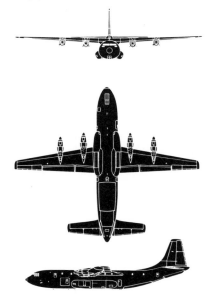

Development and Service:

Design of the Shorts Belfast was based upon that of the Bristol Britannia (the RAF version of which was built by Shorts in Belfast) and the type was known initially as the Britannic. The name was changed in December 1960 when the RAF finalised its contract for 10 examples to serve in the strategic freighting role, the Belfast eventually emerging with little of the Britannia left apart from some basic wing structure. Construction of the first Belfast began in October 1959 and it flew for the first time on January 5, 1964. Deliveries to the RAF began on January 20, 1966, when the first Belfast C.Mk 1 was handed over to No 53 Squadron, RAF, at Brize Norton; in January 1970 the Belfast became the first military transport aircraft in the world to be cleared for "hands-off" automatic landing in fully-operational conditions. The Belfasts served with No 53 Squadron until 1976, having first undergone a series of drag-reduction modifications around the rear fuselage. They were then phased out of RAF service as part of economy cuts, and early in 1977 the entire fleet was acquired for civil use by Pan-African Air Freight-Liners, an American-owned company formed to operate low-cost freight services in the ex-colonial territories of West Africa, including Upper Volta, Chad, Mauritania, Mali, Senegal, Niger, Cape Verde Islands and the Gambia.

Shorts 330   UK

Commuter and local-service passenger and freight transport, in production and service.

Accommodation: Flight crew of 2, and 30 passengers, 7,500lb (3,400kg) of freight, or mixed passenger/cargo loads.
Powered by: Two 1,120shp Pratt & Whitney (Canada) PT6A-45 turboprops.
Span: 74ft 9in (22.78m).
Length: 58ft 0½in (17.69m).
Gross weight: 22,000lb (9,980kg).
Max payload: 5,850lb (2,655kg) in passenger configuration.
Max cruising speed: 228mph (367km/h) at 10,000ft (3,050m).
Range: 455 miles (732km) at 228mph (367km/h) with 30 passengers and baggage.

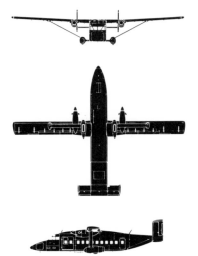

Development and Service:
Derived from the Skyvan, the SD3-30 embodies the same outer wings, tail unit and large cabin cross-section. By lengthening the cabin 12ft 5in (3.78m), Shorts have produced a suitable replacement for the current generation of 18/20-seat commuter transports on routes where traffic is expanding rapidly. Passengers enter through a rear door on the port side. This is supplemented on freight-carrying versions by a door at the front large enough to admit standard "D" size containers. Seven containers of this size can be packed into the cabin, with ample room around them for other freight. The floor is only 3ft (0.91m) above the ground, for easy loading, and the aircraft can be supplied with a large Skyvan-type ramp-door under the rear fuselage if required. Two prototypes of the SD3-30 were built initially; the first of these flew on August 22, 1974 and the second on July 8, 1975. The first production aircraft flew on December 15, 1975, and British certification was obtained on February 18, 1976. Initial orders, for three aircraft each, had been placed by Time Air of Canada and Command Airways of the USA, and the first commercial service was flown by the SD3-30 on 24 August 1976, in Time Air colours. Other customers include Golden West Airlines of the USA (2), Hanson Airways (2), and DLT of Germany (1).

Transall C-160P

Mail carrier, in service.

Accommodation: Flight crew of three and up to 29,735lb (13,500kg) load of mail.
Powered by: Two 6,100ehp Rolls-Royce Tyne RTy 20 Mk 22 turboprops.
Span: 131ft 3in (40.0m).
Length: 106ft 3½in (32.40m).
Gross weight: 112,440lb (51,000kg).
Max payload: 35,270lb (16,000kg).
Cruising speed: 306mph (492km/h) at 26,250ft (8,000m).
Range: 730 miles (1,175km) with max payload.

Development and Service:

The C-160 was developed as a medium-sized tactical transport to meet the requirements of the *Luftwaffe* and the *Armèe de l'Air*, and the AG Transall concern was set up in January 1959 to handle its production as a joint effort in France and Germany. The first prototype flew on 25 February 1963, and production aircraft followed the completion of three prototypes and six pre-series C-160s. The *Luftwaffe* acquired 110, delivered from April 1968 onwards, of which 20 were later transferred to the Turkish Air Force. The *Armèe de l'Air* bought 50, delivered from October 1967 onwards, and the South African Air Force bought nine, delivered between July 1969 and July 1970. During 1973, four of the French C-160Fs were modified by SOGERMA for the carriage of mail; re-designated C-160Ps, they were loaned to the Centre d'Exploitation Postal Metropolitain (CEPM), to be operated by Air France on night mail services within France, supplementing a fleet of Fokker F.27 Mk. 500s. By late 1976, these four Transalls had flown a total of 10,000 hrs, with a regularity factor of 98 per cent, carrying an average of 1.8 million letters each night. Modifications made to the Transalls allow the 13.5 ton load to be emplaned in 12 minutes. Two of the C-160Ps are based in Paris and two at Bastia, Corsica, and they operate each night in opposite directions over the route Paris-Lyons-Nice-Corsica.

Tupolev Tu-124 (and Tu-104)

USSR

Medium-range airliner, in service.
Photo: Tu-104.
Data and silhouette: Tu-124V.

Accommodation: Flight crew of 4, and 56 passengers.
Powered by: Two 11,905lb (5,400kg) st Soloviev D-20P turbofans.
Span: 83ft 9½in (25.55m).
Length: 100ft 4in (30.58m).
Gross weight: 83,775lb (38,000kg).
Normal payload: 13,225lb (6,000kg).
Max cruising speed: 540mph (870km/h).
Range: 760 miles (1,220km) with max payload at 497mph (800km/h) at 33,000ft (10,000m), with reserves.

Development and Service.

Andrei Tupolev's design bureau developed the Tu-124 from the earlier Tu-104 design for service on the more important short-range routes in Russia. First flown in 44-seat prototype form in June 1960, the design was developed into the 56-seat production model Tu-124V which entered service in October 1962 and became one of Aeroflot's standard short-range airliners during 1965–66. Three were delivered to CSA in 1964, and two to Interflug of East Germany, these being the only examples exported for airline use. Two other versions of the Tu-124 have been reported in service with Aeroflot, with a higher standard of cabin furnishing and fewer seats. These are the Tu-124K, with a 24-seat main cabin and two other compartments for four and eight passengers respectively; and the Tu-124K2, with individual cabins for four and two, and a 16-seat rear compartment.

Aeroflot continued to operate a few Tu-124s in 1976. The Soviet airline also employs considerable numbers of veteran Tu-104s on domestic services, mostly equipped to Tu-104V standard, with 100 seats, 21,385lb (9,700kg) st Mikulin AM-3M-500 turbojets and range of 1,305 miles (2,100km) at 497 mph (800km/h) with max payload. The Tu-104 was the Soviet Union's first jet transport, and only the second in the world to enter commercial service, after the Comet. The design was based on that of the Tu-16 bomber, using the same wings and power plant, with a new fuselage and modified tail unit. Over 200 are reported to have been built.

Tupolev Tu-134

USSR

Short/medium-range jet airliner, in production and service.
Photo and data: Tu-134A.

Accommodation: Flight crew of 3, and up to 80 passengers.
Powered by: Two 14,990lb (6,800kg) st Soloviev D-30-2 turbofans.
Span: 95ft 2in (29.00m).
Length: 122ft 0in (37.10m).
Gross weight: 103,600lb (47,000kg).
Max payload: 18,000lb (8,200kg).
Cruising speed: 466–559mph (750–900km/h).
Typical range: 1,243 miles (2,000km) with 18,108lb (8,215kg) payload at 466mph (750km/h) at 32,800ft (10,000m), with reserves.

Development and Service:

Operationally in the same class as the BAC One-Eleven and Douglas DC-9, the Tu-134 is a development of the Tu-124 and was referred to at first as the Tu-124A. The principal difference is relocation of the engines on the aft fuselage and the use of a 'T'-tail; many other detail changes and improvements have also been made. First flight of the Tu-134 is believed to have been made early in 1964 and Aeroflot put 72-seat production aircraft into service in 1967 on domestic and international routes in Europe. During 1969, a developed version designated the Tu-134A was publicly demonstrated; this has a fuselage lengthened by 6ft 11in (2.10m), 76–80 seats, increased baggage space, thrust reversers, APU and improved electronics. Originally, both the Tu-134 and Tu-134A had the distinctive Tupolev nose with a navigator's station, but later examples—particularly those for export—have radar in a conical nose fairing. Users of the Tu-134 and Tu-134A, apart from Aeroflot, include Aviogenex with five, Balkan Bulgarian (7), CSA (11), Interflug (12), LOT (10) and Malev (7). Aeroflot is reported to have at least 200 in service.

Tupolev Tu-144

USSR

Medium/long-range supersonic airliner, in production and service.

Accommodation: Flight crew of 3–4, and up to 140 passengers.
Powered by: Four 44,090lb (20,000kg) st (with afterburning) Kuznetsov NK-144 turbofans.
Span: 94ft 6in (28.80m).
Length: 215ft 6½in (65.70m).
Gross weight: 396,830lb (180,000kg).
Normal cruising speed: Mach 2.2 (1,452mph; 2,336km/h) at 52,500–59,000ft (16,000–18,000m).
Max range: 4,030 miles (6,500km) with 140 passengers at Mach 1.9 (1,243mph; 2,000km/h).

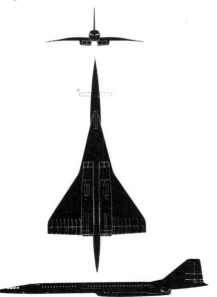

Development and Service:

In general conception, size and performance, the Tu-144 resembles the Concorde, although Russia chose to use turbofan rather than turbojet engines, with afterburners for continuous operation in flight, and designed the Tu-144 for a higher cruising speed. The development programme for the Tu-144 included flight testing of a scale model of the ogival wing on a modified MiG-21. The first flight of the Tu-144 was made on December 31, 1968, to make it the world's first SST in the air. The first supersonic flight was made on June 5, 1969 and Mach 2 was achieved for the first time in May 1970.

This aircraft was followed by a second, similar, prototype. The design then underwent a radical revision. The wings were increased in span by nearly 4ft (1.15m) and cambered over the full area, giving a curved trailing-edge. The fuselage was lengthened by nearly 19ft (5.7m), and the engines were moved outboard into paired ducts. The undercarriage was redesigned, and "moustache" retractable foreplanes were added to improve take-off and landing characteristics. The second production Tu-144 in this configuration was lost while taking part in the 1973 Paris Air Show, but at least three other examples were flying by 1975, and on December 26 that year, Aeroflot inaugurated a regular scheduled operation between Moscow and Alma Ata. Following Soviet custom with brand-new commercial aircraft, this operation was intended primarily as a proving trial and only freight was carried. No details of Aeroflot's plans for a passenger service had been announced up to mid-1977.

Tupolev Tu-154   USSR

Medium/long-range jet airliner, in production and service.
Photo: Tu-154B.
Data and silhouette: Tu-154A.

Accommodation: Flight crew of 3–4, and up to 167 passengers.
Powered by: Three 20,950lb (9,500kg) st Kuznetsov NK-8-2 turbofans.
Span: 123ft 2½in (37.55m).
Length: 157ft 1¾in (47.90m).
Gross weight: 198,416lb (90,000kg).
Max payload: 44,090lb (20,000kg).
Cruising speed: 528–605mph (850–975km/h) at 36,000ft (11,000m).
Range: 2,360 miles (3,800km) with max payload at 528mph (850km/h), with reserves.

Development and Service:

The Tu-154 is a second-generation aircraft that was designed to replace the Tu-104 from the same design bureau, and the Il-18 and An-10 on those routes where traffic growth required a larger aeroplane. Whilst retaining several features of the Tupolev family of jet transports, the Tu-154 also breaks with Tupolev tradition in some aspects of fuselage design, such as the nose, which no longer contains a navigation station, and the small close-pitched windows replacing the former generously-sized transparencies at each seat row. Location of the three engines at the rear of the fuselage matches Western practice, and the Tu-154 is in the same general bracket of size and performance as the HS Trident Three and the Boeing 727-200. The prototype made its first flight on October 4, 1968 and a pre-production model was under test by 1970. Aeroflot proving flights, carrying freight and mail, began in August 1971, and scheduled services started in February 1972.

A version designated Tu-154A, with three 25,350lb (11,500kg) st NK-8-2U engines, entered service with Aeroflot in 1974 and this was followed in 1975 by the Tu-154B, with changes in the navigation equipment and other details; both of these models operate at a gross weight of 207,000lb (94,000kg) and have a centre-section fuel tank which is not usable in flight but can be used to recharge the main tanks at turn-round points where fuel may be expensive or unavailable. Aeroflot has about 100 Tu-154 variants in service and exports have been made to Balkan Bulgarian (7) and Malev (6).

Boeing 737-200 in the colourful insignia of Royal Brunei Airlines, which bought two of these twin-turbofan transports as its initial equipment.

Braniff was the first airline to declare that it wanted
'No more plain planes'. This Boeing 727-200 leaves
little doubt that Air Jamaica feels the same way.

Now seen throughout the Air France fleet, its new
blue, white and red insignia was evolved initially for
French Concordes.

During its delivery flight, this first McDonnell Douglas DC-10 Srs 30 for Malaysian Airline System set a new point-to-point record by covering the 6,936.8 miles (11,163.7km) between Honolulu and Kuala Lumpur, Malaysia, in 12hr 26min 14.5sec non-stop, an average of 547.92mph (881.79km/h).

British Airways' insignia, seen here on a Super VC10 at London Heathrow, seems to blend features of the Union Jack and BOAC's old 'Speedbird'.
/ Peter J. Bish

Line-up of 747s for Aerolineas Argentinas,
Lufthansa, Alia Royal Jordanian Airline and Avianca
of Colombia, awaiting delivery at Boeing's Everett
plant. At rear is the 747-123 (NASA 905) from
which the Space Shuttle Orbiter was air-launched
during early flight trials.

Newcomer into the top ten of world aircraft
manufacturers, in terms of number of aircraft built
annually, is EMBRAER of Brazil. This EMB-110C
Bandeirante twin-turboprop transport is operated by
the Brazilian local-service operator TAM (Taxi Aéreo
Marilia).

Rare visitor to Fairoaks, Surrey, was this US-
registered Antonov An-2 biplane, built in Poland.
/ Peter J. Bish

Built in Belfast, the Shorts SD3-30 commuter transport is fast gaining favour with operators such as Golden West Airlines of California.

Like Japanese cars, the Mitsubishi MU-2 twin-turboprop utility transport has found a worldwide market. This MU-2N is one of the larger-capacity models, on which the main landing gear retracts into bulged fairings instead of into the fuselage.

One of the less familiar US four-seat light aircraft is
the Rockwell Commander 112TCA, turbocharged
version of the basic Commander 112B.

VFW-Fokker 614

Germany

Short-range airliner, in service.

Accommodation: Flight crew of 2, and 36–44 passengers.
Powered by: Two 7,760lb (3,520kg) st Rolls-Royce M.45H Mk 501 turbofans.
Span: 70ft 6½in (21.50m).
Length: 67ft 6in (20.60m).
Gross weight: 44,000lb (19,950kg).
Max payload: 17,547lb (7,976kg).
Max cruising speed: 457mph (735km/h) at 25,000ft (7,620m).
Range: 978 miles (1,574km) with max payload, no reserves.

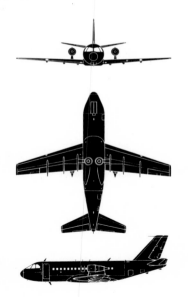

Development and Service:

The VFW-614, distinguished by its novel engine arrangement with over-wing nacelles, had been under development for several years when construction began in August 1968, following German government backing. Risk-sharing partners in the programme include Fokker-VFW in the Netherlands, SABCA and Fairey in Belgium and MBB in Germany. The first of three prototypes made its first flight at Bremen on July 14, 1971. It was lost in the following February, but two more prototypes flew on February 1 and October 10, 1972 respectively, and VFW-Fokker received a full production go-ahead from the Federal German government on December 13, 1972. A number of options for VFW-614s were announced, but few of these were, in the event, taken up and the first firm order proved to be that from Cimber Air of Denmark. German certification of the VFW-614 was obtained on August 23, 1974 and the first production aircraft flew on April 28, 1975, entering service with Cimber Air towards the end of the year. Other operators by mid-1977 were Air Alsace and TAT; the German government has ordered three for VIP duties. In mid-1977, VFW-Fokker and the Romanian government signed an agreement to set up a jointly-owned company, Romavia, to build 97 VFW-614s in Romania, for domestic use and export; three German-built VFW-614s were also being supplied to Romania.

Vickers (BAC) VC10 and Super VC10   UK

Medium /long-range airliner, in service.
Photo: V1103 VC10.
Silhouette and data: Super VC10.

Accommodation: Flight crew of 3 to 5, and up to 174 passengers.
Powered by: Four 22,500lb (10,205kg) st Rolls-Royce Conway 550 turbofans.
Span: 146ft 2in (44.55m).
Length: 171ft 8in (52.32m).
Gross weight: 335,000lb (151,950kg).
Max cruising speed: 568mph (914km /h) at 38,000ft (12,460m).
Typical range: 4,630 miles (7,450km) with max payload at 550mph (885km /h).

Development and Service:

Vickers' development of this 'second-generation' jet transport was begun to meet a BOAC requirement for an aeroplane to operate over the Empire routes, where long stages and hot and high airfields made operating conditions especially difficult. BOAC indicated, in May 1957, that it would order 35 of these aeroplanes, and a further development of the design made it possible to offer transatlantic capability by the time the contract was signed in January 1958. In June 1960, an enlarged version of the VC10 was announced, known as the Super VC10, and in 1961 BOAC announced that it had reduced its VC10 order to 12 (Model 1101) and would also take 30 Super VC10s with a 13ft longer fuselage, more fuel and higher weights. The BOAC contract for Super VC10s was eventually reduced to 17 (Model 1151) with deliveries stretched out until 1969. Other airline customers for VC10s and Super VC10s were BUA, Ghana Airways, and EAA. One of the Ghana Airways aircraft was leased to MEA and was destroyed in the Israeli attack on Beirut Airport. Laker Airways purchased the prototype VC10 early in 1968, following its modification to production standard as Model 1109, and sold it subsequently to BUA. One BOAC VC10 was sold to Nigeria Airways and was subsequently destroyed, and one BOAC Super was destroyed by hijackers at Dawson's Field in 1970. British Airways had retired its last Standard VC10s by the end of 1976, five of these having been sold to Gulf Air; but in 1977 it still had 15 Supers in its Overseas Division. Ghana Airways had one Standard in use, and East African still had four Supers.

Vickers Vanguard and Merchantman UK

Short/medium-range airliner and freighter, in service.
Photo: Type 952.
Data: Vanguard.
Silhouette: Merchantman.

Accommodation: Crew of 7, including cabin staff, and 76–139 passengers.
Powered by: Four 5,545ehp Rolls-Royce Tyne 512 turboprops.
Span: 118ft 7in (36.15m).
Length: 122ft 10½in (37.45m).
Gross weight: 146,500lb (66,448kg).
Max payload: 37,000lb (16,783kg).
Max cruising speed: 425mph (684km/h) at 20,000ft (6,100m).
Typical range: 1,830 miles (2,945km) with max payload at 420mph (676km/h).

Development and Service:

The Vanguard was evolved from a series of design studies to meet a BEA requirement for a 'big brother' to the Viscount. The design finally adopted, although new in almost every respect, relied heavily on Viscount design experience. The first Vanguard, a Vickers-owned prototype, flew for the first time on January 20, 1959, and was followed by the first of 20 ordered by BEA (G-APEA) on April 22, 1959. The first six aircraft for BEA were Type 951, with 4,985ehp Tyne 506 engines and 135,000lb (61,235kg) weight. They went into full service with BEA on March 1, 1961. Vickers built 23 Type 952s for TCA (Air Canada), with Tyne 512s and 146,500lb (66,448kg) weight. The first of these went into service on February 1, 1961. The BEA order was completed with 14 Type 953s, which had the higher weight and payload of the 952, but Tyne 506 engines. The first of these flew on May 1, 1961, and was in service on BEA routes by the end of the same month. In October 1968, BEA began a programme to convert nine Vanguards to Merchantman freighters, with cargo door and other modifications designed by Aviation Traders. The first conversion was flown at Southend on October 10, 1969 and five remained in service with British Airways in 1977, all passenger Vanguards having been retired. Air Canada has also retired its Vanguards, and the principal operator is Europe Aero Service, with 16 in use. Merpati Nusantara in Indonesia has three.

Vickers Viscount

UK

Short/medium-range airliner, in service.
Photo: Viscount V.814.
Data apply to Viscount 810.

Accommodation: Flight crew of 3–4, and 52–75 passengers.
Powered by: Four 1,990ehp Rolls-Royce Dart 525 turboprops.
Span: 93ft 8½in (28.56m).
Length: 85ft 8in (26.11m).
Gross weight: 72,500lb (32,886kg).
Max payload: 14,500lb (6,577kg).
Max cruising speed: 358mph (576km/h) at 15,000ft (4,575m).
Range: 1,760 miles (2,830km) with 14,500lb (6,575kg) payload at 343 mph (552km/h).

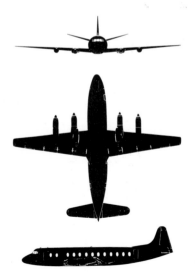

Development and Service:
The first Viscount, the Type 630 G-AHRF (first flown on July 16, 1948) was smaller than all examples which followed, but all the 700 Series are dimensionally similar to the prototype 700, G-AMAV (flown on August 28, 1950). Initial production aircraft had Dart 505s or 506s and operated at a lower gross weight. With Dart 510s, provision for slipper tanks on the wings and 64,500lb (29,250kg) weight, the type was known as the 700D. 285 Series 700s were ordered by airlines, in addition to several VIP and executive variants. Each initial-customer model was distinguished by a separate type number between 700 and 799. The 810 Series was developed later from the 700 Series, with greater length and more powerful engines. The first of these (G-AOYV) flew on December 23, 1957. The first of the 800 Series was the 802 for BEA (first flown on July 27, 1956); this had the same power plant as the 700D Series but the longer fuselage of the 810 Series, and was able to carry a bigger payload over shorter ranges. Large-scale production of the Viscount ended in 1959, but Vickers continued to work on a small quantity of Viscounts until the spring of 1964, the last aircraft on the line at Hurn being six for airline use in China. The grand total of all Viscount variants built was 444. Most major airline users of the Viscount have retired most or all of their fleets; but about 100 remain in airline service with subsequent owners. Others are used for executive transport by private companies, Governments and air forces.

Yakovlev Yak-40

USSR

Short-range jet airliner, in production and service.

Accommodation: Flight crew of 2, and 27–32 passengers.
Powered by: Three 3,300lb (1,500kg) st Ivchenko AI-25 turbofans.
Span: 82ft 0$\frac{1}{4}$in (25.00m).
Length: 66ft 9$\frac{1}{2}$in (20.36m).
Gross weight: 35,275lb (16,000kg).
Payload: 6,000lb (2,720kg).
Cruising speed: 292–342mph (470–550km/h).
Range: 1,118 miles (1,800km) with max payload (with reserves).

Development and Service:

First flown on October 21, 1966, the Yak-40 is the smallest of the current range of jet airliners manufactured in Russia. It is of particular interest as the first civil transport to come from the Yakovlev design bureau, after many years of specialisation on high-performance attack bombers and fighters. Use of three engines is also of interest in so small an aircraft; it can take off and climb on any two engines, and maintain height in cruising flight with two engines shut down. Production of the Yak-40 began in 1967, for Aeroflot use as a replacement for the several hundred Li-2s still in service. More than 200 were in service by April 1970, when production of 300 more was authorised, with a further 300 authorised by 1976. An executive version has also been displayed, primarily for the export market. Aertirrena in Italy acquired an agency to market the Yak-40 in Europe and took delivery of the first European-registered Yak-40 (I-JAKA) at the end of 1970; this company had three in service in 1976. Two have been supplied to Bakhtar Afghan Airlines, six to Balkan Bulgarian, five to General Air in Federal Germany, 11 to CSA and four to North Vietnam, with others in military service in various countries. During 1976, a Yak-40 was demonstrated in the UK and steps were being taken to obtain British certification in view of the interest shown by several UK operators. The practicability of fitting US engines for sale on the American market was also being investigated.

Yakovlev Yak-42

USSR

Short-to-medium-range airliner, under development.

Accommodation: Flight crew of 3–4. Either 100 or 120 passengers six-abreast in a single-class layout; typical mixed-class layout, 40 four-abreast and 60 six-abreast.
Powered by: Three 14,200lb (6,440kg) st Lotarev D-36 high by-pass turbofans.
Span: 112ft 2½in (34.20m).
Length: 119ft 4¼in (36.38m).
Gross weight: 114,640lb (52,000kg).
Max payload: 30,850lb (14,000kg).
Cruising speed: 510mph (820km/h).
Range: 1,150 miles (1,850km) with max payload.

Development and Service:

First news of the development of the Yak-42 was given in mid-1973, by which time a mock-up existed in Yakovlev's works near Moscow and detail design was under way. The aircraft is designed to operate into the less well-developed airfields in the Soviet Union, away from the trunk routes, with the ability to operate onto and off grass and to fly from runways less than 3,000ft (915m) in length. In overall configuration, the Yak-42 resembles the Yak-40, with three engines grouped in the tail; in passenger capacity it resembles the DC-9 Series 40 and 50. The fact that it has almost 50 per cent more power than the latter aircraft is indicative of the premium placed upon airfield performance. The Yak-42 is designed to airworthiness standards comparable with those of FAR 25 in the USA and is expected to be one of the major civil aircraft exports of the Soviet Union in the 'eighties, once Aeroflot's immediate needs have been met. The total domestic requirement is said to be for 2,000 aircraft of this type. The first Yak-42 prototype flew on March 7, 1975 and had a wing sweepback of 11 deg. The second aircraft, flown in April 1976, had 25 deg. of sweep-back and this standard applies to production aircraft, the first of which flew in spring 1977.

Part Two

Aerocom Skyliner

USA

Utility transport and commuter airliner, in production (original name: Volpar Centennial).

Accommodation: Crew of two and up to 19 passengers.
Powered by: Two 750shp Pratt & Whitney (Canada) PT6A-34 turboprops.
Span: 54ft 0in (16.47m).
Length: 54ft 4in (16.57m).
Gross weight: 12,500lb (5,575kg).
Cruising speed: Over 253mph (407km/h).

The Skyliner is a distant relative of the Beech 18, making use of the basic Model 18G or 18H fuselage with new front and rear sections that add 13ft 5in (4.1m) to the overall length. A new single tail unit, originally designed by Pacific Airmotive, is used, and a completely new wing with modified supercritical characteristics based on the GAW-2 series of aerofoils developed by NASA. A fully retractable tricycle undercarriage is fitted and provision made for large freight-loading doors in the rear fuselage. The first Skyliner flew at Reno, Nevada, in March 1977, followed by certification in May, by which time two more examples had flown and plans had been made to produce 15–20 a year.

Aérospatiale Corvette

France

Executive jet and air taxi, in service.
Data for SN 601.

Accommodation: Crew of 1 or 2, and 6 to 13 passengers.
Powered by: Two 2,300lb (1,043kg) st Pratt & Whitney JT15D-4 turbofans.
Span: 42ft 2½in (12.87m).
Length: 45ft 4½in (13.83m).
Gross weight: 13,890lb (6,300kg).
Max payload: 2,248lb (1,000kg).
Max cruising speed: 472mph (760km/h) at 30,000ft (9,144m).
Range: 910 miles (1,465km) with 12 passengers at 391mph (628km/h) (with reserves).

The Corvette is a multi-purpose light transport suitable for business use or as an air taxi, ambulance, freighter or training aircraft. The prototype (with JT15D-1 engines) made its first flight on July 16, 1970, but was destroyed in March 1971. It was followed by two pre-production models, the first of which flew on December 20, 1972, with JT15D-4 engines, and the first production example flew in November, 1973. Initial orders included four for Air Alpes, one for Air Alsace, one for *Protection Civile* and one for Africair; deliveries began in September 1974 following certification on May 28. Production ended in 1976 when 40 had been built.

Ahrens AR-404

USA

Utility transport, under development.

Accommodation: Crew of two and up to 30 passengers.
Powered by: Four 420eshp Allison 250-B17B turboprops.
Span: 66ft 0in (20.12m).
Length: 52ft 9in (16.08m).
Gross weight: About 17,000lb (7,710kg).
Max cruising speed: 195mph (315km/h).
Range: 978–1,473 miles (1,575–2,370km).

A prototype of the AR-404 light utility transport was designed and built by Ahrens Aircraft Corp at Oxnard, California, in 1976, and it made its first flight on December 1, 1976. After a brief period of flight testing in the USA, the prototype was transferred to Ramey AFB, Puerto Rico, where certification was to be completed and production launched. The Puerto Rican government was providing finance for an initial batch of 18 aircraft, the first of which was to fly in the late summer of 1977. The AR-404 is designed for civil or military use in the general category of a DC-3 replacement, featuring a rear-loading ramp and a rectangular section fuselage that can seat three-abreast or carry mixed loads of passengers and freight. Production aircraft, to which the data apply, have a 1ft (0.30m) greater span and are 4ft 5in (1.35m) longer than the prototype, with twice as many cabin windows.

American Jet Model 400 Hustler

USA

Business transport, under development.
Photo: Hustler mockup.

Accommodation: Crew of one or two, plus five passenger seats in cabin.
Powered by: One 850shp Pratt & Whitney PT6A-41 turboprop.
Span: 32ft 7½in (9.95m).
Length: 37ft 11½in (11.57m).
Gross weight: 6,500lb (2,948kg).
Max cruising speed: 380mph (610km/h).
Range: 2,970 miles (4,780km) at 343mph (552km/h).

The Hustler was conceived by American Jet Industries as a new-type business aircraft, with a basic turboprop engine plus a turbojet in the rear fuselage to provide power for emergency use. By mid-1977 the original turbojet had been superseded by a Williams Research WR19-3-1 turbofan, giving 718lb (325kg) st and now available optionally. The prototype Model 400 Hustler flew for the first time in January 1978, powered by the turboprop only and the aircraft will enter production in this form. Customers will have the option of adding the WR 19-3-1 turbofan retrospectively, to give the aircraft improved STOL take-off and climb performance and a max cruising speed of 435 mph (700km/h). The twin-engined Hustler will be designated Model 400A. Orders totalled 51 in June 1977.

Antonov An-2   USSR /Poland

General-purpose and utility transport.
Data for An-2P built in Poland.
Photo: WSK-Mielec An-2R.

Accommodation: One or two pilots, plus 12 adult passengers and 2 small children.
Powered by: One 1,000hp Shvetsov ASh-62IR piston-engine.
Span: 59ft 8¼in (18.18m).
Length: 40ft 8¼in (12.40m).
Gross weight: 12,125lb (5,500kg).
Normal cruising speed: 115mph (185km/h).
Range: 560 miles (900km) with 1,102lb (500kg) payload.

Designed primarily for agricultural duties, the An-2 appeared in 1947 and has subsequently been adopted for various utilitarian tasks, more than 5,000 having been built in the Soviet Union by 1962. The basic light transport for Aeroflot was the An-2P and the initial agricultural version was the An-2S. The latter was superseded by the An-2M with a number of external changes and improved performance. Other versions included the An-2V floatplane and An-2L water-bomber, also a floatplane. With the local name of Fong Chou, the An-2 was built in China, where the first example flew in December 1957. In Poland, the type has been in large-scale production since 1960 and over 7,200 had been built by 1977, at which time the WSK-Mielec factory was the sole source. Polish variants have included the An-2R (similar to Soviet An-2S), the An-2S ambulance, the An-2T (basic passenger or freight version), the An-2P passenger carrier and An-2M (as An-2V).

Antonov An-14   USSR

General-purpose light transport, in production and service.

Accommodation: Pilot and up to 8 passengers.
Powered by: Two 300hp Ivchenko AI-14RF piston-engines.
Span: 72ft 2in (21.99m).
Length: 37ft 6¼in (11.44m).
Gross weight: 7,935lb (3,600kg).
Cruising speed: 112mph (180km/h) at 6,560ft (2,000m).
Range: 404 miles (650km) with max payload.

First flown on March 15, 1958, the An-14 underwent a prolonged flight development and improvement programme, eventually going into service in the form illustrated during 1965. Changes since the prototype appeared include the use of uprated engines (the 260hp AI-14R was used initially), an enlarged wing and revised fins and rudders. The An-14 is used by Aeroflot for air-taxi, ambulance (six stretchers), and agricultural duties and can be operated on floats. An executive version has been developed, seating five passengers. More than 300 An-14s had been built by 1976, including some for the armed forces of the Soviet Union, its allies and friends.

Antonov An-28

USSR

General-purpose light transport, in production and service.

Accommodation: Flight crew of one or two and up to 15 passengers.
Powered by: Two 960hp Glushenkov TVD-10A turboprops.
Span: 72ft 2in (21.99m).
Length: 42ft 7in (12.98m).
Gross weight: 12,566lb (5,700kg).
Max cruising speed: 217 mph (350km/h).
Range: 620 miles (1,000km).

First flown in September 1969, but revealed outside Russia only in 1972, the An-14M was a derivative of the earlier An-14, from which it differed in having 810shp Isotov TVD-850 turboprops and a new, larger fuselage. In the course of prototype flight trials, various changes were made: the undercarriage, retractable on the first An-14M, is now fixed, and the size and shape of the vertical tail surfaces has been varied. With the definitive designation An-28, the type was re-engined with TVD-10As in 1975 and was expected to enter production as a replacement for the An-2 biplane.

Beagle B.206

UK

Business twin, in service.
Data apply to B.206S.
Photo: B.206 Series I.

Accommodation: 5 to 8 seats.
Powered by: Two 340hp Rolls-Royce/Continental GTS10-520 tubo-supercharged piston-engines.
Span: 45ft 9½in (13.96m).
Length: 33ft 8in (10.26m).
Gross weight: 7,500lb (3,400kg).
Cruising speed: 187–209mph (301–336km/h).
Max range: 1,600 miles (2,575km) at 187mph (301km/h) (no reserves).

First aircraft of original design produced by Beagle, the prototype B.206X (G-ARRM) had 260hp Continental IO-470-A engines and spanned 38ft (11.58m). Deliveries of production 5/8-seat B.206Cs began in 1965, together with the first of 20 similar B.206Rs for the RAF, which named them Basset C.C. Mk 1. The B.206S (or Series II) with supercharged engines first flew on June 23, 1965, and features an enlarged rear door as well as other refinements. Forty civil Beagle 206s were sold and to these have been added most of the Bassets, sold by the RAF in 1975.

Beechcraft Model 18   USA

Light transport, in service.
Photo: Beech 18S.
Data for Super H18.

Accommodation: 2 pilots, and 5–7 passengers.
Powered by: Two 450hp Pratt & Whitney R-985-AN-14B piston-engines.
Span: 49ft 8in (15.14m).
Length: 35ft 2½in (10.70m).
Gross weight: 9,900lb (4,490kg).
Max cruising speed: 220mph (354km/h) at 10,000ft (3,050m).
Range: 1,530 miles (2,460km).

First flown on January 15, 1937, the Beech 18 remained in production continuously until the end of 1969, almost certainly a record of longevity for any aircraft type; over 9,000 were built. The last three aircraft left Wichita for Japan Air Lines on November 26, 1969. Many changes were introduced in the Super 18 series of post-war business aircraft, over 700 of which were built, and a Volpar nosewheel gear was made available as an alternative to the tail-down type. The Beech 18 also provided the basis of a number of major modification schemes, with turboprop engines and other features. Resulting variants included the Dumodliner, lengthened to carry 14 passengers; the PAC Tradewind with single fin and rudder; and the turboprop Volpar Turbo 18 and Turboliner (see page 104), all with Volpar nosewheel gear; and the Hamilton Westwind (see page 89), usually with original tail-down undercarriage.

Beechcraft Model 76 Duchess   USA

Light twin transport, in production.

Accommodation: Pilot plus three passengers.
Powered by: Two 180hp Lycoming O-360 piston-engines.
Span: 38ft 0in (11.59m).
Length: 29ft 5in (8.96m).
Gross weight:
Cruising speed: 185mph (298km/h).
Range: Over 800 miles (1,287km).

Beech Aircraft Corp developed the Model 76 under the project designation PD 289 during 1974 as an addition to its twin-engined range of aircraft at the lighter end of the scale, providing competition for the Piper Seneca and Cessna 310. Following the adoption of a T-tail for the Beech Super King Air 200, this same feature was used on the PD 289, which first flew in the late summer of 1974 with 160hp engines. After 180hp engines had been substituted, Beech decided to launch production of the new light twin as the Model 76 Duchess, first deliveries being scheduled for the end of 1977. More than 200 Model 76s were ordered by Beech distributors at the annual international sales meeting in 1976.

Beechcraft Baron

USA

Business twin, in production and service.
Photo: Baron B55.
Data: Baron 58.

Accommodation: 4–6 seats.
Powered by: Two 285hp Continental IO-520-C piston-engines.
Span: 37ft 10in (11.53m).
Length: 29ft 10in (9.09m).
Gross weight: 5,400lb (2,449kg).
Cruising speed: 207–230mph (333–370km/h).
Cruising range: 1,212 miles (1,950km).

Beech introduced the Model 95-55 Baron in November 1960 to succeed the lower-powered Model 95 Travel Air (719 built), which had an unswept fin and rudder. Originally a 4/5-seater, the Baron evolved into the 4/6-seat B, C, D and E55, with more powerful engines. Introduced in late 1969, the Baron 58 is 10in (25cm) longer and has the same engines as the E55. Subsequently, the pressurised Baron 58P and turbo-supercharged Baron 58TC have been added to the range. Over 4,400 Barons of all types had been built by October 1977.

Beechcraft Duke

USA

Business twin, in production and service.
Data for B60.

Accommodation: 4–6 persons in individual seats.
Powered by: Two 380hp Lycoming TIO-541-E1C4 piston-engines.
Span: 39ft 3in (11.96m).
Length: 33ft 10in (10.31m).
Gross weight: 6,775lb (3,073kg).
Cruising speed: 197–278mph (317–447km/h).
Typical cruising range: 1,175 miles (1,891km) at 15,000ft, (4,570m).

First flown on December 29, 1966, the Duke was designed to complete the Beech twin-engined range and fits between the Baron light twin and the heavier family of Queen Airs. It is pressurised for operation above 20,000ft and has turbo-supercharged engines. Deliveries began early in 1968, following certification on February 1, and 403 had been built by January 1977. The current model is designated B60 and introduced a number of refinements including an improved pressurisation system.

Beechcraft Twin Bonanza

USA

Light business twin, in service.
Photo: E50.
Data for J50.

Accommodation: 6 seats.
Powered by: Two 340hp Lycoming IGSO-480-A1B6 piston-engines.
Span: 45ft 11½in (13.99m).
Length: 31ft 6¼in (9.61m).
Gross weight: 7,300lb (3,311kg).
Cruising speed: 172–223mph (277–359km/h).
Max range: 1,650 miles (2,655km).

The first example of the Twin Bonanza was flown on November 15, 1949, as a straightforward development of the Bonanza (page 113) and became the first light twin of modern configuration to achieve production status after the War. The early models had 260hp engines, successive development bringing 275hp, 295hp and eventually 340hp engines. The final production version, J50, had a more pointed nose than its predecessors, and other refinements. The type eventually gave way to the Travel Air and Baron after 974 had been built. Modernised variants include the Excalibur 800, a Twin Bonanza D50 with 400hp Lycoming IO-720 engines and other refinements.

Beechcraft Queen Air

USA

Business twin, in production and service.
Photo: Queen Air B80.
Data for Model B80.

Accommodation: Crew of 1 or 2 and 4–9 passengers.
Powered by: Two 380hp Lycoming IGSO-540-A1D piston-engines.
Span: 50ft 3in (15.32m).
Length: 35ft 6in (10.82m).
Gross weight: 8,800lb (3,992kg).
Cruising speed: 183–224mph (294–360km/h).
Max range: 1,517 miles (2,441km).

The first Queen Airs were 6/9-seaters designated Model 65 (first flight August 28, 1958), followed by A65s with swept-back fins; both had 340hp Lycoming IGSO-480-A1E6 engines. Queen Air 70s had greater span and the same power plant as the A65s. Production of these models ended in 1971 with a total of 444 built, including 71 military U-8Fs, and some 11-seat Queen Airliner versions. A prototype Queen Air 80 flew on June 22, 1961 with more power and went into production as the A80 and B80 with increased span. Over 500 of the Queen Air 80 series, including Queen Airliners, had been built by early 1977. Excalibur Aviation offer a modified version of the Queen Air 65 and 80 as the Queenaire 800, with 400hp Lycoming IO-720 engines and other refinements.

69

Beechcraft King Air   USA

Business twin and third-level airliner, in production and service.
Photo: King Air B100.
Data: King Air B100.

Accommodation: 2 pilots and up to 13 passengers.
Powered by: Two 715shp Garrett AiResearch TPE331-6-252B turboprops.
Span: 45ft 10½in (13.98m).
Length: 39ft 11¼in (12.17m).
Gross weight: 11,800lb (5,352kg).
Max cruising speed: 306mph (493km/h) at 10,000ft (3,050m).
Cruising range: 1,575 miles (2,438km).

Beech developed the pressurised King Air as an outgrowth of the piston-engined Queen Air, by way of the military NU-8F, which had PT6A turboprops. A production prototype of the commercial model flew on January 20, 1964, and entered production during the same year as the Model 90 with PT6A-6 engines. A switch to -20 engines was made in the Model A90, announced in 1966. The current King Air C90 is the economy member of the family, with 550shp PT6A-21 engines, a span of 50ft 3in (15.32m), length of 35ft 6in (10.82m) and gross weight of 9,650lb (4,377kg). The King Air 100 appeared in 1969 with 680shp PT6A-28 engines and dimensions as quoted alongside. The same PT6A-28 engines crossed with the earlier airframe produced the King Air E90 in 1972; TPE331 engines in the A100 airframe produced the B100 in 1975. The C100, introduced in 1978, has 750shp PT6A-135s.

Beechcraft Super King Air 200   USA

Business transport, in production and service.

Accommodation: Two seats on flight deck and 6–8 passengers in the cabin.
Powered by: Two 850shp Pratt & Whitney PT6A-41 turboprops.
Span: 54ft 6in (16.6m).
Length: 43ft 10in (13.36m).
Gross weight: 12,500lb (5,670kg).
Max cruising speed: 320mph (515km/h) at 25,000ft (7,620m).
Range: 1,370–2,172 miles (2,204–3,495km).

The Super King Air was developed by Beech (with the engineering designation of Model 101) over a period of four years and was marketed as an addition to the King Air range, starting in 1974. Compared with the King Air (see above) the Super has more powerful engines, moved out from the fuselage sides to reduce cabin sound levels, a T-tail, lengthened fuselage and increased wing span, more fuel capacity and a higher cabin pressurisation level. Two prototypes were used for flight development, first flights being made on October 27 and December 15, 1972 respectively. FAA certification was obtained on December 14, 1973. Deliveries totalled 205 civil and 55 military Super King Airs by early 1977.

Beechcraft 99   USA

Light transport and third-level airliner, in production and service.
Data for B99.

Accommodation: Pilot and 15 passengers.
Powered by: Two 680shp Pratt & Whitney PT6A-27 turboprops.
Span: 45ft 10½in (14.00m).
Length: 44ft 6¾in (13.58m).
Gross weight: 10,900lb (4,944kg).
Max cruising speed: 283mph (455km/h).
Max range: 838 miles (1,348km).

Beech Aircraft developed the Model 99 from the Queen Air by lengthening the fuselage and fitting turboprop engines. The long-fuselage prototype first flew, with piston-engines, in December 1965 and with the new engines in July 1966. A production prototype flew early in 1968 and deliveries began on May 2 of that year, with 550hp PT6A-20 engines. The Model 99A and A99A introduced the PT6A-27 engines derated to 550shp, and the B99 followed, with the same engines fully rated. Nearly 200 have been built.

Britten-Norman BN-2 Islander   UK

Light feeder-line transport, in production and service.
Data for BN-2A.

Accommodation: Pilot and up to 9 passengers.
Powered by: Two 260hp Lycoming O-540-E4C5 piston-engines.
Span: 49ft 0in (14.94m).
Length: 35ft 7¾in (10.86m).
Gross weight: 6,300lb (2,857kg).
Cruising speed: 160mph (257km/h).
Max range: 1,193 miles (1,920km).

Over 750 of these simple and sturdy light transports had been ordered by September 1976. The prototype first flew on June 13, 1965, with 210hp Continental IO-360-B engines, but production

aircraft, the first of which flew on August 20, 1966, had 260hp Lycomings as standard equipment. The BN2A, starting with the 25th aircraft, has increased payload and gross weight, and is available in several configurations, the most distinctive of which has extra fuel in tanks forming extensions to the wing-tips. Also available are a 'hot and high' version with 300hp Lycoming IO-540-K1B5 engines, and a supercharged version with TIO-540-H engines rated at 270hp each. Other optional modifications include a longer nose with extra baggage space, crop-spraying or dusting equipment, a water-bombing installation, amphibious floats or skis. Islander production was based originally in the Isle of Wight, later being transferred to Belgium, with a licence production line in Romania and another in the Philippines.

Britten-Norman Turbo-Islander UK

Light general-purpose transport, under development.
Data for BN-2A-41.

Accommodation: Pilot and up to nine passengers.
Powered by: Two 600shp Avco Lycoming LTP101 turboprops.
Span: 53ft 0in (16.15m).
Length: 39ft 5¼in (12.02m).
Gross weight: 7,300lb (3,311kg).
Cruising speed: 220mph (354km/h).
Max range: 783 miles (1,260km).

Development of a turboprop version of the basic Islander was announced towards the end of 1975 and a prototype first flew on April 6, 1977. An increase in the gross weight has required some structural strengthening of the wing and fuselage, and of the landing gear. The Turbo-Islander has the lengthened nose introduced on some models of the Islander, and can have the extended fuel-carrying wingtips; designations of the versions with standard and extended tips are BN-2A-40 and BN-2A-41 respectively.

Britten-Norman BN-2A Mk III Trislander UK

Light feeder-line transport, in production and service.
Data for BN-2A Mk III-2.

Accommodation: 1 or 2 crew, and 16-17 passengers.
Powered by: Three 260hp Lycoming O-540-E4C5 piston-engines.
Span: 53ft 0in (16.15m).
Length: 47ft 6¼in (14.48m).
Gross weight: 10,000lb (4,536kg).
Max cruising speed: 166mph (267km/h).
Max range: 1,000 miles (1,610km).

Britten-Norman developed the Mk III Islander by adding a third engine and extending the fuselage.

The extra length is provided by inserting a 7ft 6in (2.29m) portion of standard parallel-section fuselage, and the third engine is located in a nacelle on the fin. Apart from some structural strengthening, the remainder of the airframe remains substantially unchanged. The second prototype Islander (G-ATWU) was converted to this configuration and flew as the Islander III prototype (now named Trislander) on September 11, 1970. A production prototype Trislander flew on March 6, 1971, and deliveries began in June that year. Production was transferred to Belgium in 1973 after the Fairey Group acquired Britten-Norman. Over 40 had been ordered by mid-1976, including some Mk III-2 versions with lengthened nose and extra baggage space.

Canadair CL-215

Canada

Water-bomber and general-purpose amphibian, in production and service.

Accommodation: Crew of 2—4 and water tanks or up to 19 passengers.
Powered by: Two 2,100hp Pratt & Whitney R-2800-83AM-12AD/CA3 piston-engines.
Span: 93ft 10in (28.60m).
Length: 65ft 0¼ in (19.82m).
Gross weight: 43,500lb (19,728kg).
Cruising speed: 181mph (291km/h) at 10,000ft (3,050m).
Range: 1,405 miles (2,260km) with 3,500lb (1,587kg) payload.

The CL-215 was evolved as a specialised water-bomber, following several years' close study by Canadair of the requirements for this type of operation. In the water-bomber role the aircraft can carry 12,000lb (5,440kg) of water in a fuselage tank which can be emptied in less than a second, and refilled in 12 seconds during a high-speed taxi across a lake. The prototype CL-215 made its first flight on October 23, 1967 and the first four of 19 purchased by the French *Protection Civile* went into use during 1969. Fifteen have been delivered to the Ontario Provincial Government, 10 for use in Spain, including eight with search and rescue duties with nose radar, and eight have gone to the Greek Air Force.

Canadair CL-600 Challenger

Canada

Business twin-jet and light transport, under development.

Accommodation: Flight crew of two and 10—30 passengers according to rôle.
Powered by: Two 7,500lb (3,405kg) st Avco Lycoming ALF 502 turbofans.
Span: 61ft 10in (18.85m).
Length: 68ft 6in (20.88m).
Gross weight: 32,500lb (14,740kg).
Cruising speed: 562mph (904km/h).
Range: 3,700 miles (5,926km) with eight passengers.

The original version of this aircraft, known as the LearStar 600, was designed by William P Lear in the USA in 1974/75, and an option on design and manufacturing rights was acquired by Canadair in mid-1976. Following an extensive market survey, some re-design of the airframe and final selection of the power plant, Canadair received Canadian government approval on October 29, 1976 to proceed with full-scale development and production of what is now named the Challenger. This is intended primarily for the top end of the biz-jet market and also has applications in the third level/commuter market. By late 1977, more than 100 firm orders for Challengers had been placed, including five freighters for Federal Express, a small-package cargo transporter in the USA. First flight was set for early 1978, with initial certificated deliveries in early summer 1979.

Canadian Car and Foundry Norseman   Canada

Utility transport, in service.
Data for Norseman V.

Accommodation: Pilot and 7–9 passengers.
Powered by: One 600hp Pratt & Whitney S3H1 or R-1340-AN-1 Wasp piston-engine.
Span: 51ft 8in (15.74m).
Length: 33ft 4in (10.16m).
Gross weight: 7,400lb (3,357kg).
Cruising speed: 141mph (227km/h).
Range: 464 miles (747km).

The rugged Norseman was designed in 1934 specifically for Canadian 'bush' flying, and a prototype flew in 1935 with a 450hp engine. Pre-war production models were the Norseman II and IV, built by the Noorduyn company, which also produced 746 of these aircraft for the USAAF during the war, with the designation UC-64. In 1946, CCF acquired the design and produced an improved version, the Norseman V, until 1950, by which time about 850 of all models had been built. Many still operate in Canada, often on floats or skis.

Cessna Stationair and Skywagon   USA

Single-engined utility aircraft, in production and service.
Photo: Skywagon 207.
Data for Model 206 Stationair.

Accommodation: Pilot and up to five passengers.
Powered by: One 300hp Continental IO-520-F flat-six piston engine.
Span: 35ft 10in (10.92m).
Length: 28ft 0in (8.53m).
Gross weight: 3,600lb (1,633kg).
Cruising speed: 169mph (272km/h).
Range: 518–869 miles (833–1,398km).

The Cessna U206 and turbo-charged TU206 (with 285hp Continental TSIO-520-C engine) were originally known as Skywagons but were renamed to distinguish them from the smaller Model 185 Skywagon (see page 119). They incorporate double cargo doors to facilitate freight loading. By early 1976, 3,724 Model 206s had been delivered, including 643 *de luxe* versions known as Super Skylanes, no longer in production. The Model 207 Skywagon and T207 Turbo-Skywagon (the latter with 300hp Continental TSIO-520-G) are generally similar but have a lengthened centre fuselage and can seat up to seven including the pilot. The prototype Model 207 flew on May 11, 1968, and over 320 have been built.

Cessna 310 /340　　　　　　　　　　USA

Business twin, in production and service.
Data for Model 340.
Photo: Model 340.

Accommodation: 5 or 6 seats.
Powered by: Two 285hp Continental TSIO-520-B piston-engines.
Span: 38ft 1½in (11.62m).
Length: 34ft 4in (10.46m).
Gross weight: 5,975lb (2,710kg).
Cruising speed: 221–241mph (356–388km/h).
Max range: 1,640 miles (2,640km) (no reserves).

Cessna's popular Model 310 made its first flight on January 3, 1953, and went into production in 1954, since when more than 4,000 have been built. Early models had an unswept fin; the present swept fin was introduced on the Model 310D in 1960 and the current 310P has 285hp Continental IO-520-M engines and a ventral fin. The similar Turbo-System T310 has turbo-supercharged TS10-520-B engines. This variant took the place of the Model 320 Skyknight, production of which ended in 1968 after 575 had been delivered. In 1972, Cessna introduced the pressurised Model 340, derived from the basic 310 design with the Model 414's wing and Turbo-System 310's power plant. The Model 340A, which followed in 1976, has 310hp Continental TSIO-520-N engines.

Cessna 337 Skymaster　　　　　　USA

Light transport, in production and service.
Photo and data: Pressurised Skymaster.

Accommodation: 4–6 seats.
Powered by: Two 225hp Continental TSIO-360-C piston-engines.
Span: 38ft 2in (11.63m).
Length: 29ft 10in (9.09m).
Gross weight: 4,700lb (2,132kg).
Cruising speed: 228mph (367km/h) at 16,000ft (4,877m).
Range: 1,320–1,810 miles (2,124–2,913km).

The prototype of this revolutionary 'push-and-pull' twin-boomed four-seat business aircraft flew on February 28, 1961, and production deliveries began in May 1963. Powered by two 210hp Continental IO-360 engines, the Skymaster combined all the advantages of a normal light twin with simpler handling characteristics, especially after a failure of one engine. The original Model 336 Skymaster had a fixed undercarriage and 195 were built. The Model 337, with retractable undercarriage, replaced it in 1965 and introduced a number of other new features. A cargo pack can be carried externally under the fuselage. The Turbo-System Skymaster, with turbo-supercharged engines, was announced in April 1967, and over 2,500 Model 337s had been built by 1976, including 510 O-2 military versions. Added to the range in 1972 was a pressurised version, data for which are quoted here. Reims Aviation assembles the standard versions in France. In addition, it offers a STOL version, with special high-lift flaps, as the FA-337.

Cessna 401 /402　　　　　　　　　USA

Business twin and air taxi, in production and service.
Data for Model 402B.
Photo: Model 402 Businessliner.

Accommodation: Up to 10 seats.
Powered by: Two 300hp Continental TSIO-520-E turbo-supercharged piston-engines.
Span: 39ft 10½in (12.15m).
Length: 36ft 1in (11.0m).
Gross weight: 6,300lb (2,858kg).
Cruising speed: 215–240mph (346–386km/h) at 20,000ft (6,100m).
Range: 633–1,639 miles (1,018–2,637km).

Cessna announced these additions to its twin-engined range late in 1966, having flown the 401 prototype on August 26, 1965. They were closely related to the Model 411, which was subsequently dropped, but are lighter and cheaper. The 6/8-seat Model 401 was aimed specifically at the executive market and production ended in 1973 with more than 400 built. The Model 402 Businessliner and Utililiner, with similar dimensions, weights and performance, has a re-designed interior for use as a 9/10-seat commuter or for light freighting. The Model 402B, introduced in 1971, has a longer nose than the original Model 401. Over 700 have been built to date. American Jet Industries produced a small number of turboprop conversions of the Model 402, with 400shp Allison 250-B17 engines, as the Turbo Star 402A.

Cessna 404 Titan　　　　　　　　　USA

Business twin and commuter / light freighter, in production and service.

Accommodation: Up to 10 including pilot.
Powered by: Two 375hp Continental GTSIO-520-M turbo-supercharged piston-engines.
Span: 46ft 0in (14.02m).
Length: 39ft 5in (12.04m).
Gross weight: 8,300lb (3,765kg).
Cruising speed: 246mph (396km/h) at 20,000ft (6,100m).
Range: 1,020–2,060 miles (1,641–3,315km).

The Model 404 Titan joined the Cessna range of business twins during 1976, being similar in general size and characteristics to the Model 421 but without cabin pressurisation. Consequently, the type was expected to appeal more especially to the commuter/air cargo market, with its large cabin and its ability to fly good loads out of short, rough fields. A large cargo door was available as an option, permitting the loading of freight containers or items of unusual size. Two versions of the Model 404 were offered: the Ambassador for the business/executive market and the Courier for the commuter and freighting operator. In common with other recent Cessna types, the Model 404 makes use of a bonded wing structure.

Cessna 411 /414 /421   USA

Business twin and air taxi, in production and service.
Photo: Model 414.
Data: Model 421C Golden Eagle.

Accommodation: 6–8 seats.
Powered by: Two 375hp Continental GTSIO-520-H turbo-supercharged piston-engines.
Span: 41ft 1½in (12.53m).
Length: 36ft 4½in (11.09m).
Gross weight: 7,450lb (3,379kg).
Max cruising speed: 276mph (445km/h) at 25,000ft (7,620m).
Range: 1,080–1,716 miles (1,740–2,761km).

First flown on July 18, 1962, the Cessna 411 entered production as the largest member of the Cessna range and deliveries began in February 1965. Production ended in June 1968, when 301 had been built, and the top end of the range was filled instead by the Model 421 which was similar but with pressurisation. The 421B had tip-tanks but was followed in 1976 by the 421C with a new wing incorporating extra fuel capacity. First flown on November 1, 1968, the Model 414 combines the pressurised fuselage and tail unit of the Model 421 with the wing and power plant of the Model 401. Cessna has sold over 1,000 Model 421s to date, and about 400 Model 414s.

Cessna 441 Conquest   USA

Business twin and light transport, in production.

Accommodation: Up to 10 including pilot.
Powered by: Two 620shp Garrett AiResearch TPE331-8-401 turboprops.
Span: 49ft 4in (15.05m).
Length: 39ft 0½in (11.89m).
Gross weight: 9,850lb (4,468kg).
Cruising speed: 328mph (528km/h).
Range: 2,106 miles (3,389km) with five passengers at 33,000ft (10,058m) at an average 312mph (502km/h).

The Cessna 441 was first flown on 26 August 1975 and was added to the company's range of business twins in 1977 as its first turboprop aircraft. Of typical Cessna configuration and similar in overall appearance to the 404 Titan, it originally had an almost identical wing, but after initial specifications had been released, the aspect ratio was increased by adding 18in (46cm) to each semi-span; this also allowed an increase in fuel capacity and improved the service ceiling and cruising speed. The Conquest's cabin is pressurised to a differential of 6.3psi (0.44kg/cm²), permitting a comfortable cruising ceiling of 33,000ft (10,058m).

Cessna 500 Citation I & II

USA

Business jet transport, in production and service.
Data for Citation I.
Photo: Citation II.

Accommodation: Crew of 2 and up to 6 passengers.
Powered by: Two 2,200lb (998kg) st Pratt & Whitney JT15D-1A turbofans.
Span: 47ft 1in (14.36m).
Length: 43ft 6in (13.26m).
Gross weight: 12,850lb (5,834kg).
Max cruising speed: 404mph (650km/h).
Normal range: 1,540 miles (2,478km).

Cessna announced preliminary details of its first jet-powered design for the commercial market in October 1968, when the type was known as the Fanjet 500. The prototype made its first flight on September 15, 1969, and production deliveries began late in September 1971 following certification to FAR Pt 25 standards. Engines were JT15D-1s and span 43ft 9in (13.33m). After production of 349 Citations, a switch was made at the end of 1976 to the Citation I with increased span and uprated engines. The Citation II, for introduction early in 1978, has a stretched fuselage for 8–12 seats, span of 51ft 8½in (15.76m), and 2,500lb (1,135kg) st JT15D-4 engines; the prototype first flew on 31 January 1977.

Cessna Citation III

USA

Business jet transport, under development.

Accommodation: Crew of 2 and up to 13 passengers.
Powered by: Two 3,650lb (1,655kg) st Garrett AiResearch TFE 731-3 turbofans.
Span: 53ft 3½in (16.25m).
Length: 51ft 7in (15.73m).
Gross weight: 17,000lb (7,711kg).
Max cruising speed: 540mph (868km/h).
Range: 2,190–2,875 miles (3,525–4,625km) (with reserves).

Cessna announced in late-1976 that it would proceed with development of the Citation III for 1980 deliveries, after earlier studies for Citation derivatives that had included the Citation 600 and the three-engined straightwing Citation 700. The Citation III is larger than those projects, with stand-up aisle height, and retains little of the basic Citation beyond the name. The wing has a super-critical section and, with the different turbofan engines, helps to give the aircraft an intercontinental range.

Dassault-Breguet Falcon 10 (Mystère 10) France

Business jet transport, in production and service.

Accomodation: Crew of 2, and 4–7 passengers.
Powered by: Two 3,230lb (1,465kg) st Garrett AiResearch TFE 731-2 turbofans.
Span: 42ft 11in (13.08m).
Length: 45ft 5in (13.85m).
Gross weight: 18,740lb (8,500kg).
Max cruising speed: 572mph (920km/h).
Range: 2,210 miles (3,555km) with 4 passengers (with reserves).

Development of the Mystère 10 was first announced by Dassault in June 1969, when the type was known as the Minifalcon. As that name suggested, it is a scaled-down version of the Mystère/Falcon 20, of about three-quarters the power and two-thirds the weight. First flight of the prototype was made on December 1, 1970, with 2,954lb st General Electric CJ610-6 engines, pending availability of the AiResearch turbofans planned for production models and fitted in the second prototype, flown on October 15, 1971. This aircraft subsequently became a test-bed for the Larzac, flying with one of these engines (and one TFE 731) on May 22, 1973. Falcon Jet Corporation markets the Falcon 10 in North America and placed an initial order for 40 with options on 120 more. By late 1977, over 140 Falcon 10s had been delivered.

Dassault-Breguet Falcon 20 (Mystère 20) France

Business jet transport, in production and service.
Data for Falcon F.

Accommodation: Crew of 2, and up to 14 passengers.
Powered by: Two 4,315lb (1,960kg) st General Electric CF700-2D-2 turbofans.
Span: 53ft 6in (16.30m).
Length: 56ft 3in (17.15m).
Gross weight: 28,660lb (13,000kg).
Cruising speed: 466–536mph (750–862km/h).
Max range: 2,220 miles (3,570km) with 1,600lb (725kg) payload (with reserves).

Construction of a prototype Mystère 20 executive jet transport was started by Dassault in January 1962, and the first flight was made on May 4, 1963, with 3,300lb st Pratt & Whitney JT12A-8 turbojets; a switch to G.E. turbofans was made later, and the prototype flew in this form on July 10, 1964. The aircraft is known in the USA, and generally outside of France, as the Falcon. The Standard Falcon was followed by the C, D, E and F versions, the latest of these having uprated engines, more fuel, new high-lift devices and other improvements. Several special-purpose versions have been produced, and a Falcon G was launched late in 1976, with 5,050lb (2,250kg) st AiResearch ATF 3-6 turbofans. Some 430 Falcon 20s had been ordered by mid-1977.

Dassault-Breguet Falcon 50 (Mystère 50) France

Business jet transport, under development.

Accommodation: Flight crew of two and up to ten passengers.
Powered by: Three 3,700lb (1,680kg) st Garrett AiResearch TFE 731-3 turbofans.
Span: 61ft 10½in (18.86m).
Length: 60ft 9in (18.52m).
Gross weight: 37,480lb (17,000kg).
Cruising speed: 541mph (870km/h).
Range: 3,450 miles (5,560km) at Mach 0.80 with eight passengers.

The Dassault-Breguet company decided to add the Falcon 50 to its range of biz-jets during 1974, finding that the market for such an aircraft was more promising than for the larger Falcon 30 twinjet, which was then dropped. The Falcon 50, a prototype of which made its first flight on November 7, 1976, uses many components of the Falcon 20, having the same basic fuselage cross-section, but introduced an improved wing, and a third engine in the rear fuselage. The latter is lengthened, to provide extra space for fuel and baggage; passenger accommodation remains unchanged, and the Falcon 50 differs from the 20 primarily in having much greater range and somewhat better economics. Further improvement in performance followed replacement of the original wing with one of supercritical aerofoil section, with which the prototype resumed flight trials on May 6, 1977. Forty Falcon 50s had been ordered by mid-1977.

De Havilland DHC-2 Beaver and Turbo-Beaver Canada

Light utility transport, in service.
Data: DHC-2 Mk. III Turbo-Beaver.
Photo: Beaver Mk. I.

Accommodation: Pilot and up to 10 passengers.
Powered by: One 578ehp Pratt & Whitney PT6A-6 or -20 turboprop.
Span: 48ft 0in (14.64m).
Length: 35ft 3in (10.75m).
Gross weight: 5,370lb (2,435kg).
Cruising speed: 140–157mph (225–252km/h).
Range: 260–677 miles (418–1,090km) (with reserves).

The Beaver was the first of de Havilland's family of STOL utility aircraft, and made its first flight in August 1947. It was designed particularly to meet local Canadian requirements for a rugged 'bush' aircraft, but found a wide market overseas. A total of 1,657 Mk 1s were built, with 450hp P&W R-985 engine, including 968 for the US Army and USAF and 46 for the British Army. A single Beaver Mk II had an Alvis Leonides engine. On December 30, 1963, DHC flew the prototype Mk III Turbo-Beaver, powered by a PT6A turboprop, and a few examples were built. A Garrett AiResearch TPE 331 has been fitted in a Beaver in New Zealand.

De Havilland DHC-3 Otter

Canada

Utility transport, in service.

Accommodation: Pilot and up to eleven passengers.
Powered by: One 600hp Pratt & Whitney R-1340-S1H1-G piston-engine.
Span: 58ft 0in (17.69m).
Length: 41ft 10in (12.80m).
Gross weight: 8,000lb (3,629kg).
Cruising speed: 121–132mph (195–212km/h).
Range: 875 miles (1,410km) with 2,100lb (953kg) payload.

Second of the de Havilland utility line, the Otter was first flown on December 12, 1951, and was an extrapolation of the successful Beaver formula into a larger size. Deliveries began at the end of 1952 and 460 were built, including large batches for the US Army and the RCAF. Land, sea and snow undercarriages can be fitted and a later development was an amphibious version, featuring retractable wheels in standard Edo floats.

De Havilland DHC-6 Twin Otter

Canada

General-purpose light STOL transport, in production and service.
Photo and data: Series 300.

Accommodation: One or two pilots, and up to 20 passengers.
Powered by: Two 652ehp Pratt & Whitney PT6A-27 turboprops.
Span: 65ft 0in (19.81m).
Length: 51ft 9in (15.77m).
Gross weight: 12,500lb (5,670kg).
Max cruising speed: 210mph (338km/h) at 10,000ft (3,050m).
Range: 794 miles (1,277km) at 210mph (338km/h).

As suggested by its name, the Twin Otter was derived from the single-engined Otter, retaining much of the latter's fuselage and wing structure but having two turboprop engines. Developed as a private venture, the first Twin Otter flew on May 20, 1965, and deliveries began in July 1966. The initial Series 100 production version (115 built), with 579ehp PT6A-20 engines, was superseded by the Series 200 (115 built), with a lengthened nose and higher operating weights, followed in turn by the Series 300 described alongside. More than 500 Twin Otters have been built for civil and military use, and four delivered to the US Army and Air Force in 1976/77 were designated UV-18s. Float and ski versions of the Twin Otter are in service also.

Dominion Skytrader 800

USA

Utility transport, under development.

Accommodation: Crew of two and up to 12 passengers.
Powered by: Two 400hp Lycoming IO-720-B1A flat-eight engines.
Span: 55ft 0in (16.76m).
Length: 41ft 0in (12.50m).
Gross weight: 8,500lb (3,855kg).
Cruising speed: 177mph (285km/h) at 10,000ft (3,050m).
Range: 930–2,450 miles (1,495–3,940km).

The Skytrader 800 was developed at Renton, Washington, as a utility and general-purpose transport particularly for operation in underdeveloped areas, and with production in Canada as one of the objectives of the design team. A number of options were built into the design, including use of 475hp Lycoming TIO-720-C engines, provision for extra fuel in wing roots and drop tanks, provision for JATO and provision for amphibious twin float or wheel/ski landing gear. Several alternative interior layouts were designed, including one for use as a water bomber. The prototype first flew on April 21, 1975, at which time it was reported that Macmillan-Bloedel Forest Products had ordered two.

Dornier Do 27

Germany

Light utility transport, in service.
Data for Do 27A–4.

Accommodation: 2 pilots, and up to 6 passengers.
Powered by: One 270hp Lycoming GO-480-B piston-engine.
Span: 39ft 4½in (12.00m).
Length: 31ft 6in (9.6m).
Gross weight: 4,070lb (1,850kg).
Cruising speed: 109–130mph (175–210km/h).
Max range: 685 miles (1,100km) (no reserves).

Dornier's Do 27, a development of the Do 25 which was built in Spain to Prof. Dornier's designs in 1954, was the first aircraft of indigenous design to be produced in Germany after the Second World War. The prototype, built by CASA in Spain, flew on June 27, 1955, followed by the first genuine German specimen on October 17, 1956. A total of 620 were built, of which 478 were for the Luftwaffe and Spanish Air Force (the latter built in Spain). Prototypes were flown on floats and with an Astazou turboprop engine.

Dornier Do 28   Germany

Utility transport, in service.
Data for Do 28B-1.

Accommodation: Pilot and up to 7 passengers.
Powered by: Two 290hp Lycoming IO-540-A piston-engines.
Span: 45ft 3½in (13.80m).
Length: 29ft 6in (9.00m).
Gross weight: 6,000lb (2,720kg).
Cruising speed: 150–170mph (242–274km/h).
Normal range: 768 miles (1,235km) with max payload (no reserves).

Derived from the Do 27, the Do 28 has virtually the same fuselage and an extended version of the same wing. The two engines are carried on stub wings. The prototype, with a standard Do 27 wing and 180hp Lycoming O-360 engines, flew on April 29, 1959. The first production model was the Do 28A-1 with 250hp O-540 engines; 60 were built. First flown in April 1963, the Do 28B-1 has more power, a larger tailplane, higher weights and other changes. A total of 60 were built, of which six were converted to Do 28B-1-S floatplane configuration by the Jobmaster Company for service in Canada, following one Do 28A-1-S prototype.

Dornier Do 28 D-1 and D-2 Skyservant   Germany

STOL utility transport, in production and service.
Data for Do 28 D-2.

Accommodation: Pilot and up to 14 passengers.
Powered by: Two 380hp Lycoming IGSO-540-A1E piston-engines.
Span: 51ft 0½in (15.55m).
Length: 37ft 5¼in (11.41m).
Gross weight: 8,470lb (3,842kg).
Cruising speed: 150–170mph (241–273km/h).
Max range: 1,255 miles (2,020km) (no reserves).

Despite its designation, the Skyservant inherits only the basic configuration of the Do 28 which pre-ceded it. The wing is similar but of greater span. The new fuselage is much longer and of bigger cross-section than that of the Do 28, and embodies a larger freight loading door. Developed with financial assistance from the German government, the prototype flew for the first time on February 23, 1966, and certification was obtained in February 1967. Following delivery of seven initial production aircraft designated Do 28 D, manufacture switched to the D-1, with a small increase in wing span and other refinements, and then to the further-developed Do 28 D-2. Deliveries of more than 220 civil and military versions have been made to 25 countries, with production continuing.

Embraer EMB-110 Bandeirante

Brazil

Short-haul feeder-line transport, in production and service.
Photo and data: EMB-110P.

Accommodation: Flight crew of two and 18 passengers.
Powered by: Two 680hp Pratt & Whitney PT6A-27 turboprops.
Span: 50ft 2½in (15.30m).
Length: 46ft 8¼in (14.23m).
Gross weight: 12,345lb (5,600kg).
Max cruising speed: 263mph (424km/h).
Range: 287–1,266 miles (463–2,037km) according to payload.

The EMB-110 was developed to meet a Brazilian Air Force requirement for a general-purpose light transport, and the prototype first flew on October 26, 1968, followed by the first production C-95 on August 9, 1972. Several versions have been developed for commercial use, including the EMB-110C, EMB-110P and EMB-110P2 (with lengthened fuselage and 22 seats) as used by Transbrasil, VASP and other Brazilian third-level operators; the EMB-110F and EMB-110K1 (with lengthened fuselage) freighters; the EMB-110B photo-survey version; EMB-110S geo-physical survey version; and EMB-110E(J) executive transport with de luxe interior. Over 200 Bandeirantes had been sold for military and civil use by the summer of 1977.

Embraer EMB-121 Xingu

Brazil

Business twin-jet, in production and service.

Accommodation: Flight crew of two and up to six passengers.
Powered by: Two 680shp Pratt & Whitney PT6A-28 turboprops.
Span: 45ft 11½in (14.02m).
Length: 41ft 1in (12.52m).
Gross weight: 11,466lb (5,200kg).
Cruising speed: 292mph (470km/h).
Range: 1,428 miles (2,300km).

The Brazilian state factory EMBRAER has been steadily expanding the family of designs based on the Bandeirante since this light transport was first developed for the Brazilian Air Force. In addition to the variants of the EMB-110 itself (see previous entry), the family has been expanded to include pressurised versions in the EMB-120 series. The first of these, flown in prototype form in November 1976, is the EMB-121 Xingu, which has essentially the same wing and powerplant as the EMB-110, but a shortened, pressurised fuselage and a T-tail. This first production Xingu flew on May 20, 1977, and eight more were scheduled for completion by the end of the year. For future development, the EMB-123 Tapajos and EMB-120 Araguaia have two different fuselage lengths, the same T-tail, uprated 1,120shp PT6A-45 engines and a supercritical wing with optional tip tanks.

Evangel 4500-300   USA

Light passenger/cargo aircraft, in service.

Accommodation: Pilot and 8 passengers.
Powered by: Two 300hp Lycoming IO-540-K1B5 piston-engines.
Span: 41ft 3in (12.52m).
Length: 31ft 6in (9.60m).
Gross weight: 5,500lb (2,495kg).
Cruising speed: 171–182mph (275–293km/n).
Max range: 637–750 miles (1,025–1,207km).

Designed specifically for heavy-duty operations in underdeveloped areas, the Evangel 4500-300 has a performance which belies its rugged, boxlike appearance. In particular, it will take off with a full load in only 500ft (152m) and land in 475ft (145m). Design was started in 1962 and the proto-type flew for the first time in June 1964. Little was heard about the Evangel until the first production model had flown in January 1969; but certification followed only 18 months later and seven production Evangels had been completed by February 1974.

Gates Learjet Models 23, 24 and 25   USA

Business twin-jet, in production and service.
Photo: Model 25.
Data: Model 25F.

Accommodation: Two pilots, and up to 6 pas-sengers.
Powered by: Two 2,950lb (1,340kg) st General Electric CJ610-6 turbojets.
Span: 35ft 7in (10.84m).
Length: 47ft 7in (14.50m).
Gross weight: 15,000lb (6,804kg).
Cruising speed: 481–534mph (774–859km/h).
Max range: 1,902 miles (3,060km) with reserves.

The Learjet is one of the smallest and fastest of the modern business jets. The prototype was first flown on October 7, 1963, and deliveries began in October 1964. A total of 104 of the original Model 23 were built before a switch was made to the

Model 24, with modifications to meet Part 25 of the Federal Air Regulations. The Model 24 first flew on February 24, 1966, and 80 were built. In 1968 the company progressed to the Model 24B, with -6 engines replacing the lower-rated -4s and a higher gross weight. This version was followed in 1970 by the 24D, with greater range and without the bullet fairing at the junction of the tailplane and fin. Current versions are the short-field 24E and, with increased fuel capacity, 24F. Lengthened by 4ft 2in (1.27m), to seat 8 passengers, the Model 25 flew for the first time on August 12, 1966. Current versions are the improved Learjet 25D and the Model 25F with extra fuel. Under development in 1977 was the prototype of a new version known as the Learjet Model 28/29 Longhorn, with long-span wings carrying NASA winglets above the tips, and powered by 3,100lb (1,380kg) st CJ610-8A turbojets.

Gates Learjet Models 35 and 36   USA

Business twin-jet, in production and service.
Photo: Model 36.
Data: Model 35A.

Accommodation: Two pilots, and up to 7 passengers.
Powered by: Two 3,500lb (1,588kg) st Garrett AiResearch TFE 731-2 turbofans.
Span: 39ft 4in (12.04m).
Length: 48ft 8in (14.83m).
Gross weight: 17,000lb (7,711kg).
Max cruising speed: 534mph (859km/h).
Max range: 2,775 miles (4,466km).

Announced at the 1973 Paris Air Show, the Learjet 35 and 36 differ only in payload/range charac-

teristics. The Model 35A carries seven passengers in its main cabin, plus an eighth on the flight deck when flown with a single pilot. The Model 36A carries only five passengers in its cabin but has an increased fuel capacity, to extend its range to 3,305 miles (5,318km) with four passengers. Both aircraft represent slightly 'stretched' versions of the basic Learjet airframe. The switch to turbofans enables them to offer both improved payload/range and lower noise levels. First to fly with TFE 731 engines, on January 4, 1973, was a modified Learjet 25, followed by the Model 35 prototype on August 22, 1973. Deliveries began in the Summer of 1974 and by mid-1977 a total of over 700 Learjets of all models (including 23s and 24s) had been delivered.

Government Aircraft Factories Nomad   Australia

Twin-turboprop STOL utility transport, in production.
Photo: N24A.
Data: N24.

Accommodation: Crew of 1 or 2, and 15 passengers or freight.
Powered by: Two 400shp Allison 250-B17B turboprops.
Span: 54ft 0in (16.46m).
Length: 47ft 1¼in (14.36m).
Gross weight: 8,500lb (3,855kg).
Normal cruising speed: 193mph (310km/h).
Max range: 840 miles (1,352km), with reserves.

This light STOL transport has been under development since 1965, when the Fishermen's Bend headquarters of the GAF began design studies for a turboprop utility aircraft. The first of two N2 prototypes, produced with government funds, flew on July 23, 1971 and the second on December 5. The basic N22 production version for military and civil use is similar to the prototypes, although the military version has provision for armour protection, self-sealing fuel tanks and external weapons. A higher-capacity commercial model is also produced as the N24 and six of these were delivered to the Northern Territory Aeromedical Service. Of 95 Nomads authorised for production by early 1977, the majority are for military use, with a smaller number of commercial N22s.

Grumman (and McKinnon) Goose   USA

Light transport amphibian, in service.
Photo: Standard Goose.
Data: G-21G Turbo-Goose.

Accommodation: Pilot and up to 11 passengers.
Powered by: Two 680shp Pratt & Whitney (Canada) PT6A-27 turboprops.
Span: 50ft 10in (15.49m).
Length: 39ft 7in (12.07m).
Gross weight: 12,500lb (5,670kg).
Max speed: 243mph (391km/h).
Max range: 1,600 miles (2,575km).

The Grumman G-21 first flew in June 1937 and production was initiated to meet orders from commercial users. The majority of over 250 built,

however, were for military use during the Second World War, although many of these were later sold in the civil market. McKinnon Enterprises engineered a conversion scheme for the Goose, soon after the War, in which four 340hp Lycoming GSO-480s replaced the original pair of 450hp R-985 Wasps, and many other changes were made to improve the performance of the Goose and its suitability as an executive aircraft. In 1966, McKinnon flew the prototype of a further refined conversion, with PT6A turboprops. This conversion is available to owners of Goose amphibians, current versions being the G-21C, with short bow, and the lengthened G-21G (data above), with further improvements to enhance comfort and performance.

Grumman (and McKinnon) Widgeon   USA

Light transport amphibian, in service.
Photo: Standard Widgeon.
Data for Super Widgeon.

Accommodation: 2 pilots, and 3 or 4 passengers.
Powered by: Two 270hp Lycoming GO-480-B1D piston-engines.
Span: 40ft 0in (12.19m).
Length: 31ft 1in (9.47m).
Gross weight: 5,500lb (2,500kg).
Cruising speed: 175–180mph (282–290km/h).
Max range: 1,000 miles (1,600km) with reserves.

First produced in 1940, the G-44 was the second light amphibian of similar configuration designed by Grumman, being rather smaller than the Goose. Over 200 were built, including 176 for the US Navy and Air Force, and shortly after the war ended SCAN built 40 in France. Most of the latter were later re-engined with 300hp Lycoming R-680s in place of the original Ranger L-440s, while McKinnon Enterprises engineered the Super Widgeon conversion of the Grumman-built G-44s, also with Lycoming engines and optional retractable wingtip floats. More than 70 Widgeons have been converted into Super Widgeons.

Grumman Gulfstream I

USA

Business transport, in service.

Accommodation: Crew of 2, and 10–14 passengers.
Powered by: Two 2,210ehp Rolls-Royce Dart 529-8X turboprops.
Span: 78ft 4in (23.88m).
Length: 63ft 9in (19.43m).
Gross weight: 36,000lb (16,330kg).
Cruising speed: 357mph (575km/h).
Max range: 2,740 miles (4,410km).

The Gulfstream was developed as the first of the larger, long-range corporate transports to take advantage of turbine power plants. In all respects a 'baby airliner', with standards of comfort and performance equal to those experienced on scheduled airline flights, the Gulfstream was intended primarily for the US domestic market, where it gained a ready acceptance. The first flight was made on August 14, 1958 and certification was obtained in the following year. Production ended early in 1969, when the 200th aircraft had been delivered; throughout the production run, no substantial changes were made in the configuration or specification of the aircraft.

Grumman Gulfstream II

USA

Business twin-jet, in production and service.

Accommodation: Crew of 2 or 3, and up to 19 passengers.
Powered by: Two 11,400lb (5,171kg) st Rolls-Royce Spey Mk 511-8 turbofans.
Span: 68ft 10in (20.98m).
Length: 79ft 11in (24.36m).
Gross weight: 65,500lb (29,711kg).
Max cruising speed: 581mph (936km/h).
Max range: 4,275 miles (6,880km).

Although named to stress continuity from the Gulfstream I, the Gulfstream II was in fact a completely new design and not just a jet version of the earlier business twin. The fuselage was optimised for only 19 seats, and the Gulfstream consequently has a much greater range than that of many airliners of similar size, making non-stop transcontinental operation possible. The first Gulfstream II flew on October 2, 1966 and 141 production aircraft had been delivered by early 1974. The first 82 aircraft had a lower gross weight of 57,500lb (26,080kg) and with effect from aircraft No. 166 delivered July 1975, hush-kits are fitted on the engines. During 1977, Grumman developed wing-tip tanks for the Gulfstream II, adding 3,120lb (1,415kg) of fuel; data alongside are for this version.

Grumman GA-7 Cougar

USA

Light business and private twin, in production.

Accommodation: Pilot plus 3—5 passengers.
Powered by: Two 160hp Lycoming O-320-D1D piston-engines.
Span: 36ft 10½in (11.25m).
Length: 29ft 10in (9.10m).
Gross weight: 3,800lb (1,725kg).
Max cruising speed: 190mph (306km/h).
Max range: 1,265 miles (2,030km).

The Cougar is the first twin-engined aircraft developed by Grumman American, designed, like the Beech Model 76, to meet the requirements of that portion of the market left unfilled when Piper stopped production of the Twin Comanche. A four-seat prototype of the Cougar first flew on December 20, 1974, and a pre-production prototype flown on January 14, 1977 differed from this prototype in having a wider fuselage, outward rather than inward retracting undercarriage, and a cabin entry door in place of a sliding canopy. Production Cougars were expected to be ready for delivery by the Autumn of 1977, with optional fifth and sixth seats. Versions with 180hp and 200hp engines are planned.

Hamilton Westwind

USA

Light passenger/cargo transport, in production and service.
Photo: Westwind II.

Accommodation: Flight crew of one or two and eight passengers.
Powered by: Two 579ehp Pratt & Whitney (Canada) PT6A-20 turboprops.
Span: 46ft 0in (14.02m).
Length: 35ft 7¼in (10.85m).
Gross weight: 11,230lb (5,094kg).
Cruising speed: 235—250mph (378—402km/h).
Range: 933 miles (1,500km) with max payload.

The Westwind family of aircraft is derived from the Beech 18, using the same basic fuselage, wings and tail unit, with a modified tailwheel-type under-carriage and turboprop power. The data above refer to the Westwind III, which can also be powered by PT6A-27 or PT6A-28 engines derated to 630ehp each, or 610ehp Lycoming LTP-101s. The West-wind II STD is similar but has a lengthened fuse-lage to seat up to 17 passengers in third-level/commuter type operations, and is powered by 840shp PT6A-34 engines, with 776ehp AiResearch TPE 331-6-251 or 1,000ehp Lycoming T5307A turboprops as optional alternatives; a tricycle undercarriage is also optionally available for this model. Versions of the Westwind were still being produced by Hamilton in 1977.

Hawker Siddeley (D.H. 104) Dove and Riley Turbo-Exec 400

UK/USA

Light transport and business twin, in service.
Photo: Riley Turbo-Exec 400.
Data for Dove 8.

Accommodation: Crew of 2, and 8–11 passengers.
Powered by: Two 400hp Gipsy Queen 70 Mk 3 piston-engines.
Span: 57ft 0in (17.37m).
Length: 39ft 3in (11.96m).
Gross weight: 8,950lb (4,060kg).
Cruising speed: 187–210mph (301–338km/h).
Range: 880 miles (1,416km) at 187mph (301km/h) with reserves.

The Dove was the first civil transport to fly in Britain after the second World War, on September 25, 1945; production eventually totalled about 540, mostly for export. The early series had 340hp Gipsy Queen 7-3 (Dove 1 and 2) or Gipsy Queen 70-4 (Dove 1B and 2B) engines and 8,500lb (3,855kg) gross weight. Dove 5 and 6 executive versions have 380hp Gipsy Queen 70 Mk 2s and 8,800lb (3,991kg) weight. Doves 7 and 8 have ejector exhausts, a Heron-type canopy and, respectively, airline-type and executive interiors. Known also as the Dove Custom 600, the executive 8A was built for the US market. US conversions built in small numbers included the Riley Turbo-Exec 400 with 400hp Lycoming IO-720s and other refinements, with an optional swept fin; and the Carstedt Jet Liner 600 with 605ehp AiResearch TPE 331-101E turboprops and a longer fuselage seating 18 passengers; the latter variant was being marketed as the CJ600 by Texas Airplane Mfg. Co. in 1977.

Hawker Siddeley (D.H. 114) Heron and Riley Turbo Skyliner

UK/USA

Short-range transport, in service.
Photo: Riley Turbo Skyliner.
Data for Heron 2.

Accommodation: Crew of two, and 14–17 passengers.
Powered by: Four 250hp Gipsy Queen 30 Mk 2 piston-engines.
Span: 71ft 6in (21.79m).
Length: 48ft 6in (14.78m).
Gross weight: 13,500lb (6,123kg).
Cruising speed: 183–191mph (295–307km/h).
Range: 1,180 miles (1,900km) with 2,100lb (952kg) payload.

The Heron was developed as a larger-capacity four-engined partner to the Dove; more than 140 were built eventually for feeder-line, local service and executive duties. The Heron 1, of which the prototype (G-ALZL) flew on May 10, 1950, has a fixed tricycle undercarriage. The Heron 2 (prototype G-AMTS flown on December 14, 1952) has a retractable undercarriage and could be fitted optionally with feathering airscrews. Final production versions of both series carried the suffix 'B'. The 'C' and 'D' suffixes indicated specially furnished executive models. Conversions included the US Riley Turbo Skyliner, re-engined with four 290hp supercharged Lycomings, giving a max speed of 285mph (459km/h); and the turboprop Saunders ST-27 (see page 101).

Hawker Siddeley HS 125   UK

Business jet transport, in production and service.
Photo and data: Series 700.

Accommodation: Crew of two, and 8–14 passengers.
Powered by: Two 3,700lb (1,680kg) st Garrett AiResearch TFE731-3-1H turbofans.
Span: 47ft 0in (14.33m).
Length: 50ft 8½in (15.46m).
Gross weight: 24,200lb (10,977kg).
Cruising speed: 464–502mph (747–808km/h).
Range: 2,210 miles (3,556km) with max payload and reserves.

A prototype of the HS 125 Series 700 made its first flight on June 28, 1976, followed by the first production model before the end of the year and

deliveries in the first half of 1977. This variant of the well-known Hawker Siddeley biz-jet differed from its predecessors primarily in having turbofan engines, which together with a number of drag-reducing refinements and other improvements give the Srs 700 a marked superiority in range, noise levels and passenger appeal. The original 125 prototype (as a de Havilland product) flew on August 13, 1962 and 378 of all versions had been sold by mid-1977, all except the Srs 700 with Rolls-Royce (Bristol) Viper turbojets. From the original Srs 1 evolved the Srs 3A and 3B (A = North American market, B = rest of the world) with increased power, the 3A-RA and 3B-RA with flush-fitting ventral fuel tank, the Srs 400A and 400B with uprated Vipers and higher weights, and the Srs 600A and 600B with lengthened fuselage and other refinements.

Helio Courier and Super Courier   USA

STOL utility transport, in production and service.
Photo and data: H-295 Super Courier.

Accommodation: 6 seats.
Powered by: One 295hp Lycoming GO-480-G1D6 piston-engine.
Span: 39ft 0in (11.89m).
Length: 31ft 0in (9.45m).
Gross weight: 3,400lb (1,542kg).
Cruising speed: 150–165mph (241–265km/h).
Range: 660–1,380 miles (1,062–2,220km).

Helio Aircraft Corporation was founded to develop and market a light aircraft with STOL characteristics and above-average safety. After flight tests of a converted Piper Vagabond, the company produced the prototype Courier incorporating full-span automatic leading-edge slats and high-lift flaps. More than 500 single-engined Couriers have been built, including 150 for the USAF, many of which were used for clandestine CIA-backed operations in SE Asia. Principal commercial version was the H-295 Super Courier, first flown on February 24, 1965; the HT-295, introduced in 1974, differed in having a nosewheel undercarriage.

Israel Aircraft Industries 1123/1124 Westwind   Israel

Business twin-jet transport, in production and service.
Photo and data: 1124.

Accommodation: 1 or 2 pilots, and up to 10 passengers.
Powered by: Two 3,700lb (1,680kg) st Garrett AiResearch TFE 731-3 turbofans.
Span: 44ft 9½in (13.65m).
Length: 52ft 3in (15.93m).
Gross weight: 22,850lb (10,364kg).
Max level speed: 542mph (872km/h) at 19,400ft (5,900m).
Range: 2,764 miles (4,447km) with seven passengers.

The Aero Commander company in the USA flew the prototype of its Model 1101 Jet Commander business transport on January 27, 1963. The second prototype, with longer fuselage and higher weights, flew on April 14, 1964; deliveries of production aircraft, to the same standard with General Electric CJ610 turbojets, began in January 1965. The complete programme was sold by Rockwell International to Israel Aircraft Industries which renamed the aircraft the Commodore Jet and began developing 'stretched' and improved models. A total of 150 Jet Commanders and Commodore Jets were built in three models, the 1121, 1121A and 1121B. They were superseded by the 1123 Westwind with uprated engines, wingtip tanks, lengthened fuselage and other improvements. Deliveries totalled 36 by mid-1976, when the 1124 Westwind was introduced in its place, with turbofan engines and some equipment improvements. The prototype 1124 flew on July 21, 1975.

L-200 Morava   Czechoslovakia

Light business twin, in service.
Data: L-200D.

Accommodation: 4–5 seats.
Powered by: Two 210hp M337 piston-engines.
Span: 40ft 4½in (12.31m).
Length: 28ft 3in (8.61m).
Gross weight: 4,300lb (1,950kg).
Normal cruising speed: 159mph (256km/h) at 8,200ft (2,500m).
Max range: 1,063 miles (1,710km).

First flown on April 8, 1957, the Morava was developed as a successor to the Aero 145, and like the earlier type was sold in quantity to the Soviet Union for use as an air taxi. The original L-200 had 160hp Walter Minor 6-III engines. The M337 engines were introduced on the L-200A, and three-blade vp propellers and other refinements distinguished the L-200D. More than 1,000 examples of the L-200 were built, but few examples are seen outside of the Eastern European countries.

Let L-410 Turbolet

Czechoslovakia

Twin-turboprop light passenger/freight transport, in production and service.
Photo: L-410A.
Data for L-410M.

Accommodation: Crew of 1–2, and 15–19 passengers.
Powered by: Two 730ehp Walter M601A turboprops.
Span: 57ft 4¼in (17.48m).
Length: 44ft 7¾in (13.61m).
Gross weight: 12,566lb (5,700kg).
Cruising speed: 227mph (365km/h) at 9,850ft (3,000m).
Max range: 720 miles (1,160km), with reserves.

This twin-turboprop light transport is a product of the Let National Corporation at Kunovice. Design began in 1966, with the object of producing an aircraft suitable for operation from grass airfields. The L-410 prototype flew for the first time on April 16, 1969, with 715ehp Pratt & Whitney PT6A-27 turboprops, which are standard on production L-410As. Deliveries began in September 1971, initially to Slov-Air, a newly-formed Czechoslovakian internal airline. Others have been supplied to Aeroflot for evaluation. The L-410M with Czech-built M601 engines first flew in 1974 and deliveries began in 1976. The L-410AF is a special photo-survey version with enlarged and extensively glazed nose. A version with lengthened fuselage is also under development, but the prototype was lost during flight testing in 1977.

Lockheed JetStar and JetStar II

USA

Business twin-jet, in production and service.
Photo and data for JetStar II.

Accommodation: Crew of 2, and up to 10 passengers.
Powered by: Four 3,700lb (1,680kg) st Garrett AiResearch TFE 731-3 turbofans.
Span: 54ft 5in (16.60m).
Length: 60ft 5in (18.42m).
Gross weight: 43,750lb (19,844kg).
Cruising speed: 508–547mph (817–880km/h).
Range: 2,994–3,189 miles (4,818–5,132km), with reserves.

Lockheed developed the JetStar as a private venture, to meet a USAF requirement for a utility jet transport, and flew two prototypes each powered by two Bristol Siddeley Orpheus turbojets. The first flight was made on September 4, 1957. Production models switched to four JT12As, initially in the 2,400lb (1,088kg) st -6 version and later the 3,300lb (1,497kg) JT12A-8. Production totalled 162 by 1973. In 1974, Garrett AiResearch developed the JetStar 731 conversion with TFE 731 turbofans (first flown on July 10, 1974) and Lockheed subsequently put a similar version back into production as the JetStar II, first flown on August 18, 1976.

Messerschmitt-Bölkow-Blohm HFB 320 Hansa Germany

Business twin-jet and light transport, in service.

Accommodation: Crew of 2, and up to 12 passengers.
Powered by: Two 3,100lb (1,406kg) st General Electric CJ610-9 turbojets.
Span: 47ft 6in (14.49m).
Length: 54ft 6in (16.61m).
Gross weight: 20,280lb (9,200kg).
Cruising speed: 420–513mph (675–825km/h).
Range: 1,472 miles (2,370km) with 6 passengers (with reserves).

Development of the Hansa began in 1961 as the first original product of the resurrected Blohm und Voss concern in Hamburg. The company was then known as Hamburger Flugzeugbau and the new aircraft, identified as HFB 320, made its first flight on April 21, 1964. Although having the typical rear-engine layout of other business jets, the HFB 320, later named Hansa, was distinguished by its unique swept-forward wings—a feature used previously by the Hansa's designer, Richard Vogt, on the wartime Junkers Ju 287. Certification of the Hansa was obtained during 1967, and the first commercial delivery was made on September 26 in that year. Among Hansa users is the Dutch Training School at Eelde. The first 15 Hansas had CJ610-1 engines and the next 20 had CJ610-5s. Subsequent aircraft have -9s as indicated above. Production totalled 46 aircraft, of which 12 were for Luftwaffe use.

Mitsubishi MU-2 Japan

General-purpose and business transport, in production and service.
Photo: MU-2P.
Data for MU-2M.

Accommodation: 2 pilots, and up to 12 passengers.
Powered by: Two 724ehp AiResearch TPE 331-6-251M turboprops.
Span: 39ft 2in (11.95m).
Length: 33ft 3in (10.13m).
Gross weight: 10,470lb (4,750kg).
Max range: 1,680 miles (2,705km), with reserves.

The Mitsubishi company began studies of a small business twin in September 1959. The first of four prototypes, with Astazou engines, flew on September 14, 1963. Two more with French engines followed as MU-2A; the MU-2B switched to TPE 331 engines, and first flew on March 11, 1965. Production totalled 34, of which 28 were for the US market, where they were sold by Mooney Aircraft Inc. The MU-2D (18 built) introduced integral tanks and higher weights, and the MU-2F (95 built) had uprated engines and larger wingtip tanks. On January 10, 1969 Mitsubishi flew the prototype MU-2G, which differed from the 7/9-seat MU-2F primarily in having a 6ft 2¼in (1.90m) stretch in length and external fairings on the fuselage sides to house the main undercarriage. The MU-2J has the same long fuselage, with uprated engines. The MU-2K is an 'F' with these same engines, while the MU-2L and MU-2M are respectively similar to the 'J' and 'K' with increased gross weights. The MU-2N and MU-2P are again respectively similar but have larger diameter, slow-running propellers to reduce cabin noise. Orders for all versions totalled 500 by the Autumn of 1977.

Partenavia P.68 Victor

Italy

Twin-engined light transport, in production and service.
Photo: P.68R.
Data for P.68B.

Accommodation: Pilot and 5 passengers.
Powered by: Two 200hp Lycoming IO-360-A1B6 piston-engines.
Span: 39ft 4½in (12.00m).
Length: 30ft 8in (9.35m).
Gross weight: 4,320lb (1,960kg).
Cruising speed: 168–188mph (270–302km/h).
Max range: 1,045 miles (1,681km) at 9,000ft (2,750m).

Partenavia developed this light twin to supplement its well-established Oscar family of single-engined 2/4-seaters. The first of two prototypes flew on May 25, 1970. Thirteen pre-production aircraft, three of them equipped for air survey, were manufactured initially, pending completion of a new works in Naples where series production of the type began in 1974. The front fuselage of the production version is lengthened by 6in (15cm). Sportavia-Pützer in Germany developed the P.68 Observer variant with a new Plexiglas nose and observation position. Other variants available from Piaggio have a retractable undercarriage (P.68R, first flown December 1976), turbo-supercharged engines (P.68T) and turboprop engines. More than 100 Victors had been built by Summer 1977.

Piaggio P.166

Italy

Light transport, in production and service.

Photo: P.166-DL3.
Data: P.166-DL3.

Accommodation: Pilot and 5–9 passengers.
Powered by: Two 587hp Avco Lycoming LTP 101 turboprops.
Span: 48ft 2½in (14.69m).
Length: 39ft 3in (11.90m).
Gross weight: 9,480lb (4,300kg).
Cruising speed: 186–250mph (300–404km/h) at 10,000ft (3,050m).
Range: 460–1,667 miles (741–2,687km) according to payload, with reserves.

Powered by two 340hp Lycoming GSO-480 engines, the original 6/8-seat P.166 was a development of the P.136 amphibian and flew for the first time on November 26, 1957. Several of the total of 94 built were purchased for use as executive transports and for service as feeder and charter airliners. The improved P.166B Portofino (five built) has more power and up to 10 seats. The prototype P.166B first flew on March 27, 1962, and was followed on October 2, 1964, by the 12-passenger P.166C (two built) with modified under-carriage. The P.166-BL2 (first flown on May 2, 1975) introduced wing-tip tanks and higher gross weight, but was superseded by the P.166-DL3 (first flown July 3, 1976) with larger cabin windows and turboprop engines.

Pilatus PC-6 Porter

Switzerland

Light utility transport, in service.
Data for PC-6-H2.

Accommodation: Pilot plus 7–9 passengers.
Powered by: One 340hp Lycoming GSO-480-B1A6 piston-engine.
Span: 49ft 10½in (15.20m).
Length: 33ft 5½in (10.20m).
Gross weight: 4,850lb (2,200kg).
Cruising speed: 118–134mph (190–216km/h) at 10,000ft (3,050m).
Max range: 932 miles (1,500km) with normal fuel.

The Porter was designed as a STOL transport with the ability to operate safely from small, high air-fields in Switzerland; this gave it characteristics that led to wide acceptance throughout the world. The first of five prototypes flew on May 4, 1959, and deliveries began at the end of that year. Production models are the PC-6 with 340hp engine, as shown above, and the PC-6/350, with 350hp Lycoming IGO-540-A1A engine, which flew for the first time in December 1961. Variants of both versions with H1 or H2 suffix in their designations have increased gross weights. First flown on April 2, 1970, the PC6/D-H3 was a prototype only, with 500hp Lycoming TIO-720 engine, swept fin, modified wingtips and longer range.

Pilatus PC-6 Turbo-Porter

Switzerland

Light utility transport, in production and service.
Photo: PC-6/B2.
Data for PC-6/B2-H2.

Accommodation: Pilot plus 7–9 passengers.
Powered by: One 550shp Pratt & Whitney (Canada) PT6A-27 turboprop.
Span: 49ft 10½in (15.20m).
Length: 36ft 1in (11.00m).
Gross weight: 4,850lb (2,200kg).
Cruising speed: 150–161mph (240–259km/h) at 10,000ft (3,050m).
Max range: 634 miles (1,020km) with normal fuel.

Three different types of turboprop engine were available in the Turbo-Porter which, apart from the power plant and consequent improvement in per-formance, is identical with the Porter. First to fly, on May 2, 1961, was the PC-6/A with 523shp Astazou IIE or IIG; the A1 and A2 have 573shp Astazou XII and XIVE respectively. The PC-6/B, with 550shp PT6A-6A engine, first flew on May 1, 1964, and was followed by the PC-6/B1 with PT6A-20 and B2 (data above). The PC-6/C and C1 have 575shp AiResearch TPE 331-25D and TPE 331-1-100 respectively. Variants of all models with H1 or H2 suffix have increased gross weights. Overall production of Porters and Turbo-Porters exceeded 360 by the end of 1976, including those built under licence in the USA as Fairchild Indus-tries Porters and military Peacemakers.

Piper PA-23 Aztec (and Apache)   USA

Light business twin, in production and service.
Data: Turbo Aztec F.
Photo: Aztec F.

Accommodation: Pilot and 5 passengers.
Powered by: Two 250hp Lycoming TIO-540-C1A piston-engines.
Span: 37ft 2½in (11.34m).
Length: 31ft 2¾in (9.52m).
Gross weight: 5,200lb (2,360kg).
Cruising speed: 179–241mph (289–389km/h).
Max range: 1,018–1,317 miles (1,639–2,120km).

The Apache was Piper's first major entry in the twin-engined market, the prototype making its first flight on March 2, 1952, when it was known as the Twin-Stinson. Successive development of the type led to the Apache H by 1962. The more powerful Aztec was developed from the later models of the Apache, both types sharing the Piper PA-23 designation. As a 5-seater, the Aztec could originally be distinguished by its angular swept-back fin and was originally type-approved by the FAA in September 1959, the 6-seat version following two years later. The Aztec's tail unit and some other features were adopted on the Apache 235, from which the Aztec could be distinguished primarily by a longer nose. Normally-aspirated and turbosupercharged versions of the Aztec were still in production in late 1977, by which time more than 4,500 Aztecs had been built.

Piper PA-30 and PA-39 Twin Comanche   USA

Light private and business twin, in service.
Data: PA-39 Twin Comanche C/R.
Photo: PA-30B Twin Comanche B.

Accommodation: Pilot and 3–5 passengers.
Powered by: Two 160hp Lycoming IO-320-B1A piston-engines.
Span: 36ft 9½in (11.22m) over tip-tanks.
Length: 25ft 2in (7.67m).
Gross weight: 3,725lb (1,690kg).
Cruising speed: 178–198mph (286–319km/h).
Max range: 1,200 miles (1,930km) at 178mph (286km/h).

As the name suggests, this aircraft was based on the design of the Comanche, especially in respect of the main fuselage structure and cabin layout. The prototype flew on November 7, 1962, and the PA-30 Twin Comanche entered production to supersede the Apache H in 1963. Twin Comanches B and C followed in 1965 and 1968 respectively, before being superseded in 1970/71 by the PA-39 series with opposite-rotating propellers. All variants had the same power plant and were available in Standard, Custom and Sportsman models with different standards of equipment. PA-30/ PA-39 Turbo Twin Comanches differed in having 160hp IO-320-C1A engines and Rajay turbosuperchargers. Production has now ended.

Piper PA-31T Cheyenne   USA

Twin-turboprop executive aircraft and air taxi, in production and service.
Photo: Cheyenne II.
Data: Cheyenne II.

Accommodation: Pilot and 5–7 passengers.
Powered by: Two 620shp Pratt & Whitney (Canada) PT6A-28 turboprops.
Span over tip-tanks: 42ft 8¼in (13.01m).
Length: 34ft 8in (10.57m).
Gross weight: 9,000lb (4,082kg).
Cruising speed: 244–326mph (393–524km/h).
Typical range: 1,620 miles (2,605km) at 326mph (525km/h) with reserves.

Top aircraft in the Piper range, the original Cheyenne combined the basic airframe of the Pressurised Navajo with PT6 turboprop engines. A prototype first flew on August 20, 1969; preliminary details were announced in August 1973, but full specification data and photographs were not released until March 1974. Production was under way by then, the first production Cheyenne having flown on October 22, 1973. Deliveries began on March 27, 1974. The basic Cheyenne II now has wingtip tanks as standard equipment. The Cheyenne I, introduced in 1978, is a low-cost model with 500shp PT6A-11s and optional tip-tanks. The stretched 6/10-seat Cheyenne III has 680shp PT6A-41 engines and a T-tail.

Piper PA-31 Navajo and Navajo Chieftain   USA

Twin-engined executive aircraft and air taxi, in production and service.
Data: PA-31-325 Navajo C/R.
Photo: Navajo C/R.

Accommodation: Pilot and 5–8 passengers.
Powered by: Two 325hp Lycoming TIO-540-F2BD piston-engines.
Span: 40ft 8in (12.40m).
Length: 32ft 7½in (9.94m).
Gross weight: 6,500lb (2,948kg).
Cruising speed: 227–253mph (365–407km/h).
Max range: 1,082 miles (1,740km) at 244mph (393km/h) at 20,000ft (6,100m).

Piper flew the prototype PA-31 on September 30, 1964 and deliveries began in April 1967. Original versions, no longer in production, were the 6/9-seat PA-31-300 Standard Navajo, the Executive Navajo, furnished to VIP standards, and the Commuter Navajo, seating 8 persons. These three models had 300hp IO-540-M engines. The current Navajo C differs in having 310hp supercharged TIO-540-A engines Lycoming, while the Navajo C/R has 325hp counter-rotating TIO-540-F2BD engines. Also in production are the PA-31P Pressurised Navajo and the Navajo Chieftain, which is lengthened by 2ft (0.61m), to seat up to 10 persons, and has 350hp Lycoming TIO-540-J2BD counter-rotating engines. More than 2,000 Navajos had been built by Autumn 1977.

Piper PA-34 Seneca   USA

Twin-engined light transport and trainer, in production and service.
Data for Seneca II.

Accommodation: Pilot and 5 or 6 passengers.
Powered by: Two 200hp Continental TSIO-360-E piston-engines.
Span: 38ft 10¾in (11.85m).
Length: 28ft 7½in (8.73m).
Gross weight: 4,570lb (2,073kg).
Cruising speed: 187–228mph (301–367km/h).
Typical range: 830 miles (1,335km) at 187mph (301km/h).

Announced in September 1971, the Seneca is a light twin developed from the Cherokee Six. Piper claimed that it was the lowest-priced aircraft of its class on the US market and uses it as a standard twin-engine transition trainer at its Flite Centers, now numbering well over 400. The centre and rear rows of seats are removable for cargo-carrying. With the seats in place, 200lb of baggage or freight can be carried in nose and rear-cabin compartments. As in the PA-39 Twin Comanche, the propellers are opposite-rotating. The 1974 model introduced a fourth window on each side of the cabin and the 1975 model, Seneca II, switched from Lycoming to Continental engines.

Rockwell Sabreliner Series   USA

Business twin-jet, in production and service.
Photo and data: Sabreliner 75A.

Accommodation: 2 crew and 6–10 passengers.
Powered by: Two 4,500lb (2,043kg) st General Electric CF700-2D-2 turbofans.
Span: 44ft 8in (13.61m).
Length: 47ft 2in (14.38m).
Gross weight: 23,000lb (10,432kg).
Max cruising speed: 528mph (850km/h).
Max range: 1,957 miles (3,149km) with 4 passengers (with reserves).

The Sabreliner was developed as a private venture to meet USAF requirements for a combat readiness trainer and utility aircraft. The prototype flew on September 16, 1958, with General Electric J85 engines. Subsequent production has included the Sabreliner 40, with JT12A turbojets and similar to the initial military variants; the Sabreliner 60 with fuselage lengthened by 3ft 2in (0.97m); the Sabreliner 75 with deepened cabin and similar Sabreliner 75A with CF700-2D turbofans. First flown on June 29, 1977, the Sabreliner 65 has 3,700lb (1,680kg) st Garrett AiResearch TFE 731-3 turbofans and Raisbeck Mark Five System wing modifications for improved take-off and landing characteristics. The same wing is fitted to the Sabreliner 60A with JT12A-8 engines. The Sabreliner 80A will have the Raisbeck-modified wing on a 75A fuselage with CF700 engines, giving a range of 2,533 miles (4,077km).

Rockwell Shrike Commander, Courser Commander and Commander 685

USA

Twin-engined light transport, in production and service.
Photo and data for Commander 685.

Accommodation: Pilot and up to eight passengers.
Powered by: Two 435hp Continental GTSIO-520-F flat-six engines.
Span: 46ft 6½in (14.19m).
Length: 42ft 11¾in (13.10m).
Gross weight: 9,000lb (4,082kg).
Cruising speed: 175–256mph (281–412km/h).
Max range: 1,766 miles (2,842km) at 175mph (281km/h) at 20,000ft (6,100m) with reserves.

Since the merger which brought together the former Rockwell Aero Commander and North American Aviation companies, the twin-engined Aero Commander transports have been marketed under new names. The Shrike Commander 500S with 290hp Lycoming IO-540-E1B5 engines is the current production version of the original Aero Commander 500; the Shrike Commander Esquire was a de luxe 6-seat executive version. Until production was suspended, the former Grand Commander was produced as the Courser Commander, with 380hp IGSO-540 engines and up to 11 seats in a lengthened fuselage. The newer Commander 685 is a 7/9-seater, combining the Turbo Commander 690 airframe with piston-engines.

Rockwell Turbo Commander

USA

Business twin, in production and service.
Photo: Turbo Commander 690B.
Data: Turbo Commander 690A.

Accommodation: Up to 11 persons, including 1 or 2 pilots.
Powered by: Two 700ehp AiResearch TPE 331-5-251K turboprops.
Span: 46ft 8in (14.22m).
Length: 44ft 4½in (13.52m).
Gross weight: 10,250lb (4,649kg).
Cruising speed: 289–322mph (465–518km/h).
Max range: 1,693 miles (2,725km), with reserves.

First flown on December 31, 1964, the original Turbo Commander made use of a Grand Commander (Courser Commander) airframe in all major respects other than the engines. Production deliveries began in April 1965. After the Aero Commander/North American merger, the nose was lengthened and the name changed for a time to Hawk Commander. The name Turbo Commander was revived in 1971, when the basic Model 681B, with 605ehp engines and up to nine seats, was joined by the new Turbo Commander 690, with increased span and uprated engines, weights and performance. Over 150 Model 690/690As have been built.

Rockwell Commander 700/710

USA/Japan

Business twin, in production.
Photo and data: Commander 700.

Accommodation: Two pilots and up to 6 passengers.
Powered by: Two 325hp Lycoming TIO-540-R2AD piston-engines.
Span: 42ft 5½in (12.94m).
Length: 39ft 4½in (12.00m).
Gross weight: 6,600lb (2,993kg).
Cruising speed: 252mph (405km/h) at 24,000ft (7,315m).
Range: 810 miles (1,303km).

Fuji in Japan began development of this business twin in 1971, and three years later concluded an agreement with Rockwell International for the latter to market an Americanised version in the USA as the Commander 700, using Japanese-built components assembled and furnished in the USA. The prototype, known as the Fuji FA-300, first flew on November 13, 1975 in Japan, followed by a second on February 25, 1976 in the USA. Deliveries of certificated aircraft began early in 1977 and on December 22, 1976, a more powerful version made its first flight. Known as the FA-300-Kai or Commander 710, it has 450hp Lycomings.

Saunders ST-27 and ST-28

Canada

Short-range third-level and commuter transport, in service.
Photo and data: ST-27.
Accommodation: Two crew, and up to 23 passengers.
Powered by: Two 783ehp Pratt & Whitney (Canada) PT6A-34 turboprops.
Span: 71ft 6in (21.79m).
Length: 59ft 0in (17.98m).
Gross weight: 13,500lb (6,124kg).
Cruising speed: 210–230mph (338–370km/h) at 7,000ft (2,135m).
Range: 115–817 miles (185–1,315km), with reserves.

The ST-27 is a 'stretched' re-manufacture of the Hawker Siddeley (D.H. 114) Heron, with turboprop engines, designed by Saunders Aircraft Corporation of Canada. The prototype conversion was produced by Aviation Traders of Southend, England, and flew for the first time on May 28, 1969. By early 1976, Saunders had completed 13 ST-27 conversions, including one ST-27A prototype for the ST-28 (originally ST-27B) which was a completely new-build airframe to meet current FAA requirements. The ST-27A flew on July 18, 1974 and the first ST-28 on December 12, 1975, but financial problems then forced termination of production.

Scottish Aviation Jetstream 200   UK

Feeder-liner and business transport, in service.
Photo: Century Jetstream III.
Data: Jetstream 200.

Accommodation: Crew of 1–2, and 12–18 passengers.
Powered by: Two 996ehp Turbomeca Astazou XVI C2 turboprops.
Span: 52ft 0in (15.85m).
Length: 47ft 1½in (14.37m).
Gross weight: 12,566lb (5,700kg).
Cruising speed: 269–282mph (433–454km/h).
Max range: 1,380 miles (2,224km) with reserves.

Development of the Jetstream was undertaken by the former Handley Page company early in 1966 and the first of four test aircraft flew on August 18, 1967. Deliveries of the Jetstream Mk 1, with Astazou XIV engines, began in the Spring of 1969, and 36 had been completed for customers in the UK, USA, Canada and Germany by the time of the Handley Page closure. Scottish Aviation subsequently acquired design and production rights and built 26 more as multi-engined pilot trainers for the RAF. In the USA, several original HP Jetstreams have been re-engined with Garrett AiResearch TPE 331s or Pratt & Whitney PT6A-34s, one such conversion scheme being the Century III Jetstream by Century Aircraft, with the Garrett engines.

Shorts SC.7 Skyvan and Skyliner   UK

General-purpose light STOL transport, in production and service.
Photo and data: Skyvan Srs 3.

Accommodation: Crew of 1 or 2 plus up to 19 passengers, 12 stretchers or 4,600lb (2,085kg) of freight.
Powered by: Two 715shp AiResearch TPE 331-201 turboprops.
Span: 64ft 11in (19.79m).
Length: 40ft 1in (12.21m).
Gross weight: 12,500lb (5,670kg).
Cruising speed: 173–203mph (278–327km/h) at 10,000ft (3,050m).
Range: 187–694 miles (300–1,115km), with reserves.

The Skyvan was designed as a simple, capacious utility transport able to lift a two-ton payload from any half-mile airstrip. The prototype flew originally, on January 17, 1963, with 390hp Continental GTSIO-520 piston-engines. Following the decision to switch to turboprop power, it was re-engined with Astazou IIs, flying again on October 2, 1963. Three development aircraft and 16 initial production Srs 2 Skyvans were next produced with 730ehp Astazou XIIs, before TPE 331 engines were standardised for the Srs 3, first flown on December 15, 1967. Deliveries began in the following Summer, with a few converted Srs 2 airframes preceding genuine Srs 3s. Civil and military orders for 116 TPE 331-engined aircraft had been received by January 1977, including one Srs 3A Skyvan with a gross weight of 13,700lb (6,215kg) and nine all-passenger Skyliners able to carry 19 or 22 passengers in de luxe accommodation. Customers for the VIP Skyliner Executive model have included the King of Nepal.

Swearingen Merlin II and III   USA

Business twin, in production and service.
Photo and data: Merlin IIIA.

Accommodation: Crew of 2, and 6 to 9 passengers.
Powered by: Two 904ehp AiResearch TPE 331-3U-303G turboprops.
Span: 46ft 3in (14.10m).
Length: 42ft 2in (12.85m).
Gross weight: 12,500lb (5,670kg).
Max cruising speed: 325mph (523km/h) at 16,000ft (4,875m).
Max range: 1,968 miles (3,167km) at 325mph (523km/h) with reserves.

To produce the original Merlin IIA, Swearingen Aircraft combined the basic wing structure of the Beech Queen Air and undercarriage of the Twin Bonanza with an entirely new pressurised fuselage of its own design and two 578shp Pratt & Whitney PT6A-20 turboprops instead of the Queen Air's Lycomings. The first Merlin IIA flew on April 13, 1965, and production deliveries began in August 1966. The IIA was superseded by the IIB with 665shp AiResearch engines; but production is now centred on the Merlin III, with a slightly longer fuselage, new tail unit and the wings, undercarriage and engines of the Metro. A total of over 60 Merlin IIIs and IIIAs had been delivered by the beginning of 1977.

Swearingen Metro and Merlin IV   USA

Twin-turboprop commuter airliner and corporate transport, in production and service.
Data for Metro.
Photo: Metro.

Accommodation: Crew of 2, and up to 20 passengers, or varied passenger/cargo payloads.
Powered by: Two 940shp AiResearch TPE 331-3UW-303G turboprops.
Span: 46ft 3in (14.10m).
Length: 59ft 4¼in (18.10m).
Gross weight: 12,500lb (5,670kg).
Cruising speed: 279–294mph (449–473km/h).
Range: 100–500 miles (160–804km), with reserves.

Although equipped normally as a 20-passenger airliner, the Metro has an easily-convertible passenger/cargo interior, offering maximum flexibility to operators. Unlike the company's Merlin II and III, it is not an adaptation of an existing business aircraft but a completely new design. Construction of the prototype was started in August 1968, and it flew one year later, on August 26, 1969. Operators in 1977 include Air Midwest (4), Air Wisconsin (12), Commuter Airlines (2), Crown Airways (1), Mississippi Valley Airlines (1), Sun Aire Lines (1), Jet Alaska (1), European Air Transport (1), Southeast Airlines (1), Southern Airways (7), Scenic Airlines (5) and Tejas Airlines (3). About 40 business transport versions, with standard seating for 12 passengers, are also in service as Merlin IVs.

Ted Smith Aerostar

USA

Twin-engined light transport, in production and service.
Photo: Aerostar 600A.
Data: Aerostar 601.

Accommodation: Pilot and 5 passengers.
Powered by: Two 290hp Lycoming TIO-540-S1A5 piston-engines.
Span: 34ft 2in (10.41m).
Length: 34ft 9¾in (10.61m).
Gross weight: 5,700lb (2,585kg).
Normal cruising speed: 262mph (422km/h) at 20,000ft (6,100m).
Max range: 1,420 miles (2,285km) at 20,000ft (6,100m).

The name Aerostar is common to a family of high-speed light transports designed by the late Ted R.

Smith, who was responsible for the original Aero Commander light twins. Production was undertaken initially by Butler Aviation, but was taken over by Ted R. Smith and Associates (now Ted Smith Aerostar Corp) in 1972. Manufacture was concentrated initially on the Aerostar 600 which had first flown in prototype form in October 1967, and the similar Aerostar 601 with turbochargers. The 601P is pressurised, with 300hp Lycoming TIO-541 engines and has increased span of 36ft 8in (11.18m) and gross weight of 6,000lb (2,721kg). A further development stage was represented by the slightly larger Aerostar 700, with 350hp IO-540-M engines, which flew for the first time on November 22, 1972, and its pressurised version, the 700P. In flight test late in 1976 was the Aerostar 800 with 400hp Lycomings and a 32in (0.81m) fuselage stretch.

Volpar Turbo 18 and Turboliner

USA

Light general-purpose turboprop transport, in production and service.
Photo: Turboliner II.
Data: Turboliner.

Accommodation: Crew of 2, and up to 15 passengers.
Powered by: Two 705ehp AiResearch TPE 331-1-101B turboprops.
Span: 46ft 0in (14.02m).
Length: 44ft 2½in (13.47m).
Gross weight: 11,500lb (5,216kg).
Cruising speed: 256–280mph (412–451km/h) at 10,000ft (3,050m).
Range: 346–2,076 miles (556–3,340km) with reserves.

After evolving the Volpar Mk IV nosewheel undercarriage for the Beechcraft 18 (see page 67), Volpar Inc decided to progress to a turboprop conversion of the same type. The resulting Turbo 18 aircraft has TPE 331 engines, Volpar Mk IV undercarriage, lengthened front fuselage, increased chord on the wing leading-edge over the inner sections to reduce the effective thickness/chord ratio, and smaller wingtips. Many conversion kits have been delivered to Beech 18 operators. Following on from the Turbo 18, Volpar built a prototype of the 'stretched' Turboliner, which flew for the first time on April 12, 1967. A total of 26 were in service by early 1975.

WSK-Mielec M-15

Poland

Agricultural aircraft, in production and service.

Accommodation: Pilot plus provision for two passengers in cabin for ferry flights.
Powered by: One 3,306lb (1,500kg) st Ivchenko AI-25 turbojet.
Span: 73ft 3¼in (22.33m).
Length: 41ft 8¾in (12.72m).
Gross weight: 12,456lb (5,650kg).
Max cruising speed: 124mph (200km/h).
Range: 248 miles (400km) at 9,850ft (3,000m).

The unique M-15—the world's only jet-powered biplane—was developed in Poland by a joint Soviet/Polish team under the terms of an agreement concluded in 1971 providing for Poland exclusively to develop new agricultural aircraft for use in the Soviet bloc countries. A prototype (known as the LLP-M15, or 'flying laboratory' prototype M-15) flew on May 20, 1973, followed by a fully representative prototype on January 9, 1974. Powered by a turbofan of Soviet origin, the M-15 can carry 640 Imp gal (2,900 litres) or 4,850lb (2,200kg) of insecticide in containers between the wings and produces a swath width of 197ft (60m). Five preproduction M-15s were sent to the Soviet Union for evaluation in April 1975 and series production began in the same year. About 100 were reported built by 1977, when the production rate was still increasing to meet Soviet orders for some 3,000 M-15s.

105

AAMSA Quail Commander (and Rockwell Sparrow and Snipe Commanders) / Mexico

Part Three

Photo and data: Quail Commander.

Span: 34ft 9in (10.59m).
Length: 23ft 6in (7.16m).
Gross weight: 3,600lb (1,633kg).
Operating speed: 90–100mph (145–161km/h).
Max range: 300 miles (483km).

The Commander family of agricultural sprayer/dusters have had a long and involved history. Early, lower-powered versions were developed and produced by the CallAir company, from 1956 to 1962, when CallAir was taken over by Intermountain Manufacturing Co (IMCO). IMCO evolved the A-9, with 235hp Lycoming O-540-B2B5 engine and 1,250lb (567kg) payload; the A-9 Super, with 290hp Lycoming IO-540-G1C5 and 1,600lb (726kg) payload; and the scaled-up B-1, with span of 42ft 8in (13.00m), 400hp Lycoming IO-720-A1A engine and 2,000lb (907kg) payload. After a subsequent period of production by Aero Commander as Ag Commanders, the three types became, respectively, Rockwell's Sparrow Commander, Quail Commander and Snipe Commander, the Snipe being re-engined with a 450hp Pratt & Whitney IR985 radial. The Quail programme has been transferred to Aeronautica Agricola Mexicana SA in Mexico, from where deliveries have been resumed. Production of the Sparrow and Snipe Commanders has ended.

Aero 2 and 3 / Yugoslavia

Photo: Aero 3.
Data: Aero 2D.

Span: 33ft 9½in (10.29m).
Length: 27ft 8¾in (8.45m).
Gross weight: 2,197lb (996kg).
Range: 425 miles (684km) at 99mph (160km/h).

First flown in prototype form in 1940, the Aero 2 two-seat primary trainer was put into production after the second World War, the first series-built model flying on October 19, 1946. Construction is of wood, with plywood covering. Most versions have a 160hp Walter Minor 6-III engine; but the Aero 2B and 2BE have a 145hp D.H. Gipsy Major 10. The Aero 2B, 2C and 2F have open cockpits; a transparent canopy is fitted to the 2BE, 2D, 2E and 2H, the last of which is a twin-float seaplane. The improved Aero 3 has a 190hp Lycoming engine and one-piece canopy. Aero 2s and 3s, at one time used by the Yugoslav Air Force, are now operated mainly by Yugoslav flying clubs.

Aero Boero 95/115/150/180 /Argentina

Photo and data: Aero Boero 180 RV.

Span: 35ft 2in (10.72m).
Length: 23ft 10¼in (7.27m).
Gross weight: 1,860lb (844kg).
Max cruising speed: 131mph (211km/h).
Max range: 733 miles (1,180km).

The prototype of this family of 3-seat lightplanes flew for the first time on March 12, 1959. Initial production Aero Boero 95s had a 95hp Continental C90-8F engine; they were followed by the Aero Boero 95A De Lujo and its agricultural dusting/spraying counterpart, the 95A Fumigador, each with a 100hp Continental O-200-A. Standard production model from July 1969 was the Aero Boero 95/115, with 115hp Lycoming O-235-C2A engine, followed by the AB 115 BS, with swept fin, increased span and more fuel. Twenty-five 115 BS were built. Production is now centred on the 180 RV (data above) with 180hp Lycoming O-360-A1A and higher performance; the generally similar 180 RVR glidertowing version; the 180 Ag agricultural sprayer; the 150 RV with 150hp Lycoming O-320-A2B; and its agricultural counterpart, the 150 Ag. A total of 45 of the 180hp models had been built by Spring 1977.

Aero Boero 260 Ag /
Argentina

Span: 35ft 9in (10.90m).
Length: 24ft 5¼in (7.45m).
Gross weight: 2,976lb (1,350kg).
Max cruising speed: 125mph (201km/h).
Range: 683 miles (1,100km).

The Aero Boero company, which previously had built only high-wing lightplanes, began design of this agricultural aircraft in 1971. A prototype made its first flight on December 23, 1972, powered by a 260hp Lycoming O-540 engine. A second proto- type was completed in mid-1977. Production 260 Ag sprayer/dusters will be similar, except that the fairing at the rear of the canopy will be replaced by a window, to give the pilot an all round view.

Aeronca 7 Champion (and Champion Traveler and Challenger) /USA

Photo: Model 7AC.
Data: Model 7EC.

Span: 35ft 0in (10.67m).
Length: 21ft 6in (6.55m).
Gross weight: 1,450lb (658kg).
Range: 350 miles (563km) at 100mph (161km/h).

More than 10,000 Champions were built by Aeronca in 1946-51. All were tandem 2-seaters, with engines ranging from the 65hp Continental A65-8 (Model 7AC) to the 90hp Continental C90-12F (Model 7EC). Manufacture of the 7EC was resumed by Champion Aircraft from 1955 to 1964, under the names Traveler and Traveler Deluxe. The 7FC TriTraveler is similar, but with tricycle under- carriage. Developments, built in quantity, were the 3-seat 7GC Sky-Trac with 140hp Lycoming O-290-D2B engine, and the 2-seat 7GCB Challenger with 150hp Lycoming O-320-A2B engine. The Champion-built models have shorter, more square wingtips than the original Aeronca machines (see also Bellanca Champ and Citabria).

Aeronca 15AC Sedan / USA

Span: 37ft 6in (11.43m).
Length: 25ft 3in (7.69m).
Gross weight: 2,050lb (930kg).
Max cruising speed: 114mph (183km/h).
Range: 455 miles (732km).

A very large number of these 4-seat light aircraft are still in service. First flown in 1947, the Sedan has a metal structure, with metal-skinned wings and fabric-covered fuselage. Standard power plant is a 145hp Continental C145; but a few Sedans have a 165hp Franklin engine.

Aerospace (NZAI) Airtourer /New Zealand

Photo: Airtourer T2.
Data: Airtourer T5.

Span: 26ft 0in (7.92m).
Length: 22ft 0in (6.71m).
Gross weight: 1,750lb (793kg).
Max range: 670 miles (1,075km) at 134mph (216km/h).

The Airtourer beat 103 other designs to win a Royal Aero Club design competition for a 2-seat light aircraft in 1953. A wooden prototype, with 65hp engine, flew in Australia in March 1959. Victa Ltd, of Milperra, New South Wales, then built 170 all-metal production Airtourers with 100hp Continental O-200-A or 115hp Lycoming O-235 engine. Manufacture in New Zealand by Aero Engine Services Ltd (now New Zealand Aerospace Industries) began in October 1967. Variants were the Airtourer T2 (115hp O-235-C2A), T3 (130hp engine), T4 (150hp O-320-E2A), T5 (O-320-E1A engine with constant-speed propeller and needle-type spinner) and T6, as T5 with 1,900lb (862kg) gross weight. Over 100 were built in New Zealand, in addition to similar CT/4 Airtrainers for military use.

Aerospace (NZAI) Air Parts Fletcher FU-24 (and Cresco) /New Zealand

Data and Photo: FU-24-950.

Span: 42ft 0in (12.81m).
Length: 31ft 10in (9.70m).
Gross weight: 5,430lb (2,463kg).
Max cruising speed: 122mph (196km/h).
Max range: 441 miles (709km).

The FU-24 was designed originally by Fletcher Aviation Co of America for agricultural top-dressing duties in New Zealand. The first 100 production machines were built by the parent company in 1954-64. Air Parts (NZ) Ltd then acquired all rights in the FU-24 and continued manufacture in New Zealand. The basic version is operated as a single-seater, with 300hp Continental IO-520-F and hopper for 1,610lb (730kg) of chemicals aft of the cockpit. The FU-24A is a dual-control version. Now available is the FU-24-950 with 400hp Lycoming IO-720 engine, which carries a 2,320lb (1,052kg) payload in agricultural form and has a ferry seat for a loader/mechanic. It can be flown in utility form, carrying up to 7 passengers or freight. Prototypes have flown with both AiResearch TPE 331 and Pratt & Whitney PT6A turboprops, and New Zealand Aerospace Industries hopes to put into production a turboprop version known as the Cresco. A prototype Cresco, with 700shp Avco Lycoming LTP 101, was expected to fly in Summer 1978.

Aerotec A-122B Uirapuru / Brazil

Span: 27ft 10½in (8.50m).
Length: 21ft 8in (6.60m).
Gross weight: 1,825lb (840kg).
Max cruising speed: 121mph (195km/h).
Max range: 495 miles (800km) at 108mph (174km/h).

The prototype of this side-by-side 2-seat all-metal trainer flew on June 2, 1965, with a 108hp Lycoming O-235 engine. The A-122A Uirapuru was ordered into production for the Brazilian Air Force as the T-23, with a 160hp Lycoming O-320-B2B engine, a total of 100 being delivered, followed by 18 for Bolivia and 8 for Paraguay. A 2-seat civil version has been developed as the A-122B, with a modified cockpit, and 18 were delivered to Brazilian civil flying clubs in 1975.

Aircoupe (and Ercoupe, Fornaire and Mooney M-10 Cadet) /USA

Photo and data: M-10 Cadet.

Span: 30ft 0in (9.14m).
Length: 20ft 4in (6.19m).
Gross weight: 1,450lb (657kg).
Max cruising speed: 124mph (200km/h).
Max range: 455 miles (732km).

This series of 2-seat all-metal light aircraft began with the Erco Ercoupe of 1940, featuring a then-unique two-control system without rudder pedals. Manufacturing rights passed subsequently to Forney, who produced the same design as the Fornaire, and then to Alon, who introduced several changes in the A-2 Aircoupe and offered optional conventional controls. The Alon company was acquired by Mooney in 1967, the final versions of this aircraft being produced subsequently as the A-2 with new spring-steel main undercarriage legs and the M-10 Cadet with new rear fuselage and single tail-fin. Standard engine in the later versions was the 90hp Continental C90-16F.

Air Tractor Model AT-301 (and AT-302) / USA

Span: 45ft 0in (13.72m).
Length: 27ft 0in (8.23m).
Gross weight: 6,900lb (3,130kg).
Range: 350 miles (563km) at 140mph (225km/h).

The design of this agricultural sprayer/duster originated in the Snow S-2B, certificated in 1958. Aero Commander acquired the Snow range of aircraft, which eventually formed the basis of some of Rockwell's agricultural types. Leland Snow, designer of the S-2B, began work on the AT-301 Air Tractor in 1971. The prototype flew in September 1973. By May 1977, a total of 120 production models had been ordered; 82 had been delivered, with production continuing at the rate of five aircraft a month. The AT-301 is a conventional single-seater, of all-metal construction, except for fabric-covered tail control surfaces, and powered by a 600hp Pratt & Whitney R-1340 piston-engine. A version with an Avco Lycoming LTP 101 turboprop engine is in production as the AT-302.

AISA I-11B /Spain

Span: 30ft 7in (9.32m).
Length: 21ft 3in (6.47m).
Gross weight: 1,474lb (668kg).
Range: 403 miles (649km) at 110mph (177km/h).

The prototype I-11, which flew in 1950, had a tricycle undercarriage. All production I-11Bs have a tailwheel; the first one flew on October 16, 1953, and a total of 180 have been delivered, some to the Spanish Air Force for liaison and training duties. Standard engine is the 90hp Continental C90-12F, but some I-11Bs have a 93hp ENMA Flecha of Spanish design. All are side-by-side two-seaters of wooden construction.

Anahuac Tauro /Mexico

Photo and data: Tauro 350

Span: 37ft 6½in (11.44m).
Length: 26ft 11¼in (8.21m).
Gross weight: 4,545lb (2,062kg).
Cruising speed: 85–90mph (137–145km/h).
Max range: 233 miles (375km).

The Anahuac company was founded to develop aircraft suited particularly to Mexican needs. Its first product is this single-seat agricultural aircraft, which flew on December 3, 1968. The first of a test batch of seven production Tauro 300s followed on June 5, 1970, with a 300hp Jacobs R-755-A2M1 engine. On the basis of experience with these aircraft, an improved version known as the Tauro 350, with 350hp Jacobs R-755-SM engine, was developed and Is in series production.

Arctic Aircraft Interstate S1B2 Arctic Tern /USA

Span: 35ft 6in (10.82m).
Gross weight: 1,900lb (862kg).
Max cruising speed: 117mph (188km/h).
Max range: 650 miles (1,045km).

The Arctic Tern is an updated and improved version of the Interstate S-1 Cadet, which first entered production in 1940. Cadets began life as S-1As with 65hp Continental or Franklin engines. Variants with 85hp and 90hp Franklins followed. Then, when America came into the Second World War, 250 S-1Bs were acquired for the US Army as L-6s for liaison and observation roles. As well as having a 102hp Franklin O-200-5 engine, the L-6s had their cabin glazing extended back to a point about halfway between the wing trailing-edge and the fin. Several Cadets remain airworthy in the US. In addition, Arctic Aircraft is building the tandem two-seat Arctic Tern in Alaska, with a 150hp Lycoming O-320 engine, optional underbelly cargo pack, and a removable rear seat to provide space for bulky freight inside the cabin.

Auster J/1 Autocrat (and J/1B Aiglet, J/1N Alpha, J/2 Arrow, J/4 and J/5 Adventurer) /UK

Photo and data: Autocrat.

Span: 36ft 0in (10.98m).
Length: 23ft 5in (7.14m).
Gross weight: 1,850lb (839kg).
Range: 320 miles (515km) at 100mph (161km/h).

The Autocrat was Auster's first post-war lightplane, powered by a 100hp Cirrus Minor II engine. Others have been converted from 3 to 4-seaters (J/1A), or to have a 130hp Gipsy Major I engine and larger vertical tail surfaces, when they become J/1N Alphas. Aircraft built from the start with a Gipsy Major I and enlarged tail are J/1B Aiglets; of the 90 or so built, those registered in the UK were equipped mainly for crop-spraying. The J/2 Arrow (75hp Continental) and J/4 (90hp Cirrus Minor) are similar to the J/1 but seat only two. The J/5 Adventurer differed from the Aiglet in not having enlarged tail surfaces. The J/5F Aiglet Trainer has a wider fuselage and shorter span, and is aerobatic.

Auster J/5B, J/5G and J/5P Autocar (and J/5Q and J/5R Alpine) /UK

Photo: J/5Q Alpine.
Data: J/5B Autocar.

Span: 36ft 0in (10.98m).
Length: 23ft 4in (7.11m).
Gross weight: 2,400lb (1,088kg).
Range: 260 miles (418km) at 106mph (171km/h).

First full 4-seater put into production by Auster, the Autocar made its maiden flight in August 1949 and about 100 were built, mostly for export. Variants are the J/5B with 130hp Gipsy Major I engine, J/5G with 155hp Cirrus Major 3, and J/5P with 145hp Gipsy Major 10. The somewhat similar Alpine is a cross between the Autocar and the Aiglet Trainer, offering improved performance as a 3-seater. Variants are the J/5Q with Gipsy Major I and J/5R with Gipsy Major 10.

Beagle (Auster) 'D' Series and A.113 Husky / UK

Photo and data: A.113.

Span: 36ft 0in (10.98m).
Length: 22ft 2in (6.76m).
Gross weight: 2,400lb (1,088kg).
Cruising speed: 95–110mph (153–177km/h).
Range: 580 miles (933km) at 95mph (153km/h).

The cleaned-up Auster 'D' Series, introduced in 1960, have basically identical airframes, with new metal wing spars and Lycoming engines. The D.4 2-seater has 108, 150/160 or 180hp engine and 32ft (9.75m) or 36ft (10.98m) wing. The D.5 3-seater has 150/160 or 180hp engine and 32ft or 36ft wing. D.6 4-seater has 160 or 180hp engine and 36ft wing. Production of the D.5/160 and D.5/180 was continued by Beagle, the latter aircraft, with 180hp Lycoming O-360-A2A engine, being redesignated A.113 Husky. Some were equipped with agricultural spray-gear. The specialised J-1U Workmaster agricultural aircraft, first flown in 1958, is similar, with 180hp Lycoming engine. In addition, 150 D.4/108, D.5/160 and D.5/180 aircraft were built by OGMA in Portugal for air force and local club use.

Beagle A.61 Series 2 Terrier /UK

Span: 36ft 0in (10.98m).
Length: 23ft 8in (7.21m).
Gross weight: 2,400lb (1,088kg).
Cruising speed: 108–115mph (174–185km/h).
Range: 300 miles (483km) at 108mph (174km/h).

This 2/3-seat touring and training lightplane, first flown on April 25, 1962, was produced by rebuilding and refurbishing ex-Army Auster AOP.6 and T.7 monoplanes. The normal 145hp Gipsy Major 10 Mk 1-1 engine is retained, but cabin noise is reduced by fitting a lengthy exhaust and silencer. The Terrier is an excellent glider tug and had its origin in the less-refined, but generally similar, Auster 6A Tugmaster.

Beagle A.109 Airedale / UK

Span: 36ft 4in (11.07m).
Length: 26ft 4in (8.02m).
Gross weight: 2,750lb (1,247kg).
Cruising speed: 108–115 mph (174–185km/h).
Max range: 830 miles (1,335km) at 115mph (185km/h).

First flown on April 16, 1961, the 4-seat Airedale was a refined development of the traditional Auster monoplane. The 180hp Lycoming O-360 engine gives a top speed of 141mph (227km/h). More modern features include a car-type cabin, wheel controls, swept fin, spatted tricycle undercarriage, and provision for complete airline-standard instrumentation for all-weather flying. 42 were built.

Beagle B.121 Pup / UK

Photo and data: Pup-100.

Span: 31ft 0in (9.45m).
Length: 22ft 9in (6.93m).
Gross weight: 1,600lb (726kg).
Range: 540 miles (870km) at 100mph (161km/h).

First flown on April 8, 1967, the Pup-100 is a fully-aerobatic lightplane, powered by a 100hp Rolls-Royce/Continental O-200-A engine and able to carry two adults and, optionally, two children. Deliveries of production aircraft began in April 1968. Meanwhile, the first of two prototypes of the 2/4seat Pup-150, with 150hp Lycoming O-320-A2B engine, had flown on October 4, 1967. This aircraft was re-engined subsequently with a 160hp Lycoming, to fly as the prototype Pup-160 on September 5, 1968. The first Pup-200 flew in 1969 with a 200hp Continental engine. Early in the following year the Beagle company went into liquidation and production ended. 128 Pups of all models were built. The Scottish Aviation Bulldog military trainer is derived from the same design.

Beechcraft Model 17 / USA

Data: G17S.

Span: 32ft 0in (9.75m).
Length: 25ft 9in (7.85m).
Gross weight: 4,250lb (1,928kg).
Max cruising speed: 198mph (319km/h).
Max range: 1,400 miles (2,253km).

The famous Beechcraft 'Staggerwing' first flew in 1932 and remained in production, in various versions, until 1948. Many remain in use. Early models included the 4-seat 17R (420hp Whirlwind), A17F (700hp Cyclone) and B17L (225hp Jacobs), of which the first two had fixed spatted undercarriages and the B17L a retractable gear. Hundreds built pre-war were supplemented by 270 UC-43s and GB-1s (D17S variants), delivered to the US Services with 450hp Pratt & Whitney R-985 engine. About 90 civil G17S 5-seaters were produced post-war, also with R-985 engine.

Beechcraft Bonanza (V-tail series) /USA

Photo: Model V35B.
Data: Model V35B.

Span: 33ft 5½in (10.20m).
Length: 26ft 4½in (8.04m).
Gross weight: 3,400lb (1,542kg).
Cruising speed: 164—203mph (264—327km/h).
Range: 520—1,010 miles (836—1,625km) (with reserves).

The prototype of this V-tail 4/6-seat light-plane flew on December 22, 1945, and a total of 10,000 had been built by February 1977. The design has undergone continuous refinement, with increasingly-powerful engines, and the current Model V35B Bonanza has a 285hp Continental IO-520-B fuel-injection engine. The V35B TC is similar except for having a turbosupercharger and oxygen system. Conventional-tailed Bonanzas are described below.

Beechcraft Bonanza (conventional tail) and Debonair /USA

Photo and data: Model F33A.

Span: 33ft 5½in (10.20m).
Length: 25ft 6in (7.77m).
Gross weight: 3,400lb (1,542kg).
Cruising speed: 156—200mph (251—322km/h).
Range: 515—980 miles (828—1,577km) (with reserves).

Except for having a conventional tail unit and different engine, this family of Bonanzas is generally similar to the V-tail series. The prototype flew on September 14, 1959, and production models were known as Debonairs until 1967. Production of the G33, with 260hp Continental IO-470-D engine, ended in 1973, after 49 had been delivered. Current models are the F33A with 285hp IO-520-B and aerobatic F33C. Altogether, 2,090 Model 33s had been built by the beginning of 1977. The Model A36 Bonanza is generally similar to the F33A, but is lengthened to make it a full 6-seater, and has a double-door for easier cargo loading; 969 had been built by January 1977.

Beechcraft Model 77 / USA

Span: 30ft 0in (9.14m).
Length: 23ft 10in (7.28m).
Gross weight: 1,650lb (748kg).
Performance: no details available.

In late 1974 Beech announced that it was building the prototype of a single-engined trainer designated PD 285 for potential use at its Aero Centers. New constructional methods were to be used to keep manufacturing costs to a minimum. The wing, of GAW-1 aerofoil section, resulted from combined NASA/Beech research into supercritical aerofoils with high-lift characteristics. Emphasis was also to be placed on providing a spacious cabin, with good all-round field of view, for the two side-by-side occupants. The prototype PD 285 flew for the first time on February 6, 1975, powered by a 115hp Lycoming O-235 engine. After a time, the original low-mounted tailplane was exchanged for a T-tail and the aircraft was redesignated Beech Model 77. It is expected to enter production in 1978.

Beechcraft Musketeer (and Sierra, Sundowner and Sport) / USA

Data: Sundowner.
Photo: Sierra.

Span: 32ft 9in (9.98m).
Length: 25ft 9in (7.85m).
Gross weight: 2,450lb (1,111kg).
Cruising speed: 123–143mph (198–230km/h).
Range: 685–860 miles (1,102–1,384km) (with reserves).

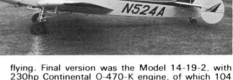

The prototype of this family of low-cost all-metal light aircraft flew on October 23, 1961. Initially, all Musketeers had a fixed undercarriage, the 1971 models of this type being the 4/6-seat Musketeer Custom with 180hp Lycoming O-360-A4G engine; 2-seat (optional 4-seat) Musketeer Sport with 150hp O-320-E2C; and 4/6-seat Musketeer Super with 200hp IO-360-A2B. There were aerobatic versions of the Custom and Sport; the Super R differed from the Super in having a retractable undercarriage and constant-speed propeller. In 1972, the Musketeer range was renamed, becoming the Sierra (Super R); the Sundowner (Custom) and Sport (Sport). Subsequently, suffix numbers were added to these names to indicate the engine power. A total of 3,533 Musketeers and later models had been built by the beginning of 1977.

Bellanca (and Downer) 14-19-2 Cruisemaster / USA

Data: Downer 14-19-2.

Span: 34ft 2in (10.41m).
Length: 22ft 10¾in (6.98m).
Gross weight: 2,700lb (1,225kg).
Range: 800 miles (1,287km) at 196mph (315km/h).

Development of this aircraft began with the 3-seat Bellanca 14-9 of 1937, with alternative 90hp Rearwin and 100hp Lycoming engines. First post-war models were the 4-seat 14-13 Cruisair and 14-19 Cruisemaster, of which large numbers are still flying. Final version was the Model 14-19-2, with 230hp Continental O-470-K engine, of which 104 were built by Downer Aircraft Co after it acquired manufacturing rights from Bellanca.

Bellanca 260 (and Viking 300) /USA

Photo: Viking 300.
Data: Super Viking 300.

Span: 34ft 2in (10.41m).
Length: 23ft 6in (7.16m).
Gross weight: 3,325lb (1,508kg).
Cruising speed: 190–194mph (306–312km/h).
Max range: 940 miles (1,513km).

On November 15, 1958, Downer Aircraft flew the prototype of an improved version of the Cruisemaster, known as the Bellanca 260 Model 14-19-3, with 260hp Continental IO470-F engine and tricycle undercarriage. After a period of quantity production, the design was refined further to substitute a single square-cut fin and rudder for the original triple-tail. Manufacturing rights in the new version were taken over by Bellanca Aircraft Corp, which is currently manufacturing a refined version as the Super Viking 300 with 300hp Continental IO-520-D or Lycoming IO540 engine and the Turbo-Viking with 310hp Lycoming TIO-540.

Bellanca Aries T-250 / USA

Span: 31ft 4in (9.55m).
Length: 26ft 2in (7.98m).
Gross weight: 3,150lb (1,430kg).
Max cruising speed: 208mph (335km/h).
Max range: 1,170 miles (1,883km).

The prototype of this four-seat lightplane was designed and built by Ben Anderson and Marvin Greenwood, who are remembered best for the AG-14 high-wing twin-boom light aircraft of 1948, with pusher engine, of which four examples were completed. Known as the AG-51, this new prototype received FAA Type Approval in July 1976.

Production, under the name Aries T-250, has been undertaken by Bellanca Aircraft Corporation, following this company's acquisition by Anderson, Greenwood & Co. Construction is all-metal, with a T-tail and retractable landing gear. Power plant is a 250hp Lycoming O-540-A4D5 engine.

Bellanca Model 7ACA Champ /USA

Span: 35ft 1½in (10.70m).
Length: 21ft 9½in (6.63m).
Gross weight: 1,220lb (553kg).
Max cruising speed: 86mph (138km/h).
Max range: 300 miles (483km).

Cheapest lightplane built in recent times in America, this wooden-sparred metal fuselage 2-seater was a 1971 reincarnation of the Aeronca 7AC, of which more than 7,200 were built in 1946–48. Main difference is the use of a 60hp Franklin 2A-120-B engine, in place of the original 65hp Continental which is no longer available. This is enclosed by a new cowling, which improves visibility; and the Champ also has lightweight cantilever spring-steel main undercarriage legs.

Bölkow (Klemm) KI 107C and Bölkow 207 /Germany

Photo and data: Bölkow 207.

Span: 35ft 6in (10.82m).
Length: 27ft 3in (8.30m).
Gross weight: 2,645lb (1,200kg).
Range: 775 miles (1,247km) at 124mph (200km/h).

The basic design of the KI 107 was evolved by Klemm during the war, but the prototype, with 90hp Continental C90 engine, did not fly until 1955. A year later, the 3-seat KI 107B appeared with 150hp Lycoming engine. Manufacturing rights were acquired by Bölkow, which built 150 improved KI 107Cs with the same engine. Final production model was the further refined 4-seat Bölkow 207, as described and illustrated, with 180hp Lycoming O-360-A1A engine, modified wing and redesigned canopy and tail unit. All of these aircraft are of wooden construction.

Bölkow BO 208/MFI-9
Junior /Germany /Sweden

Photo and data: BO 208C.

Span: 26ft 4in (8.02m).
Length: 19ft 0in (5.79m).
Gross weight: 1,390lb (630kg).
Max cruising speed: 127mph (204km/h).
Max range: 620 miles (1,000km).

The prototype of this ultra-light 2-seater was amateur-built in the USA by Bjorn Andreasson and first flew on October 10, 1958. Andreasson later became head of the Aircraft Division of the Swedish Malmo company, which put the aircraft into production as the MFI-9 Junior, with 100hp Rolls-Royce/Continental O-200 engine. Licence rights were acquired by Bölkow, which built about 200, under the basic designation BO 208, before ending production in 1969/70. Malmo completed 25 before switching to the MFI-9B Trainer variant, mainly for military use.

Bücker Bü 131B
Jungmann /Germany

Photo: CASA 1.131E.
Data: Bü 131B Jungmann.

Span: 24ft 3in (7.39m).
Length: 21ft 8in (6.60m).
Gross weight: 1,475lb (670kg).
Max cruising speed: 106mph (171km/h).
Max range: 400 miles (643km).

The prototype of this tandem 2-seat aerobatic biplane flew on April 27, 1934. Large numbers of the original Bü 131A (80hp Hirth HM.60R) were built, followed in 1936 by the Bü 131B, with 105hp Hirth HM.504A engine, which was built in Germany, Czechoslovakia, Switzerland and (both pre-war and post-war) in Spain. Many still fly, including ex-military Spanish-built examples known as CASA 1.131Es, with 125hp ENMA Tigre G-IV engines. Others have been re-engined with the 180hp Lycoming IO-360 in Switzerland, a typical conversion of this kind being the Dätwyler Bücker/Dubs Lerche, with new wings to improve inverted flight performance.

Bücker Bü 133
Jungmeister /Germany

Photo and data: Bü 133D-1.

Span: 21ft 7¾in (6.60m).
Length: 19ft 9in (6.02m).
Gross weight: 1,410lb (640kg).
Cruising speed: 87–124mph (140–200km/h).
Range: 310 miles (500km) (with reserves).

Although its design dates back to 1935, the Jungmeister is still rated so highly as a single-seater for advanced aerobatics that it was put back in production for a time in Germany by Aero Technik Canary.
Two versions were available. The Bü 133D-1 with 160hp Siemens Halske Sh-14A4 (Bramo) is virtually unchanged. The Bü 133F, first flown on October 1, 1969, has a more modern 220hp Franklin 6A-350-C1 horizontally-opposed engine and improved performance, but retains the traditional 'radial' cowling.

C.A.A.R.P./Mudry CAP 10 and CAP 20 /France

Data: CAP 10.
Photo: CAP 20L.

Span: 26ft 5¼in (8.06m).
Length: 23ft 6in (7.16m).
Gross weight: 1,829lb (830kg).
Max cruising speed: 155mph (250km/h).
Max range: 745 miles (1,200km).

Developed from the Piel Emeraude, the CAP 10 is a two-seat touring, training and aerobatic lightplane. The prototype flew for the first time in August 1968; a total of 76 had been completed by early 1977, including 30 delivered to the basic flying training school and the aerobatic team of the French Air Force. Construction is all-wooden, except for fabric covering on the fuselage and rudder. The power plant is a 180hp Lycoming IO-360?B2F. Avions Mudry's associated company, C.A.A.R.P., supplies fuselages for the CAP 10 and is responsible for the entire manufacture of a single-seat derivative of this aircraft, designated CAP 20. Intended as a specialised aerobatic type, the current CAP 20L is available with 180hp Lycoming AEIO-360 or 200hp AIO-360-B1B, in each case with fixed-pitch or variable-pitch propeller.

CERVA CE.43 Guépard / France

Span: 32ft 9½in (10.00m).
Length: 25ft 9in (7.85m).
Gross weight: 3,220lb (1,460kg).
Normal cruising speed: 174mph (280km/h).
Max range: 1,800 miles (2,900km).

The four/six-seat CE.43 Guepard is basically an all-metal version of the Wassmer WA 4/21, with the same 250hp Lycoming IO-540 engine. The prototype flew for the first time on May 18, 1971 and was exhibited at the Paris Air Show a few weeks later by the CERVA consortium, in which Wassmer-Aviation and Siren SA each had a 50 per cent holding. Deliveries totalled 43 by early 1977. Variants are the CE.44 Couguar and CE.45 Léopard, with 285hp Continental Tiara and 310hp Lycoming TIO-540 engine respectively.

Cessna Models 120, 140 and 170 /USA

Photo: Model 120.
Data: Model 140 (65hp).

Span: 32ft 10in (10.0m).
Length: 20ft 11¾in (6.39m).
Gross weight: 1,450lb (658kg).
Range: 450 miles (724km) at 102mph (164km/h).

The side-by-side 2-seat Model 120 was the first of Cessna's post-war designs for the civil market, a total of 2,164 being built in 1946-48, each powered by an 85hp Continental C85-12 or 12F engine. In parallel production was the Model 140, which differed in having manually-operated flaps, a starter and generator. The Model 140 could also be fitted, optionally, with a 90hp Continental C90-12F engine. Both the 120 and 140 were superseded in 1948 by the Model 140A, with the same choice of engines, metal instead of fabric covering on the wings and a single bracing strut each side in place of the former Vee struts. A total of 5,560 140/140As were built. A large proportion of them continue to fly, together with many hundreds of 120s. Also in production from 1948 to 1956 was the Cessna 170, a 4-seat counterpart of the Model 120/140 with 145hp Continental C145-2 engine. A large number of the 5,171 built remain airworthy.

Cessna Model 150 and 152 /USA

Data: Model A150.

Span: 32ft 8½in (9.97m).
Length: 23ft 11in (7.29m).
Gross weight: 1,600lb (726kg).
Cruising speed: 94–121mph (151–195km/h).
Range: 656–835 miles (1,055–1,343 km).

A total of 23,299 of these little side-by-side 2-seaters had been built by the beginning of 1977. The appearance of the prototype, in September 1957, had marked Cessna's re-entry into the 2-seat market after a seven-year lapse. Powered by a 100hp Continental O-200-A piston engine, it followed the familiar Cessna all-metal high-wing, tricycle undercarriage formula. Detail refinements introduced after some years have included a sweptback fin, stepped-down rear fuselage with panoramic rear window, and an optional rear 'family' seat for two small children. The Model 150 is available in standard, trainer and commuter versions, on wheels or floats, and in specialised aerobatic form as the A150K Aerobat. The Commuter has a small increase in wing span. Versions built in France by Reims Aviation are designated F-150 and FRA-150 Aerobat; others are built in Argentina. During 1977, the Cessna 150 was succeded by the Cessna 152 with a 110hp Lycoming O-235 engine operating on 100-octane low-lead fuel.

Cessna Model 172 (and Skyhawk, 175, Skylark, 182, Skylane and Reims Rocket and Hawk) /USA

Photo: Model F-172.
Data: Skylane.

Span: 35ft 10in (10.92m).
Length: 28ft 2in (8.59m).
Gross weight: 2,950lb (1,338kg).
Cruising speed: 115–160mph (185–257km/h).
Range: 690–1,160 miles (1,110–1,866km).

The 172 and other types listed above represent Cessna's 'middle line' of 4-seat allmetal aircraft with optional 'family seat' for two small children. The late-model 172 had a 150hp Lycoming O-320-E2D engine and was built in France as the F.172, by Reims Aviation. The Skyhawk is a *de luxe* version of the 172. The 175 and Skylark, no longer in production, have a 175hp GO-300 engine. The 182 and Skylane are standard and *de luxe* models with a 230hp Continental O-470-R. By January 1977, a total of 20,014 172/Skyhawks and 16,352 182/Skylanes had been delivered, plus 1,567 French-built F-172s and 590 Reims Rockets (210hp Continental IO-360-D). Only the Skylane and Skyhawk remained in production by Cessna in 1977. Reims was assembling Skyhawks and the FR 172K Hawk XP with a 195hp Continental IO-360-K.

Cessna Model 177 (and Cardinal) /USA

Photo: Cardinal II.
Data: Cardinal RG.

Span: 35ft 6in (10.82m).
Length: 27ft 3in (8.31m).
Gross weight: 2,800lb (1,270kg).
Cruising speed: 140–171mph (225–275km/h).
Range: 785–1,005 miles (1,260–1,615km).

Introduced into the Cessna range in September 1967, the Model 177 and *de luxe* Cardinal are basically 4-seaters (plus optional seat for two children) with a cantilever wing and fixed tricycle undercarriage. The original versions had a 150hp Lycoming engine, but this gave way to a 180hp Lycoming O-360-A2F in the 1969 Model 177A. The latest version has an O-360-A1F and a new wing leading-edge of gull-wing concept. The series was supplemented in December 1970 by the Cardinal RG, which differs from the standard model by having a retractable undercarriage and 200hp IO-360-A1A engine; data for this model are given here. By the beginning of 1977, 3,740 Model 177/Cardinals and 1,182 RGs had been delivered, including 166 RGs assembled by Reims Aviation.

Cessna Models 180 and 185 Skywagon /USA

Photo: Model 185.
Data: Model 180.

Span: 35ft 10in (10.92m).
Length: 25ft 9in (7.85m).
Gross weight: 2,800lb (1,270kg).
Cruising speed: 121–162mph (195–261km/h).
Range: 695–1,215 miles (1,118–1,955km).

The two versions of the Skywagon are generally similar except for power plant, the 180 having a 230hp Continental O-470-R engine, while the 185 has a 300hp Continental IO-520-D. Each can carry up to six persons, in pairs. Alternatively, all the passenger seats can be removed to permit use of the aircraft for cargo carrying. A detachable cargo pack, with a capacity of 300lb (136kg), can be carried under the fuselage of the 185, and the A185 version is for agricultural use, named the AGcarryall. Deliveries by January 1977 totalled 5,762 Model 180s, 3,120 Model 185s and 80 AGcarryalls.

Cessna Model 188 AGwagon and AGtruck / USA

Photo: AGwagon.
Data: AGtruck.

Span: 41ft 8in (12.70m).
Length: 26ft 3in (8.00m).
Gross weight: 4,200lb (1,905kg).
Range: 295 miles (475km) at 113mph (182km/h).

The prototype AGwagon flew for the first time on February 19, 1965, and two versions went into production. The basic AGwagon 'B', had a 230hp Continental O-470-R engine and a more powerful model was available optionally with a 300hp Continental IO-520-D engine and gross weight of 4,000lb. The basic model was renamed AGpickup in 1971; the 300hp version became the AGwagon and a version with enlarged hopper became the AGtruck. Deliveries totalled 1,462 AGwagons, 1,270 AGtrucks and 53 AGpickups by February 1977. AGpickup production ended in 1975.

Cessna Model 195 (and 190) /USA

Photo and data: Model 195.

Span: 36ft 2in (11.02m).
Length: 27ft 4in (8.33m).
Gross weight: 3,350lb (1,520kg).
Range: 750 miles (1,207km) at 165mph (265km/h).

Between 1947 and 1954, Cessna produced a total of 890 Model 195s and 195As, powered by a 300hp Jacobs R-755-A2 and 245hp Jacobs R-744-A2 engine respectively. Simultaneously, it built 233 Model 190s, which were generally similar except for their 240hp Continental R-670-23 engine. All were 4/5-seaters, with the now-familiar Cessna cantilever spring-steel main undercarriage legs designed by Steve Wittman. Many examples are still current in the USA.

Cessna Stationair (and Model 206 Skywagon / Super Skylane) /USA

Photo: U206 Skywagon.
Data: Stationair.

Span: 35ft 10in (10.92m).
Length: 28ft 0in (8.53m).
Gross weight: 3,600lb (1,633kg).
Cruising speed: 131–164mph (211–264km/h).
Range: 650–1,020 miles (1,045–1,640km).

In 1970 Cessna introduced the names Stationair and Turbo-Stationair in place of the earlier U206 Skywagon and TU206 Turbo-Skywagon, to emphasise the differences between these 6-seat cargo/utility aircraft and the Models 180 and 185 Skywagon. They have a swept fin, tricycle undercarriage, bigger flaps and tailplane, and a double cargo-door. The Stationair (and earlier U206) has a 300hp Continental IO-520-F engine; the Turbo-Stationair (and TU206) is similar except for its 310hp Continental TSIO-520-M. Other models, no longer in production, are the P206 and TP206 Super Skylanes, *de luxe* passenger versions minus the cargo-door and with 285hp IO-520-A and TSIO-520-C engine respectively. All of these aircraft can carry an under-fuselage cargo-pack. Deliveries by January 1977, totalled 4,221 Model 206 Skywagons and Stationairs, and 643 Super Skylanes.

Cessna Model 210 Centurion /USA

Photo and data: Centurion II.

Span: 36ft 9in (11.20m).
Length: 28ft 3in (8.61m).
Gross weight: 3,800lb (1,724kg).
Cruising speed: 154–188mph (248–303km/h).
Range: 765–1,250 miles (1,231–2,010km).

The prototype Cessna 210, flown in January 1957, was the first Cessna high-wing lightplane with a retractable undercarriage. FAA Type Approval was obtained on August 23, 1966. The 1967 models set a further new fashion by dispensing with wing-struts to give a full cantilever wing. The current basic versions are the Model 210 Centurion I with 300hp Continental IO-520-L engine and 6 seats in pairs, and the T210 Turbo-System Centurion I which differs in having a 310hp TSIO-520-R supercharged engine. The externally-identical Centurion II and Turbo-System Centurion II have as standard equipment a factory-installed avionics package, gyro panel, dual controls and other refinements. A total of 5,077 Model 210s of all types had been delivered by January 1977.

Champion Citabria (and Scout and Decathlon) / USA

Photo: Scout.
Data: Model 7KCAB Citabria.

Span: 33ft 5in (10.19m).
Length: 22ft 8in (6.91m).
Gross weight: 1,650lb (748kg).
Max cruising speed: 125mph (201km/h).
Range: 537 miles (865km) at 125mph (201km/h).

Citabria is 'airbatic' spelled backwards, emphasising the manoeuvrability of this advanced development of the old Aeronca Champion family (see page 107). It is a tandem 2-seater, with composite wood and metal wings and steel-tube fuselage, all fabric-covered. Current models are the 7ECA with 115hp Lycoming O-235-C1 engine and optional floats or skis; Model 7GCAA with 150hp Lycoming O-320-A2B; and Model 7KCAB with 150hp IO-320-E2A and fuel and oil systems for prolonged inverted flight. The Model 7GCBC Scout is a utility/crop sprayer with span of 34ft 5¼in (10.50m), flaps and O-320-A2B engine. The similar Model 8KCAB Decathlon is an unlimited aerobatic competition aircraft and has a 150hp IO-320-E1A engine and 32ft (9.75m) wing span. All Champion aircraft are marketed by Bellanca.

De Havilland D.H.82A Tiger Moth (and Thruxton Jackeroo) /UK

Photo and data: Tiger Moth.

Span: 29ft 4in (8.94m).
Length: 23ft 11in (7.29m).
Gross weight: 1,825lb (828kg).
Range: 285 miles (460km) at 90mph (145km/h).

A few pre-war civil Tiger Moths, after service with the RAF throughout the war, are still flying together with a dwindling number of the war-time trainers which were demobilised by the score after RAF use. The engine is the 130hp Gipsy Major 1. A few veteran D.H.60 Moths without wing sweepback, are also still flying. The Jackaroo is a Tiger Moth in which the centre fuselage has been widened and enclosed to accommodate two pairs of seats in an enclosed cabin. The wider fuselage increases the span to 30ft 4½in (9.25m). Relatively few were converted and only a handful remain.

De Havilland D.H.87B Hornet Moth /UK

Span: 31ft 11in (9.73m).
Length: 24ft 11½in (7.60m).
Gross weight: 2,000lb (907kg).
Range: 623 miles (1,002km) at 105mph (169km/h).

This 1934 product was virtually a side-by-side 2-seat biplane edition of the Leopard Moth, intended to replace the D.H.60 Moth. Originally the wings were sharply tapered (D.H.87A), but most of the early machines were re-fitted with the more rectangular wings of the D.H.87B in 1936. More than a dozen are still flying in Britain and a few others overseas, with 130hp Gipsy Major 1 engine.

De Havilland DHC-1 Chipmunk /Canada /UK

Photo: Chipmunk 10.

Span: 34ft 4in (10.47m).
Length: 25ft 8in (7.82m).
Gross weight: 2,200lb (997kg).
Range: 292 miles (470km) at 124mph (199km/h).

De Havilland's Canadian company designed the Chipmunk as its first exercise in original aircraft design. The prototype was first flown on May 22, 1946, and Canadian production totalled 158 for civil use and 60 for the RCAF as Chipmunk T.30. Another 60 were produced under licence in Portugal by OGMA. To meet RAF needs for a new primary trainer, the Chipmunk entered production in the UK as the T.10. The 2-seat Chipmunk 21 was built from scratch in the UK for civil use, with 145hp Gipsy Major 10 Mk 2 engine; Chipmunk 22s are ex-RAF Mk 10 trainers. Chipmunk 22As have extra fuel and the Chipmunk 23 is a modified single-seat agricultural version. Also to be seen are Bristol 'tourer conversions' of the Mk 22A with blown hood and other refinements, giving a 130mph cruising speed.

DINFIA IA 46 Model 66
Super Ranquel/Argentina

Photo: Ranquel.
Data: Super Ranquel.

Span: 38ft 1½in (11.61m).
Length: 24ft 5in (7.44m).
Gross weight: 2,775lb (1,260kg).
Range: 405 miles (652km/h) at 106mph
(171km/h).

The original prototype Ranquel flew on December 23, 1957, and 100 had been built by April 1966. Final production versions were the standard Ranquel with 150hp Lycoming O-320-A2B engine and Super Ranquel with 180hp Lycoming O-360-A2A. An 88-gallon belly tank for agricultural chemicals could be attached to the Super Ranquel without encroaching on space inside the 3-seat cabin. DINFIA flew the prototype of an improved version known as the IA 51 Tehuelche, with O-360 engine and metal skin instead of fabric on the wing; but all Ranquel production ended in December 1968, and no more IA 51s were built.

EMBRAER EMB-200 and
201 Ipanema/Brazil

Photo and data: EMB-201A.

Span: 38ft 4½in (11.69m).
Length: 24ft 4½in (7.43m).
Gross weight: 3,968lb (1,800kg).
Max cruising speed: 127mph
(204km/h).
Max range: 545 miles (878km).

Development of this single-seat agricultural aircraft was started in May 1969 by the national Aerospace Technical Centre, to specifications laid down by the Brazilian Ministry of Agriculture. When EMBRAER was formed a few months later it took over responsibility for the Ipanema. The prototype flew for the first time on July 30, 1970, and 73 of the initial EMB-200 and 200A versions, with 260hp Lycoming O-540 engine, were built before they were superseded by the EMB-201 in mid-1974. A total of 188 EMB-201s were delivered, with 300hp Lycoming IO-540 engine. This version was replaced by the current EMB-201A, with modified wings and other refinements, from March 1977. The Brazilian Air Force Academy has 3 EMB-201Rs, adapted for gliding-towing.

Fairchild F-24W/USA

Photo: F-24R.
Data: F-24W-41A.

Span: 36ft 4in (11.07m).
Length: 23ft 9in (7.24m).
Gross weight: 2,562lb (1,162kg).
Range: 640 miles (1,030km) at 117mph
(188km/h).

Many F-24Ws remain in civil use throughout the world, mostly of the F-24W-41/41A series, built during the second World War for communications duties with the USAAF and its allies, under the designation UC-61/61A. These, and post-war civil F-24W-46s, are 4-seaters with the 165hp Warner Super Scarab 165 engine. Earlier models, with 145hp Super Scarab, 175hp Ranger (F-24R) and other engines, can also be seen, particularly in the USA British name for the F-24 is Argus.

FFA AS.202 Bravo /
Switzerland

Photo and data: AS.202/15.

Span: 31ft 11¾in (9.75m).
Length: 24ft 7in (7.50m).
Gross weight: 2,202lb (999kg).
Cruising speed: 126mph (203km/h).
Max range: 553 miles (890km).

This light aircraft was intended originally to be produced in both Switzerland and Italy, with joint manufacture by Flug- & Fahrzeugwerke and SIAI-Marchetti. Instead, FFA now handles all production and marketing. First prototype to fly was an AS.202/15, with 150hp Lycoming O-320-E2A engine and 2/3 seats, on March 7, 1969. It was followed by an Italian-assembled AS.202/10 2-seater with 115hp Lycoming O-235-C2A. Two more Swiss-built prototypes flew in 1969/70. Following modification of the tail unit and other changes to improve handling qualities for training, an initial series of 25 AS.202/15s was put in hand for production at Altenrhein.

Fiat G.46 /Italy

Photo: G.46-3B.
Data: G.46-4B.

Span: 34ft 1¼in (10.39m).
Length: 27ft 10in (8.48m).
Gross weight: 3,102lb (1,406kg).
Range: 620 miles (1,000km) at 155mph (249km/h).

Fiat built a total of 150 G.46 basic trainers for the Italian Air Force in 1947–52, in five versions. These were the tandem 2-seat G.46-1B (205hp Alfa Romeo 115*bis* engine), single-seat G.46-3A and 4A, and 2-seat G.46-3B and 4B (all with 225hp Alfa Romeo 115-1 *ter*). When no longer required by the Italian Air Force, many were sold to civilian owners and quite a few examples are still on the Italian civil register.

Fleet 80 Canuck /Canada

Span: 34ft 0in (10.36m).
Length: 22ft 4½in (6.80m).
Gross weight: 1,425lb (645kg).
Range: 400 miles (644km) at 100mph (161km/h).

Designed for service in the Canadian bush and elsewhere, the Canuck is a sturdy tandem 2-seat lightplane with a fabric-covered all-metal airframe. It went into production immediately after the war and 210 were built in two years with 85hp Continental C-8512J engine. A large number are still on register, and are able to utilise alternative wheel, float and ski undercarriages.

Flight Invert Cranfield A1 /UK

Span: 32ft 10in (10.00m).
Length: 26ft 5in (8.05m).
Gross weight: 950kg (2,095lb).
Max speed: 170mph (273km/h).

Design of this specialised aerobatic aircraft was started in 1968, to a specification drawn up by one of Britain's top competition pilots, Neil Williams. Lack of finance delayed completion of the prototype, which flew for the first time on August 23, 1976. By April 1977, it had flown 50 times and was then modified to have its original 210hp Rolls-Royce Continental IO-360-D engine replaced by a 268hp Lycoming IO-540-D (Special). When flown in normal single-seat form, ultimate load factors are $+12g$ and $-9g$. A second person can be carried for training and ferrying.

Fokker S.11 Instructor (and Macchi M.416) /
Netherlands /Italy

Photo: S.12 Instructor.

Span: 36ft 1in (10.99m).
Length: 26ft 8in (8.13m).
Gross weight: 2,422lb (1,100kg).
Range: 400 miles (644km) at 102mph (164km/h).

First flown in 1947, the S.11 Instructor side-by-side 2-seat primary trainer was produced in Holland for the Dutch and Israeli air forces and in Brazil for the Brazilian air force. A tricycle undercarriage version, designated S.12, was also manufactured in Brazil. Another 150 S.11s were produced under licence in Italy as Macchi M.416s. Standard power plant for all of these machines was the 190hp Lycoming O-435-A. Having become surplus, many of the Macchi M.416s were sold to Italian flying clubs and schools, with which they continue to operate.

Fournier RF-6B Club /
France

Span: 34ft 5½in (10.50m).
Length: 22ft 11¾in (7.00m).
Gross weight: 1,631lb (740kg).
Normal cruising speed: 118mph (190km/h).

As its designation implies, this two-seat aerobatic, sporting and training aircraft is related to the four-seat Sportavia RF-6 Sportsman. The prototype flew for the first time on March 12, 1974, and was followed by five pre-production RF-6Bs, the first of which flew on March 4, 1976. About 40 aircraft had been delivered by mid-1977, the standard version being powered by a 100hp Rolls-Royce Continental O-200-A. The two seats are side by side, with dual controls. Construction is all-wooden, with plywood covered fuselage and fabric covering elsewhere. Development of a de luxe 120hp version was underway when financial difficulties brought RF-6B production to an end in late 1977.

Fuji FA-200 Aero Subaru /
Japan

Photo and data: FA-200-180.

Span: 30ft 11in (9.42m).
Length: 26ft 9½in (8.17m).
Gross weight: 2,535lb (1,150kg).
Cruising speed: 104–127mph (167–204km/h).
Max range: 835 miles (1,343km).

The prototype of this 4-seat all-metal light aircraft flew for the first time on August 12, 1965. After flight testing and some refinement of the design, two versions were put into production: the FA-200-160 has a 160hp Lycoming O-320-D2A engine; the FA-200?80 has a 180hp Lycoming IO-360-

B1B. Both types are also certificated in the Aerobatic category as 2-seaters; the FA-200-180AO has a 180hp O-360-A5AD engine and fixed-pitch propeller instead of the normal constant-speed type. A total of 274 Aero Subarus had been completed by February 1977.

Grumman American AA-1 Yankee, Trainer, T-cat and Lynx /USA

Photo: Lynx.
Data: Lynx.

Span: 24ft 6in (7.47m).
Length: 19ft 3in (5.86m).
Gross weight: 1,600lb (726kg).
Range: 344 miles (554km) at 135mph (217km/h).

The prototype of this two-seater family flew for the first time on July 11, 1963, as the Bede BD-1. American Aviation Corporation (since acquired by Grumman) was formed in 1964 to produce the type as the AA-1 Yankee, using advanced constructional techniques such as metal-to-metal bonding and aluminium honeycomb for the fuselage panels. The first production Yankee flew on May 30, 1968, with a 108hp Lycoming O-235-C2C engine; early

developments were the AA-1A/B Trainer and de luxe Tr-2. Previous models were superseded in 1977 by the AA-1C T-cat and de luxe Lynx, with a 115hp Lycoming O-235-L2C engine able to run on the new 100 octane low-lead fuel. Tailplane and elevator size were also increased. Optional extras include a spin package and 'private fighter' paint scheme.

Grumman American AA-5, Traveler, Cheetah and Tiger /USA

Photo: Tiger.
Data: Tiger.

Span: 31ft 6in (9.60m).
Length: 22ft 0in (6.71m).
Gross weight: 2,400lb (1,088kg).
Range: 637 miles (1,026km) at 160mph (258km/h).

The original AA-5, which flew on August 21, 1970, was an enlarged and more powerful four-seat version of the AA-1. It had a de luxe counterpart named the Traveler. By 1976, the standard and de luxe models had become the AA-5A and Cheetah respectively, and had been supplemented by a pair

of more powerful versions known as the AA-5B and de luxe Tiger. The basic models were dropped in 1977, leaving the Cheetah and Tiger as Grumman American's only single-engined four-seaters, with 150hp Lycoming O-320-E2G and 180hp Lycoming O-360-A4K engine respectively.

Grumman American Ag-Cat and Super Ag-Cat /USA

**Photo: Super Ag-Cat B /450.
Data for Super Ag-Cat.**

Span: 35ft 11in (10.95m).
Length: 24ft 3in (7.39m).
Gross weight: 6,075lb (2,755kg).
Working speed: 80–100mph (129–168km /h).

The original G-164 Ag-Cat flew for the first time on May 22, 1967. Quantity production was taken on by Schweizer Aircraft, and in the first six years of operation Ag-Cats logged more than one million flying hours in the USA without a fatal accident. The initial production model had a 220–225hp Continental W-670 radial engine and loaded weight of 3,600lb (1,633kg). It was followed by versions with 240hp Gulf Coast W-670 and 245–300hp Jacobs R-755 engines, and then by the G-164A Super Ag-Cat, with a Jacobs R-755, 450hp Pratt & Whitney R-985 (data above) or 600hp Pratt & Whitney R-1340 engine. Marketing is now handled by the Grumman American Aviation Division.

HAL HUL-26 Pushpak / India

Span: 36ft 0in (10.97m).
Length: 21ft 0in (6.40m).
Gross weight: 1,350lb (612kg).
Cruising speed: 70–85mph (113–137km /h).
Range: 250 miles (402km) at 70mph (113km /h).

Hindustan Aeronautics designed this 2-seat lightplane as an inexpensive locally-built trainer for use by Indian flying clubs. The prototype flew for the first time on September 28, 1958, and a total of 150 were delivered. The airframe is a fabric-covered metal structure. Standard power plant is a 90hp Continental C90-8F, but one Pushpak was fitted experimentally with a 90hp P.E.90 engine of HAL's own design. The military Krishak, used by the Indian Air Force, was a derivative.

HAL HA-31 Mk. II Basant /India

Span: 39ft 4½in (12.00m).
Length: 29ft 6¼in (9.00m).
Gross weight: 5,000lb (2,270kg).
Max cruising speed: 115mph (185km /h).
Range: 400 miles (645km).

Hindustan Aeronautics designed its first agricultural aeroplane in mid-1968. This, the HA-31 Mk I, flew as a prototype in 1969 but was not a success. A completely new design was therefore evolved as the HA-31 Mk II and this, fitted with a 400 hp Lycoming IO-720-C1B engine, made its first flight on March 30, 1972. A second prototype and 20 pre-production Basants were built subsequently; and 31 of the first series of 100 production aircraft had been completed by early 1977.

IAR-821, 822, 826 and 827 /Romania

Photo and data: IAR-826

Span: 42ft 0in (12.80m).
Length: 30ft 10in (9.40m).
Gross weight: 4,189lb (1,900kg).
Cruising speed: 103mph (165km/h).
Endurance: 1.3hrs.

The basic IAR-821 single-seat agricultural aircraft was designed at the former Industrial Aeronautica Romana works. The prototype flew for the first time in 1967. Production by IRMA (Aircraft Repair Factory) began in the following year and 20 were built in 1968–69, each with a 300hp Ivchenko AI-14RF radial engine. The prototype of a tandem 2-seat training/utility version, known as the IAR-821B, flew in September 1968. The basic design was adapted subsequently to take a 290hp Lycoming IO-540-G1D5 engine, and a prototype of the resulting IAR-822 flew in 1970. Work on a pre-series batch of five and 200 production models was started soon afterwards, primarily for agricultural duties but suitable for a wide variety of other tasks such as highway de-icing, firefighting, aerial survey, glider towing, training and mail/freight transport. The IAR-822B is a tandem 2-seat version with the same Lycoming engine, and the all-metal IAR-826, which appeared in 1973, is generally similar to the wood and metal IAR-822. The IAR-827 is a development of the 826, with a 400hp Lycoming IO-720 engine.

IAR-823 /Romania

Span: 32ft 9¾in (10.00m).
Length: 27ft 0¼in (8.24m).
Gross weight: 3,042lb (1,380kg).
Max range: 994 miles (1,600km) at 180mph (290km/h).

This two/five-seat light aircraft was designed by a team led by Dipl Ing Radu Manicatide, one of Romania's best-known designers. The prototype flew in July 1973, followed by the first pre-production IAR-823 in 1974. Power plant is a 290hp Lycoming IO-540-G1D5, enabling the aircraft to carry up to five persons in its executive, taxi and touring roles. It is fully aerobatic as a two-seater, and a military version is offered with two underwing hardpoints for drop-tanks or practice weapons.

Interceptor 400 (and Aero Commander 200 and Meyers 200) /USA

Photo: Meyers 200D.

Span: 30ft 6in (9.29m).
Length: 26ft 11½in (8.20m).
Gross weight: 4,005lb (1,815kg).
Max cruising speed: 281mph (452km/h).
Max range: 1,000 miles (1,610km) at 275mph (443km/h).

First product of Interceptor Corporation, this 4-seater was introduced as general aviation's first high-performance, pressurised, production aircraft powered by a single turboprop engine. The prototype flew on June 27, 1969, and received FAA certification in August 1971.
Power plant in production aircraft is a 665shp Ai-Research TPE 331-1-101, flat rated at 400shp. The airframe of the Interceptor 400 is based on that of the piston-engined aircraft known originally as the Meyers 200B and subsequently produced for a time by Aero Commander as their Model 200, with 285hp Continental IO-520-A engine.

Jodel D.11 Series /France

Photo: D.112.
Data: D.112.

Span: 26ft 10in (8.18m).
Length: 20ft 10in (6.35m).
Gross weight: 1,145lb (520kg).
Cruising speed: 93–105mph (150–169km/h).
Max range: 373 miles (600km).

The whole series of Jodel designs stemmed from the single-seat D.9 Bebé, an ultra-light monoplane of such simple construction that it could be built and flown easily by amateurs. The 2-seat D.11 followed and proved the starting point for a string of derivatives, including the D.112 (65hp Continental) D.117 (90hp Continental) and D.119.

Several companies acquired licences to manufacture the 2-seaters commercially. Wassmer, in France, built more than 300 D.112s and *de luxe* D.120 Paris-Nices. The improved D.1190.S Compostela was built in Spain by Aero-Difusion, with a 90hp Rolls-Royce/Continental C90-14F engine. Many home-built examples are also flying.

Jodel DR.100 Ambassadeur Series (including Sicile and Excellence) / France

Photo: DR.1050.
Data: Sicile Record.

Span: 28ft 7¼in (8.71m).
Length: 20ft 10in (6.35m).
Gross weight: 1,720lb (780kg).
Range: 775 miles (1,250km) at 133mph (214km/h).

One of the first manufacturers to realise the potential in the Jodel design was Pierre Robin of Centre Est Aeronautique (now Avions Pierre Robin). With the original designer, Jean Delemontez, he first evolved a high-performance 3-seater designated DR.100 Ambassadeur (10 built). Successive improved versions included the DR.1050 and 1051

(148 built), and DR.1050/M Sicile (114 built) and Sicile Record (58 built), with 100hp Rolls-Royce/Continental O-200-A engine. Like all Jodels, they feature all-wooden construction and considerable dihedral on the outer wings. The SAN Jodel DR.1052 Excellence is similar. Production of these types has ended.

Jodel D.140E Mousquetaire IV (and Abeille) / France

Photo and data: Mousquetaire IV.

Span: 33ft 8¼in (10.27m).
Length: 25ft 8in (7.82m).
Gross weight: 2,645lb (1,200kg).
Cruising speed: 125–149mph (200–240km/h).
Max range: 870 miles (1,400km).

Societé Aeronautique Normande (SAN), like Avions Pierre Robin, specialised in manufacturing Jodel designs. With SAN's D.140 Mousquetaire, the Jodel became a 4-seater. It could even take a fifth person on short flights and had a baggage locker aft of the cabin large enough to enable a stretcher patient to be carried. When SAN suspended operations, manufacture of the Mousquetaire IV was taken over by Robin, together with outstanding orders for the D.140R Abeille, which is similar, but is equipped as a glider-tug and has a more extensively-glazed cabin to improve rearward view. Both types have a 180hp Lycoming O-360-A2A engine.

Jodel D.150 Mascaret / France

Span: 26ft 9in (8.15m).
Length: 20ft 8in (6.3m).
Gross weight: 1,588lb (720kg).
Range: 1,000 miles (1,610km) at 120mph (193km/h).

In collaboration with Jean Delemontez, the former SAN company developed the Mascaret 2-seater as a replacement for the less-refined D.11 series. It is rather like a short-span Ambassadeur, with a more roomy fuselage than the D.112 and a 100hp Rolls—Royce/Continental O-200-A engine. Like most of the later factory-built Jodels, it has a one-piece all-moving tailplane.

Lake LA-4 Buccaneer (and Colonial Skimmer IV) /USA

Photo and data: Buccaneer.

Span: 38ft 0in (11.58m).
Length: 24ft 11in (7.60m).
Gross weight: 2,690lb (1,220kg).
Cruising speed: 150mph (241km/h).
Max range: 847 miles (1,363km).

This amphibian began life as the 3-seat Colonial C-1 Skimmer, which flew for the first time on July 17, 1948, with a 125hp Lycoming O-290 engine. The production version had a 150hp Lycoming and was joined in 1957 by the C-2 Skimmer IV 4-seater with a 180hp Lycoming O-360-A1A. Manufac-turing rights for the Skimmer IV were taken over by Lake Aircraft in 1959. From it they evolved the LA-4, with longer bow, 4-ft greater span and other improvements. Production continues, the current version being the Buccaneer, with 200hp IO-360-A1B engine, as described and illustrated.

Laverda (Aviamilano) F.8.L Super Falco /Italy

Span: 26ft 3in (8.0m).
Length: 21ft 4in (6.50m).
Gross weight: 1,808lb (821kg).
Cruising speed: 155—180mph (250—290km/h).
Max range: 870 miles (1,400km).

This side-by-side 2-seater has the typical racey lines of a design by Stelio Frati (see Procaer Picchio and SIAI-Marchetti SF.260 for others). Construction is of wood, with retractable undercarriage and 160hp Lycoming O-320-B3B engine. Earlier Falcos, built by Aviamilano and Aeromere, had 135/150hp Lycomings. Production of all versions has been completed.

129

Let Z-37 Cmelak /
Czechoslovakia

Photo and data: Z-37A.

Span: 40ft 1½in (12.22m).
Length: 28ft 0½in (8.55m).
Gross weight: 4,080lb (1,850kg).
Range: 400 miles (640km) at 114mph
(183km/h) (with reserves).

This functional-looking aircraft was designed primarily for agricultural duties, with a 143-gallon (650-litre) chemical hopper aft of the single-seat cockpit. There is a seat for a mechanic or loader aft of the hopper, and the space occupied by this seat and the hopper can be utilised for carrying mail and freight during the Winter season, when ag-planes are often unemployed. Structure is of metal, with mixed metal and fabric covering. Power plant is a 315hp M462RF radial engine of Czechoslovakian design. The first of ten prototype Cmelaks flew on March 29, 1963, and 600 production aircraft had been completed when production ended in 1975, including 27 Z-37A-2 two-seat trainers. The final operational version, the Z-37A, differed from the original Z-37 mainly in structural and anti-corrosive improvements to extend the time between major overhauls to as much as 4,000 flying hours.

Luscombe Model 8
Silvaire /USA

Photo: Model 8A.
Data: Model 8F.

Span: 35ft 0in (10.67m).
Length: 20ft 0in (6.09m).
Gross weight: 1,400lb (635kg).
Range: 500 miles (805km) at 120mph
(193km/h).

Some 2,000 all-metal 2-seat Silvaires of various models are still flying throughout the world, mostly in the USA. The original Model 8, built by Luscombe Airplane Corp, flew in 1937 and went into production with a 50hp Continental engine. It was followed by the Models 8A (65hp Continental), 8B (65hp Lycoming) and 8C and 8D (75hp Continental), and 1,200 Silvaires had been delivered by 1942, when Luscombe suspended production to meet wartime commitments. Post-war manufacture was resumed with the Models 8E (85hp Continental) and 8F (90hp Continental) by, successively, the Luscombe, Temco and Silvaire companies, the last Model 8F appearing in 1960.

Macchi M.B. 308 /Italy /
Argentina

Data: M.B.308-100.

Span: 32ft 9½in (9.98m).
Length: 21ft 5in (6.53m).
Gross weight: 1,610lb (730kg).
Range: 420 miles (676km) at 117mph
(188km/h).

The original production versions of the M.B. 308, in 1947, were 2-seaters with 85/90hp Continental engine. They were followed by the 3-seat M.B. 308G, which can be identified by a second cabin window on each side; and many still appear on the Italian civil register. In 1958, German Bianco SA of the Argentine acquired exclusive manufacturing rights, and built two versions—the standard M.B.308, with 90hp Continental C90, and the M.B.308-100 with 100hp Continental O-200-A. Production has ended.

Maule M-4 Rocket Series (and Jetasen) / USA

Photo: M-5-210C Lunar Rocket.
Data: M-4 Rocket.

Span: 30ft 10in (9.39m).
Length: 22ft 0in (6.70m).
Gross weight: 2,300lb (1,043kg).
Max cruising speed: 165mph (265km/h).
Range: 680 miles (1,095km) at 150mph (241km/h).

This high-performance 4-seat light aircraft began as an amateur 'home-built'. The prototype, known as the Maule Bee Dee B-4, flew on September 8, 1960, and several hundred production models have since been delivered, in five versions. The M-4 Jetasen has a 145hp Continental O-300-A engine; the otherwise-similar Rocket has a 210hp Continental IO-360-A, enabling it to take off in 430ft fully laden. The Astro-Rocket is a *de luxe* version of the Jetasen with 180hp Franklin 6A-335-B1A engine; the Strata-Rocket differs from the Rocket in having a 220hp Franklin 6A-350-C1. The M-5 Lunar Rocket has a 220hp engine, and larger flaps and tail unit.

MBB BO 209 Monsun / Germany

Data: BO 209-160.

Span: 27ft 6¾in (8.83m).
Length: 21ft 7¾in (6.58m).
Gross weight: 1,807lb (820kg).
Crusing speed: 151–158mph (243 –254km/h).
Max range: 745 miles (1,200km).

The prototype of this 2-seat light aircraft, known as the MHK-101, was designed by Dipl-Ing Hermann Mylius, Technical Director of the former Bölkow company, now part of Messerschmitt-Bölkow-Blohm GmbH. It flew for the first time on December 22, 1967, and was developed into the BO 209 Monsun, which first flew on May 28, 1969, and was offered in three versions. The basic BO 209-150 had a 150hp Lycoming O-320-E engine; this was replaced by a 160hp Lycoming IO-320-D1A in the BO 209-160. The BO 209S specialised trainer, first flown in June 1971, had a 130hp Rolls-Royce/Continental O-240 engine. The BO 209-150 and -160 had folding wings and an optionally-retractable nose-wheel. Production ended in 1972.

MBB 223/CASA Flamingo /Germany /Spain

Span: 27ft 2in (8.28m).
Length: 24ft 4½in (7.43m).
Gross weight: 2,315lb (1,050kg).
Max cruising speed: 136mph (219km/h).
Range: 310–715 miles (500–1,150km).

This all-metal lightplane won a design competition organised by the German Ministry of Economics in 1962, and was developed by the former SIAT company, now part of MBB. The object was to produce a standardised club and training aircraft for use in Germany, but shortage of funds delayed the first flight of the prototype until March 1, 1967. There were two basic versions: the MBB 223A1 basic 2-seat utility/trainer which could also be equipped as a '2 + 2' 3/4-seat tourer or as an agricultural aircraft; and the MBB 223K1 single-seat fully-aerobatic version with an AIO-300 engine instead of the standard 200hp Lycoming IO-360-C1B. After 50 had been built in Germany, production was transferred to CASA in Spain, where the first example flew on February 14, 1972. Subsequently, Pilatus in Switzerland acquired the tooling and continued production, primarily for military users.

Meteor F.L.55–BM /Italy

Photo: F.L.55.
Data: F.L.55-BM.

Span: 32ft 3½in (9.83m).
Length: 20ft 10½in (6.35m).
Gross weight: 1,985lb (900kg).
Range: 225 miles (362km) at 112mph (180km/h).

In 1953, Meteor SpA took over the designs of Francis Lombardi and subsequently developed from the F.L.3 the more modern F.L.53, retaining the 60hp CNA engine. Further development produced the 3-seat F.L.54, with 85 or 90hp Continental engine, and the 4-seat F.L.55, with 130 or 150hp Lycoming engine. The aircraft described is the 150hp Meteor F.L.55-BM ski-plane. Examples of all versions are still flying, plus a few of the original F.L.3s with Continental or Mikron engines.

Miles M.38 Messenger / UK

Photo and data: Messenger 2A.

Span: 36ft 2in (11.02m).
Length: 24ft 0in (7.31m).
Gross weight: 2,400lb (1,088kg).
Range: 460 miles (740km) at 112mph (180km/h).

Sixty M.38s were built, including the original Messenger Is for the RAF. Several of these are now in civil use as Messenger 4As with 145hp Gipsy Major 1D engines. Those built from scratch for the civil market are the Mk 2A with 155hp Cirrus Major III. Production ended in 1948, but a dozen or so remain on the British Civil Register. A handful of others are flying overseas.

Miles M.65 Gemini (and Aries) /UK

Photo: Gemini 3C.
Data: Gemini 1A.

Span: 36ft 2in (11.02m).
Length: 22ft 3in (6.78m).
Gross weight: 3,000lb (1,360kg).
Range: 820 miles (1,320km) at 135mph (217km/h).

Several variants of this popular post-war lightplane are still flying, including the original Gemini 1A with 100hp Cirrus Minor 2 engines; the 3A conversion with Gipsy Major 10 Mk 1, and 3C with Gipsy Major 10 Mk 2; the 3B with retractable flaps; and the 7 (and similar Aries) with Major 10 Mk 2, bigger tail and increased weight. Several Geminis and one Aries appear on the current British register. Others are flying overseas.

Mooney (and Aerostar) M-20 series /USA

Photo: Mooney 201.
Data: M-20C Ranger.

Span: 35ft 0in (10.67m).
Length: 24ft 1in (7.34m).
Gross weight: 2,575lb (1,167kg).
Max speed: 176mph (283km/h).
Max range: 1,001 miles (1,610km) (with reserves).

The Ranger (data above) is the former Mooney M-20C Mark 21 with 180hp Lycoming O360-A1D engine. The Chaparral (former M-20E Super-21) is similar except for its 200hp IO-360-A1A engine. The Executive (former M-20F) has the 200hp engine and a longer fuselage with three windows each side. Early M-20s (first flown August 10, 1953) had a metal fuselage and wooden wings. The Mooney company was renamed Aerostar Aircraft Corp in July 1970, but production was suspended in 1972, by which time total output had included over 2,000 Rangers, 1,400 Chaparrals and 1,900 Executives. Production resumed in 1974 under new management.

Navion Rangemaster (and Navion) /USA

Photo: Navion.
Data: Rangemaster.

Span: 34ft 9in (10.6m).
Length: 27ft 6in (8.38m).
Gross weight: 3,315lb (1,503kg).
Cruising speed: 185–191mph (298–307km/h).
Max range: 1,800 miles (2,900km).

The original 4-seat Navion was manufactured first by its designers, North American, and then by Ryan, each company building more than one thousand. Navion Aircraft then took over the design and, on June 10, 1960 flew the prototype of a 5-seat version named the Rangemaster, with engine power increased from 205 to 260hp and wingtip tanks for even-longer range. This was superseded by the further improved Model H, with 285hp Continental IO-520-B engine, which was taken over by Janox Corporation in 1970. The rights were sold again in 1973 to Navion Rangemaster Aircraft Corp.

Neiva Paulistinha 56 / Brazil

Photo and data: Paulistinha 56-C.

Span: 35ft 5in (10.80m).
Length: 22ft 2in (6.76m).
Gross weight: 1,455lb (660kg).
Cruising speed: 90–99mph (145–159km/h).
Max range: 560 miles (900km).

This tandem 2-seat light aircraft was produced by Neiva for many years, in several versions. Last to be manufactured in quantity was the Paulistinha 56-C, with 90hp Continental C90 engine, of which production ended in 1964, after a total of 238 had been completed. The developed 56-D, with 150hp Lycoming O-320-A1A, did not progress beyond a single prototype. Production of an updated version, known as the Paulistão, was under consideration in 1977.

Nipper (and Tipsy Nipper) /Belgium /UK

Photo: Nipper T.66 Mk 2.
Data: Nipper Mk III.

Span: 20ft 6in (6.25m).
Length: 15ft 0in (4.57m).
Gross weight: 660lb (300kg).
Cruising speed: 90–95mph (145–153km/h).
Range: 200–450 miles (322–725km).

Two versions of the diminutive Tipsy Nipper single-seater were manufactured originally by Avions Fairey in Belgium, in the form of both kits and complete aircraft. The T.66 Mk 1 Nipper had a 40hp Pollmann HEPU engine. T.66 Mk 2 had a 45hp Stark Stamo, giving a range of 525 miles (845km) when wingtip tanks were fitted. Pro-duction was taken over by Nipper Aircraft Ltd of the UK in 1966, and this company evolved two improved versions. The basic Nipper Mk III has a 45hp 1,500cc Rollason Ardem (VW) engine; the Mk IIIA has a 1,600cc Rollason Ardem. These were sold in small numbers in the form of both factory-built aircraft and kits.

Nord 1002 Pingouin II / France

Span: 34ft 5in (10.50m).
Length: 28ft 1in (8.56m).
Gross weight: 3,270lb (1,483kg).
Max cruising speed: 167mph (270km/h).
Max range: 528 miles (850km).

This light aircraft was developed from the Messer-schmitt Bf 108B, of which a few examples are also still flying. Nord built 170 standard Bf 108Bs during the war, and others under the designation Nord 1000. Change of power plant from the 240hp Argus As 10B to a 233hp Renault 6Q 11 led to the redesignation Nord 1001 Pingouin I. Finally came the Pingouin II, with four seats instead of three and a Renault 6Q 10 engine. Many still appear on the French civil register; two on the British register.

Nord 1101 Noralpha / France

Span: 37ft 8in (11.50m).
Length: 28ft 0in (8.53m).
Gross weight: 3,630lb (1,646kg).
Range: 745 miles (1,200km) at 172mph (277km/h).

This 4-seat lightplane is a development of the Messerschmitt Bf 108 with tricycle undercarriage. Two prototypes were built by Nord during the second World War, with 270hp Argus engine, as Me 208s. Post-war, the surviving prototype was redesignated Nord 1100. The Nord 1101 and 1102 production versions were similar, with 233hp Renault 6Q 10 and 6Q 11 engine respectively. A total of 200 were built for military and civilian service. Many are still flying in France and six are registered in the UK.

Nord 1203/II Norécrin
II/France

Photo and data: Norécrin II.

Span: 33ft 6¼in (10.22m).
Length: 23ft 8in (7.21m).
Gross weight: 2,313lb (1,050kg).
Max cruising speed: 137mph (220km/h).
Max range: 560 miles (900km).

Despite a family likeness to the Noralpha, the Norécrin was an original Nord design to meet a French Ministry of Transport requirement. The 2-seat Nord 1200 prototype had a 100hp Mathis engine and flew for the first time on December 15, 1945. Initial production model was the 3-seat Nord 1201 Norécrin I, with 140hp Renault 4 Pei engine. A few examples are still airworthy but are outnumbered by Nord 1203/II Norécrin IIs, with 135hp Régnier 4LO engine and four seats.

North American T-6
Texan/Harvard/USA

Span: 42ft 0in (12.80m).
Length: 29ft 6in (8.99m).
Gross weight: 5,617lb (2,547kg).
Range: 870 miles (1,400km) at 146mph (235km/h).

More than 10,000 of these famous 2-seat basic trainers were built in the USA and Canada in 1938–54 and the type still serves with about 30 world air forces. In addition, many civil-registered T-6s are flying, notably as airline pilot trainers, although some have been used for such unusual jobs as skywriting and others are privately owned. Standard power plant is a 550hp Pratt & Whitney R1340-AN-1 radial engine.

Omnipol L-40 Meta-
Sokol/Czechoslovakia

Span: 33ft 0in (10.06m).
Length: 24ft 9in (7.54m).
Gross weight: 2,062lb (935kg).
Max cruising speed: 127mph (204km/h).
Max range: 688 miles (1,107km).

An interesting feature of this Czech-built 4-seater is its 'reversed tricycle' retractable undercarriage, the third wheel of which is under the rear of the cabin. Normal engine is a 140hp Walter M332, but the 105hp Minor 4-III was installed in some aircraft. Wingtip fuel tanks may be fitted. Small numbers are in service in Western Europe, including the UK, and in Australia. All Czechoslovakian civil aircraft are marketed through the Omnipol organisation, and were usually referred to as Omnipol types during the period of Meta-Sokol production.

Partenavia P.57 Fachiro II-f /Italy

Span: 30ft 0in (9.14m).
Length: 21ft 9in (6.63m).
Gross weight: 2,420lb (1,100kg).
Cruising speed: 118–135mph (190–217km/h).
Max range: 560 miles (900km).

The prototype of the 4-seat Fachiro flew on November 7, 1958, with a 150hp Lycoming O-320 engine. A 168hp Lycoming O-360B2A was substituted in the initial production Fachiro II. This was followed by the main production series of Fachiro II-fs with 180hp Lycoming O-360-A2A engine. All have wooden wings and fabric-covered steel-tube fuselage. The Fachiro was superseded in 1966 by the P.64 Oscar.

Partenavia P.64 and P.66 Oscar and P.66C Charlie / Italy

Photo: P.66C Charlie.
Data: P.66C-160 Charlie.

Span: 32ft 9½in (9.99m).
Length: 23ft 9in (7.24m).
Gross weight: 2,183lb (990kg).
Max cruising speed: 135mph (218km/h).
Range: 486 miles (782km) at 128mph (206km/h).

The prototype of the P.64 Oscar first flew on April 2, 1965, and the type went into production as an all-metal replacement for the Fachiro. The Oscar-B of 1967 introduced a stepped-down rear fuselage and panoramic rear cabin window. Subsequently, the Oscar family was expanded to four models, and by February 1975 Partenavia had built 73 P.64B Oscar-180s with 4 seats and 180hp Lycoming O-360-A1A engine; 16 4-seat P.64B Oscar-200s with 200hp Lycoming IO-360-A1B; 107 2-seat P.66B Oscar-100s with 115hp Lycoming O-235-C1B; and 79 3-seat P.66B Oscar-150s with 150hp Lycoming O-320-E2A. The Oscar-180 was also built by AFIC in South Africa as the RSA 200 Falcon. Production of these versions has ended; but Partenavia is building for the Aero Club d'Italia a first batch of 70 P.66C Charlie basic trainers, with two/four seats and a 160hp O-320-H2AD engine.

Piaggio P.149-D /Italy

Span: 36ft 6in (11.13m).
Length: 28ft 9½in (8.78m).
Gross weight: 3,705lb (1,680kg).
Range: 680 miles (1,095km) at 145mph (233km/h).

The P.149 was designed as a 4-seat civil development of the P.148 primary trainer, using many components of the latter. It flew for the first time on June 19, 1953. Two years later, Piaggio received a contract for 72 modified versions (P.149-D) to be used as standard *Luftwaffe* training aircraft; another 190 were licence-built in Germany by Focke-Wulf. Many have been released for civilian service. Powered by a 270hp Lycoming GO-480 engine, they carry up to five persons.

Piel Emeraude (and Scintex Super Emeraude and Fairtravel Linnet) / France

Photo: CP 301B Emeraude.
Data: CP 1310 Super Emeraude.

Span: 27ft 0¼in (8.25m).
Length: 21ft 5½in (6.54m).
Gross weight: 1,550lb (703kg).
Range: 620 miles (1,000km) at 137mph (220km/h).

Many companies in France and elsewhere have manufactured versions of the little Piel Emeraude side-by-side 2-seat lightplane; others have been built by amateurs. Standard Emeraudes, with 90hp Continental C90 engine, were produced in France by Rousseau and Scintex. The CP 1310 C3 Super Emeraude was produced by Scintex with a 100hp Rolls-Royce/Continental O-200-A engine. The British Fairtravel Linnet is very similar.

Piper J-3 Cub (and J-4 Cub Coupe) /USA

Photo: Wag-Aero CUBy.
Data: J-3C-65 Cub Special.

Span: 35ft 2½in (10.73m).
Length: 22ft 4½in (6.82m).
Gross weight: 1,220lb (553kg).
Range: 300 miles (482km) at 87mph (140km/h).

First flown in 1938, the tandem 2-seat J-3 Cub became one of the most-produced aeroplanes in history. By the time production ended in 1949, a total of 14,125 civil Cubs of all versions had been delivered, plus 5,673 essentially-similar military L-4 observation aircraft. Thousands continue to fly, mainly in North America. The original J-2 Cub of 1936 had a 40hp Continental engine, and a few of these survive. The J-3 began with a 40hp Continental, but most were built with a 50hp Continental, Lycoming or Franklin engine. Post-war versions are the J-3C-65 Cub Special and PA-11 Cub Special with 65hp Continental A65 engine. Also to be seen, mainly in the USA, are J-4 Cub Coupes—more refined versions of the J-3 with side-by-side seating and a 75hp Continental A75-8 engine, built in 1939–42. Wag-Aero of Lyons, Wisconsin, markets kits of parts for an up-dated version known as the CUBy, which can be powered by Continental or Lycoming engines in the 65-125hp range.

Piper PA-12 Super Cruiser (and PA-14 Family Cruiser) /USA

Photo and data: PA-12 Super Cruiser.

Span: 35ft 5½in (10.81m).
Length: 22ft 10in (6.96m).
Gross weight: 1,750lb (793kg).
Range: 600 miles (965km) at 105mph (169km/h).

The Piper Cruiser series began with the 3-seat J-5A Cruiser of 1940, with a standard J-3 wing, revised 3-seat fuselage and 75hp A75-8 engine. It was followed within a year by the J-5C Super Cruiser, with 100hp Lycoming GO-145-C2 engine. Production was resumed post-war with the generally similar PA-12, with 104hp Lycoming O-235-C. The PA-14 Family Cruiser of 1948 differed in having 4 seats and a 115hp Lycoming O-235-C1 engine. Many PA-12s and 14s are flying.

Piper PA-15 Vagabond (and PA-17) /USA

Photo: PA-17 Vagabond.
Data: PA-15 Vagabond.

Span: 29ft 3½in (8.92m).
Length: 18ft 8in (5.69m).
Gross weight: 1,100lb (500kg).
Range: 250 miles (402km) at 90mph (145km/h).

First post-war Piper design, the side-by-side 2-seat PA-15 Vagabond entered production in 1948, with a 65hp Lycoming O-145-B engine. It was followed by the PA-17 Vagabond, with 65hp Continental A65-8 engine, intended primarily as a trainer. Many Vagabonds remain airworthy, mainly in the USA.

Piper PA-18 Super Cub / USA

Photo and data: PA-18-150 Super Cub.

Span: 35ft 2½in (10.73m).
Length: 22ft 7in (6.88m).
Gross weight: 1,750lb (793kg).
Cruising speed: 105—115mph (169—185km/h).
Max range: 460 miles (735km).

More than 6,500 Super Cubs have been built since the original versions—the PA-18-95 (90hp Continental C90) and PA-18-105 (108hp Lycoming O-235) entered production in 1949. The PA-18-135 (135hp Lycoming O-290-D2) was introduced in 1952. Current version is the PA-18-150, with 150hp Lycoming O-320, which has been in production since 1955. All versions are tandem 2-seaters. The spruce spars of earlier Piper types gave way to all-metal structure in the Super Cub, which retained the traditional welded steel-tube fuselage and overall fabric covering. Many Super Cubs are equipped for agricultural duties; others operate on floats and skis.

Piper PA-20 Pacer /USA

Photo: PA-16 Clipper.
Data: PA-20-115 Pacer.

Span: 29ft 4in (8.94m).
Length: 20ft 5in (6.22m).
Gross weight: 1,650lb (748kg).
Range: 580 miles (933km) at 112mph (180km/h).

The Pacer began life in 1949 as the PA-16 Clipper, a 4-seat counterpart of the Vagabond with a 115hp Lycoming O-235-C1 engine. The name and designation were changed in 1950 and three versions were subsequently produced: the PA-20-115 (O-235-C1), PA-20-125 (125hp Lycoming O-290-D2) and PA-20-135 (135hp O-290-D2). Several hundred Clippers and Pacers remain in service.

Piper PA-22 Tri-Pacer (and Colt and Caribbean) / USA

Photo: PA-22 Colt 108.
Data: PA-22-160 Tri-Pacer.

Span: 29ft 3¼in (8.92m).
Length: 20ft 7¼in (6.28m).
Gross weight: 2,000lb (907kg).
Max cruising speed: 134mph (216km/h).
Max range: 536 miles (862km).

This tricycle-undercarriage version of the Pacer was introduced in 1951, initially with the same 135hp O-290-D2 engine. The PA-22-150 Tri-Pacer (150hp Lycoming O-320) appeared in 1955, followed by the PA-22-160 (160hp Lycoming O-320-B) in 1957. All Tri-Pacers are 4-seaters, as is the less-elaborate Caribbean (150hp O-320), introduced in 1958. The Colt 108 is a low-price 2-seat model, with the same basic airframe and a 108hp Lycoming O-235-C1B engine, intended mainly for club and training duties. All of these types remain in large-scale use.

Piper PA-24 Comanche / USA

Photo: Turbo Comanche C.
Data: PA-24-260 Comanche C.

Span: 36ft 0in (10.97m).
Length: 25ft 0in (7.62m).
Gross weight: 3,200lb (1,451kg).
Max cruising speed: 185mph (298km/h).
Max range: 1,225 miles (1,970km).

Piper's first all-metal low-wing monoplane, the prototype 4-seat Comanche flew on May 24, 1956. It went into production as the PA24-180, with 180hp Lycoming O-360-A1A engine. Later production versions were the PA-24-250 (250hp Lycoming O-540-A1A5), PA-24-260 (260hp Lycoming O-540-E or IO-540-E) and PA-24-400 (400hp Lycoming IO-720). Final version was the PA-24-260 Comanche C, which had an IO-540 engine and could carry up to six persons. A version with Rajay supercharger was also produced as the Turbo Comanche C. Production ended in 1974, but many Comanches remain in service.

Piper PA-25 Pawnee (and PA-36 Pawnee Brave) /USA

Photo: PA-25-235 Pawnee with special wingtips.
Data: PA-25-235 Pawnee D.

Span: 36ft 2in (11.02m).
Length: 24ft 8½in (7.53m).
Gross weight: 2,900lb (1,315kg).
Max cruising speed: 114mph (183km/h).
Max range: 290 miles (467km) at 114mph (183km/h).

Specially developed as a safe and economical agricultural aircraft, the original PA-25 Pawnee was built in two versions, with 150hp Lycoming O-320 (PA-25-150) and 235hp Lycoming O-540-B2B5 (PA-25-235) engine. The more powerful model remains in production, as the improved Pawnee D, with optional 260hp Lycoming O-540-E engine and a payload of 1,200lb (544kg) of chemicals. A mechanic or loader can be carried on a temporary seat inside the hopper during staging flights. More than 4,250 Pawnees have been built by Piper and Chincul of the Argentine. The PA-25 is now supplemented by the PA-36 Pawnee Brave 285, with span of 39ft (11.89m), gross weight of 4,400lb (1,996kg), enlarged chemical hopper and 285hp Continental Tiara engine; and Pawnee Brave 375, with gross weight of 4,800lb (2,177kg), max chemical load of 1,900lb (862kg) and 375hp Lycoming IO-720-D1CD engine.

139

Piper PA-28-151 Cherokee Warrior /USA

Photo and data: Warrior II.

Span: 35ft 0in (10.67m).
Length: 23ft 9½in (7.26m).
Gross weight: 2,325lb (1,055kg).
Max cruising speed: 139mph (224km/h).
Max range: 702 miles (1,130km) at 128mph (206km/h).

This junior member of the current Cherokee family introduced a completely new wing, with tapered outer panels of increased span compared with earlier Cherokee 140s. Induced drag is reduced, boosting performance, and a reflex outboard leading-edge improves stability at stall speeds. The Warrior was intended to compete directly with the Cessna 172, and had a similar 150hp Lycoming O-320-E3D engine in its original form; the current Warrior II has a 160hp O-320-D3G. It is a full four-seater, with a maximum useful load of 989lb (448kg). The Warrior is one of 14 Piper types assembled by Chincul of the Argentine at the rate of 10 aircraft a month; a total of 204 had been built by April 1977.

Piper PA-28 Cherokee Series (except Warrior) / USA

Photo: Cherokee Pathfinder.
Data: Archer II.

Span: 35ft 0in (10.67m).
Length: 23ft 9½in (7.26m).
Gross weight: 2,550lb (1,156kg).
Max cruising speed: 144mph (232km/h).
Max range: 725 miles (1,168km) at 119mph (191km/h).

Because of its sturdy construction and low price, the all-metal Cherokee has proved even more popular than the Tri-Pacer which it superseded. The original 4-seat prototype flew on February 10, 1961, and more than 20,000 Cherokees of all types have been built, with several versions currently in production in the Argentine and Brazil, as well as by the parent company. Excluding the Warrior, which is described separately, models in the basic PA-28 range with fixed undercarriage are the simplified 2-seat Cherokee Flite Liner trainer and 4-seat Cruiser, with 150hp Lycoming O-320 engine; the PA-28-180 Cherokee Archer 4-seater with 180hp Lycoming O-360-A3A; the Archer II, introduced in 1976, with the same tapered wing as the Warrior; and the strengthened PA-28-235 Cherokee Pathfinder (Brazilian EMBRAER EMB-710C Carioca) with 235hp Lycoming O-540-B4B5 engine. Earlier names for the Archer and Pathfinder were Challenger and Charger respectively.

Piper PA-28 Cherokee Arrow Series /USA

Photo: Cherokee Turbo Arrow III.
Data: PA-28-200 Cherokee Arrow III.

Span: 35ft 0in (10.67m).
Length: 25ft 0in (7.62m).
Gross weight: 2,750lb (1,247kg).
Max cruising speed: 165mph (266km/h).
Range: 875–990 miles (1,408–1,593km) at 140mph (226km/h).

Announced on June 19, 1967, the original Cherokee Arrow (PA-28-180R) was similar to the Cherokee 180 but had a retractable undercarriage, a 180hp IO-360-B1E engine and a third window on each side. To assist pilots unaccustomed to retractable gear, the legs were designed to extend automatically if power was reduced and speed fell below 105mph (170km/h). Subsequently, the PA-28-200 appeared, with 200hp IO-360-C1C engine. Piper's 1972 range brought the similarly-powered Arrow II, with 5in longer fuselage, 26in greater span and larger tailplane. In 1977, Piper introduced the Arrow III, with tapered wing as used on the Warrior and Archer II, and the similar Turbo Arrow III with turbocharged TSIO-360-F engine. The Arrow is built by EMBRAER of Brazil as the EMB-711C Corisco, and by Chincul of the Argentine.

Piper PA-32 Cherokee Six /USA

Data: PA-32-300 Cherokee Six 300.

Span: 32ft 8¾in (9.98m).
Length: 27ft 8¾in (8.45m).
Gross weight: 3,400lb (1,542kg).
Max cruising speed: 168mph
(270km/h).
Range: 857 miles (1,379km) at 149mph
(239km/h).

First flown on December 6, 1963 the Cherokee Six is a 6/7-seat version of the Cherokee, with slightly enlarged overall dimensions. It is available in two versions, the PA-32-260 with 260hp Lycoming O-540-E engine, and the PA-32-300 with 300hp Lycoming IO-540-K. Both models are available on skis; the more powerful version can be operated as a floatplane. In addition to production by Piper, the Cherokee Six is manufactured in Brazil, as the EMB-720C Minuano, and in the Argentine by Chincul.

Piper PA-32R-300 Cherokee Lance /USA

Photo: PA-32RT-300 Cherokee Turbo Lance.
Data: Turbo Lance II.

Span: 32ft 9¾in (10.00m).
Length: 28ft 10¾in (8.81m).
Gross weight: 3,600lb (1,633kg).
Max cruising speed: 201mph
(324km/h).
Range: 938 miles (1,510km) at 155mph
(250km/h) (with reserves).

First flown on August 30, 1974, the six/seven-seat Cherokee Lance combines a basic Cherokee Six 300 fuselage with a wing similar to that of the Arrow but embodying Seneca spars, fuel tanks and main landing gear. The nose-wheel unit is like that of the Arrow, the other 'retractable' member of the Cherokee family. The first production Lance flew on July 17, 1975; within ten months Piper had sold 186 and delivered 127 of them. For 1978, Piper introduced a T-tail and changed the name of the basic model, with 300hp Lycoming IO-540-K1G5 engine, to Lance II. It also offered for the first time a turbocharged version, the Turbo Lance II, with 300hp TIO-540-S1 AD engine. When assembled by EMBRAER in Brazil, the Lance is known as the EMB-721 Sertanejo. It is also produced in the Argentine, by Chincul.

Piper PA-38 Tomahawk /USA

Span: 34ft 0in (10.36m).
Length: 23ft 1¼in (7.04m).
Gross weight: 1,670lb (757kg).
Max cruising speed: 125mph
(202km/h).
Range: 502 miles (807km) at 117mph
(189km/h).

When announcing the Tomahawk, in October 1977, Piper claimed that it embodied the answers on questionnaires sent to more than 10,000 flying instructors, who were asked to describe the ideal trainer. It is an aerobatic side-by-side two-seater, powered by a 112hp Lycoming O-235-L2C engine. The wing utilises NASA's new Whitcomb aerofoil section; other features include a T-tail, 360 degree field of view from the cabin, and an engine cowling which can be removed completely without detaching the propeller. Deliveries were expected to begin in early 1978, to meet initial orders for 1,400 Tomahawks.

Pitts Special /USA

Photo: S-1S.
Data: S-2A.

Span: 20ft 0in (6.10m).
Length: 18ft 3in (5.56m).
Gross weight: 1,500lb (680kg).
Max cruising speed: 140mph (225km/h).
Max range: 450 miles (725km).

The Pitts Special began as a 90hp custombuilt aerobatic single-seater, first flown in September 1944. Its designer, Curtis Pitts, developed the design to accept more powerful engines, of up to 180hp, and then evolved the two-seat S-2 Special (180hp Lycoming IO-360-B4A) and S-2A (200hp Lycoming). A major success was achieved in 1972, when the US national team, flying Pitts Specials, gained both the men's and women's individual prizes and the team prize at the 7th World Aerobatic Championships, in France. Britain's famous Rothman's Aerobatic Team flies S-2As, which are available only in factory-built form. Many single-seaters have been amateur-built from plans supplied by Curtis Pitts. Construction is mixed wood (wings) and metal (fuselage and tail unit), with fabric covering.

Procaer /General Avia F15 Picchio (and Delfino) / Italy

Photo and data: F15E Picchio.

Span: 32ft 5¼in (9.90m).
Length: 24ft 7¼in (7.50m).
Gross weight: 3,000lb (1,360kg).
Cruising speed: 166–190mph (267–306km/h).
Max range: 994 miles (1,600km) at 166mph (267km/h).

Designed by Stelio Frati, the original versions of the Picchio were unique in having an allwood structure covered with plywood panels which had an outer skin of aluminium bonded to them. This was claimed to combine an unrivalled surface finish with the easy maintenance of wood structures and the durability of metal skinning. The prototype Picchio flew on May 7, 1959. Successive production models were the F15 with 3 seats and 160hp Lycoming engine (15 built), F15A with 4 seats and 180hp Lycoming (54 built) and F15B with increased wing area (35 built). A prototype F15C flew, with 260hp Continental IO-470-E engine, followed by the all-metal F15E, with 300hp Continental IO-520-F, on December 21, 1968. Latest in the series is the all-metal two-seat F15F Delfino, with 200hp Lycoming IO-360-A engine, which was under development by Ing Frati's General Avia company in 1977.

Pützer Elster B /Germany

Photo and data: Elster B.

Span: 43ft 4in (13.20m).
Length: 23ft 3¼in (7.10m).
Gross weight: 1,543lb (700kg).
Range: 280 miles (450km) at 93mph (150km/h).

Three versions of this all-wood side-by-side 2-seat light aircraft were built. The original Elster A prototype had a 52hp Porsche 678/3 engine. First production model was the Elster B, with 95hp Continental C90-12F engine, which was selected for use by sporting aviation groups of the *Luftwaffe*. It was followed by the Elster C, with 150hp Lycoming O-320 engine, which was intended mainly for glider towing.

PZL-101A Gawron /Poland

Span (over end-plates): 41ft 7½in (12.68m).
Length: 29ft 6½in (9.00m).
Gross weight: 3,660lb (1,660kg).
Cruising speed: 75–81mph (120–130km/h).
Max range: 708 miles (1,140km) with external tanks.

Developed from the Soviet-designed Yak-12, the PZL-101 Gawron flew for the first time in April 1958 and was adopted subsequently as the standard agricultural aircraft for the countries of eastern Europe. The improved PZL-101A was in continuous production from 1961 to 1973, with 260hp Ivchenko AI-14R engine. Used mainly for agricultural work, it can be equipped also for ambulance and 4-seat communications duties. Agricultural payload is 1,100lb (500kg). A prototype designated PZL-101AF, with 300hp AI-14RF engine, flew on August 30, 1966, but did not enter production. Late production Gawrons have laminar-flow wingtips instead of the former end-plates, increasing the span to 42ft 9in (13.03m).

PZL-104 Wilga (and Lipnur Gelatik) /Poland

Photo and data: Wilga 35A.

Span: 36ft 6in (11.12m).
Length: 26ft 6¼in (8.10m).
Gross weight: 2,711lb (1,230kg).
Cruising speed: 80–120mph (128–193km/h).
Max range: 422 miles (680km).

The original prototype Wilga 1 flew on April 24, 1962, with a 180hp Narkiewicz WN-6B engine. The fuselage and tail unit were then redesigned completely, and the resulting Wilga 2 flew on August 1, 1963, with a 195hp WN-6RB engine. It was followed on December 30 by the Wilga C, with 225hp Continental O-470, and a modified version of this type was put into production in Indonesia as the Lipnur Gelatik. A total of 39 Gelatiks were built, the final models as Gelatik 32 with 230hp O-470-L engine. First Polish production versions were the Wilga 3A utility 4-seater for club use and Wilga 3S for ambulance duties, both with 260hp Ivchenko AI-14R radial engine. Improved versions, introduced in 1967, were the Wilga 32 (O-470-L or R) and Wilga 35 (AI-14R), built in 32A/35A club, 32P/35P passenger/liaison and 32S/35S ambulance models. About 360 Wilgas had been built by the end of 1977. Only the 35A/P/S remain in production.

PZL-106A Kruk /Poland

Span: 48ft 6½in (14.80m).
Length: 29ft 10¼in (9.10m).
Gross weight: 6,614lb (3,000kg).
Range: approx 248 miles (400km) at 112mph (180km/h).

As a successor to the PZL-101 Gawron, the WSK-Okecie design team developed and flew the much modified PZL-101M Kruk (Raven), with a 260hp AI-14R engine. By early 1972 it was clear that better results would be obtained by switching to a more powerful engine and the braced low-wing monoplane layout that has become conventional for agricultural duster/sprayers. The result was the PZL-106, of which two prototypes were flown with 400hp Lycoming engine (the first on April 17, 1973) followed by four more with the 600hp PZL-3S radial that is fitted in production PZL-106As. These are basically single-seaters, but have a rearward-facing seat behind the pilot to enable a mechanic/loader to be carried between operating sites. Chemical load is 308 Imp gallons (1,400 litres) of liquid or 2,204lb (1,000kg) of solids.

PZL M-18 Dromader / Poland

Span: 58ft 0¾in (17.70m).
Length: 31ft 2in (9.50m).
Gross weight: 11,685lb (5,300kg).
Operating speed: 105–115mph (170–185km/h).
Range: 323 miles (520km).

What appears to be a close relative of the PZL-106A Kruk is, in fact, a completely new design, powered by a 1,000hp Polish-built ASh-62IR engine and able to carry a 5,732lb (2,600kg) payload. Needing an agricultural duster/sprayer to fill the gap between the now-small Kruk and the big turbofan M-15, PZL-Mielec saved time and effort by embodying the cabin, outer wings and other components of the US Rockwell Thrush Commander into the cantilever Dromader (Dromedary). The result may inherit the ungainliness of its namesake, but offers high standards of efficiency, maintainability in the field and pilot safety. The cockpit will withstand forces of up to 40g in a crash, and all fuel is contained in the outer wings. The prototype put in a first appearance at the 1977 Paris Air Show.

RFB/Grumman American Fanliner / Germany

Span: 31ft 6in (9.60m).
Length: 21ft 7½in (6.59m).
Gross weight: 1,984lb (900kg).
Max cruising speed: 155mph (250km/h).
Max range: 621 miles (1,000km).

Rhein-Flugzeugbau has been experimenting with ducted fan propulsion for several years, with particular emphasis on integrating the duct into the aircraft's structure. After flying a prototype powered sailplane with a ducted fan built into its rear fuselage, it designed a two-seat lightweight aircraft named the Fanliner with a Dowty Rotol ducted fan in a similar location. This aircraft flew for the first time on October 8, 1973, powered by a 114hp Audi/NSU Ro 135 Wankel type engine. It was followed on September 4, 1976, by a second prototype, with a 150hp Audi/NSU KM 871 engine and a considerably refined airframe styled by industrial designer Luigi Colani, as illustrated. The wings and tailplane of this second aircraft are those of a Grumman American Cheetah, and this US manufacturer is expected to partner RFB in any future Fanliner production programme.

Robin (CEA) DR 220 '2 + 2' (and DR 221 Dauphin and DR 250) / France

Photo: DR 221 Dauphin.
Data: DR 220 '2 + 2'.

Span: 28ft 7¼in (8.72m).
Length: 22ft 11½in (7.00m).
Gross weight: 1,720lb (780kg).
Cruising speed: 125–130mph (201–209km/h).
Max range: 600 miles (965km).

The DR 220 is a much-refined development of the Jodel DR 1050 family. It retains the latter's plywood and fabric-covered wooden airframe and 100hp Rolls-Royce/Continental O-200-A engine; but, as its designation '2 + 2' implies, can carry one adult or two children in the rear of the cabin in addition to the pilot and passenger. Eighty-four had been built by January 1972, including strengthened DR 220As and DR 220/108s with 108hp Lycoming engine. The 3/4-seat DR 221 Dauphin (62 built) and DR 250 (102 built) are similar in construction and appearance, but have 115hp Lycoming O-235-C2A and 160hp Lycoming O-320 engine respectively. Production of all three types has ended.

Robin (CEA) DR 253
Regent/France

Span: 28ft 7¼in (8.72m).
Length: 23ft 6¼in (7.18m).
Gross weight: 2,425lb (1,100kg).
Cruising speed: 149–162mph (240–259km/h).
Range: 727–969 miles (1,170–1,560km).

First Centre Est (now Robin) production aircraft to have a tricycle undercarriage, the Regent flew for the first time on March 30, 1967. The cabin normally seats four, but is large enough to carry five persons on short flights. Standard power plant is a 180hp Lycoming O-360-A2A. Full blind-flying instruments and radio nav/com equipment can be fitted for all-weather flying. The DR 400/180 superseded the DR 253.

Robin (CEA) DR 300
Series/France

**Photo: DR 300/140 Petit Prince.
Data: DR 340.**

Span: 28ft 7¼in (8.72m).
Length: 22ft 10in (6.96m).
Gross weight: 2,205lb (1,000kg).
Cruising speed: 143–158mph (230–254km/h).
Range: 850 miles (1,367km) at 158mph (254km/h).

DR 300 designations cover a series of eight interrelated aircraft, of similar construction to the DR 220/221/250 but with fixed tricycle undercarriage and refinements such as modified wing camber to improve performance and handling. The DR 300/108 '2+2 tricycle', based on the DR 220, has a 108hp Lycoming O-235-C2A engine, and first flew on May 29, 1970. The DR 300/125 Petit Prince 3/4-seater has a 125hp Lycoming O-235 and flew in June 1970. The DR 300/140 Petit Prince 4-seater flew on March 25, 1970. The DR 300/180R Remorqueur 4-seat tourer/glider-tug has a 180hp Lycoming O-360-A2A and flew on May 26, 1970. The DR 315 Cadet is a 3/4-seater with 108/115hp O-235-C2A which flew on March 21, 1968. The 4-seat DR 340 Major, with 140/150hp Lycoming O-320-E, flew on February 27, 1968. The DR 360 Major 160 is a *de luxe* version with 160hp O-360-E; and the DR 380 Prince, first flown on October 15, 1968, is similar but with a 180hp O-360-D. All were superseded in production by the DR 400 series.

Robin (CEA) DR 400
Series/France

**Photo: DR 400/125 Petit Prince.
Data: DR 400/180 Regent.**

Span: 28ft 7¼in (8.72m).
Length: 23ft 6¼in (7.18m).
Gross weight: 2,425lb (1,100kg).
Cruising speed: 155–166mph (249–267km/h).
Max range: 913 miles (1,470km) at 155mph (249km/h).

The DR 400 Series differ from the DR 300 Series, which they replaced in 1972/73, mainly in having a forward-sliding canopy and lowered cabin sidewalls to improve access and visibility. Variants continuing in production in 1977 were the DR 400/100 2+2 2/4-seater with 100hp Lycoming O-235-H2C engine; 3/4-seat DR 400/120 Petit Prince with 118hp O-235-L2A; 4-seat DR 400/140B Major with 160hp Lycoming O-320-D; 4-seat DR 400/160 Chevalier with 160hp O-320-D; 4/5-seat DR 400/180 Regent (data above) with 180hp Lycoming O-360-A; and 4-seat DR 400/180R Remorqueur glider-tug with an O-360-A.

Robin (CEA) HR 100 Series/France

Photo and data: HR 100/285 Tiara

Span: 29ft 9½in (9.08m).
Length: 24ft 10¾in (7.59m).
Gross weight: 3,086lb (1,400kg).
Max cruising speed: 193mph (310km/h).
Max range: 1,456 miles (2,344km) at 182mph (293km/h).

Production of the original all-metal HR 100/200, with 200hp Lycoming IO-360-A1D6, began in 1971. After 31 had been built, it was superseded by the HR 100/210 Safari, a four-seater with 210hp Continental IO-360-D engine of which 78 were built. The four/five-seat HR 100/285 Tiara, first flown on November 18, 1972, was the first Robin lightplane with retractable undercarriage. The prototype had a 320hp engine but, as their designation implies, production models have a 285hp Continental Tiara 6-285B engine. Variants are the HR 100/250TR, with 250hp Lycoming IO-540 engine, and the HR 100/4 + 2, similar to the HR 100/285 Tiara but with lengthened cabin seating up to six persons without baggage.

Robin (CEA) HR 200 Series/France

Photo and data: HR 200/100.

Span: 27ft 4in (8.33m).
Length: 21ft 9½in (6.64m).
Gross weight: 1,719lb (780kg).
Max cruising speed: 122mph (197km/h).
Range: 652 miles (1,050km).

Intended specifically for use by clubs and flying schools, this all-metal two-seater first flew on July 29, 1971. It entered production in 1973 and deliveries by February 1975 totalled 53 HR 200/100s (data above) with 108hp Lycoming O-235-H2C; 19 HR 200/120s with 118-125hp O-235; and 1 HR 200/160 with 160hp Lycoming O-320-D. Production has ended.

Robin R 1180/France

Span: 29ft 9½in (9.08m).
Length: 24ft 10¾in (7.59m).
Gross weight: 2,535lb (1,150kg).
Range: 932 miles (1,500km) at 130mph (210km/h).

Intended as a replacement for the HR 100/210 Safari II, this fixed-undercarriage all-metal four-seat light aircraft flew for the first time in late 1976. It was expected to receive certification before the end of 1977 and to be the forerunner of a family of touring aircraft with R 1000 designations. The R 1180 is powered by a 180hp Lycoming O-360-A3AD engine, as the last three figures of its designation confirm.

Robin R 2160 /France

Span: 27ft 4in (8.33m).
Length: 23ft 3½in (7.099m).
Gross weight: 1,764lb (800kg).
Range: 590 miles (950km) at 145mph
(234km/h).

To overcome certain shortcomings in the aerobatic performance of the HR 200, Robin evolved from that design a new family of two-seat trainers under the basic designation of R 2000. These are conventional all-metal light aircraft with non-retractable landing gear. The wing is completely new by comparison with the HR 200; the rudder has been enlarged and the aircraft are distinguished by a long ventral fin to improve spinning characteristics. First to fly, on January 15, 1976, was a prototype built to R 2100 standard, with a 108hp Lycoming O-235-H engine. The same airframe was then re-engined to R 2160 standard, with a 160hp Lycoming O-320-D, with which it flew for the first time on July 15, 1976. The AEIO-320 version of the same engine powers the aerobatic R 2160A Acrobin, with fuel and oil systems for inverted flight.

Rockwell Commander Models 111 and 112 /USA

Photo: Model 112B.
Data: Model 112A.

Span: 32ft 10¾in (10.03m).
Length: 25ft 0in (7.62m).
Gross weight: 2,650lb (1,202kg).
Max cruising speed: 161 mph
(259km/h).
Max range: 1,028 miles (1,655km)

The four-seat, single-engined Aero Commander Model 112 flew on December 4, 1970, as the first of an entirely new range of light aircraft utilising many common components. The 112 is powered by a 200hp Lycoming IO-360-C1D6 engine, and has a retractable undercarriage. Deliveries began late in 1972, and this version has been followed by the improved Model 112A, described and illustrated. The Model 111, first flown in 1971, is similar except for having a fixed undercarriage.

Rockwell Thrush Commander /USA

Span: 44ft 5in (13.54m).
Length: 29ft 4½in (8.95m).
Gross weight: 6,900lb (3,130kg).
Operating speed: 95–110mph (153–177km/h).
Max range: 470 miles (756km).

Largest of the former range of Rockwell (North American) agricultural aircraft, and the only one still manufactured by the parent company, this aircraft was produced originally with a variety of engines by the former Snow Aeronautical Corp from 1958 until 1965. Snow was then taken over by Aero Commander, which continued building the S-2D version, with 600hp Pratt & Whitney R-1340-S3H1 engine, as the Ag Commander S-2D. Following Aero Commander's merger with North American, the same basic design became the Thrush Commander, with R-1340-AN-1 engine and payload of 3,280lb (1,488kg). Also still in service are many 220hp Snow S-2As, 450hp S-2Bs and 450/600hp S-2Cs.

Rollason Beta /UK

Photo and data: Beta B2.

Span: 20ft 5in (6.22m).
Length: 16ft 8in (5.08m).
Gross weight: 850lb (385kg).
Max cruising speed: 166mph (267km/h).
Max range: 320 miles (515km) at 166mph (267km/h).

The original Beta design was produced by five BAC design engineers, who called themselves the Luton Group, as an entry for the Midget Racer Design Competition organised by Mr Norman Jones, a director of the Rollason company. The Beta won the competition, against 41 other entries; a prototype, designated Beta B1 and fitted with a 65hp Continental A65 engine, was built by Rollason and flew for the first time on April 21, 1967. It was later converted to Beta B2 standard, with 90hp Continental C90. The first genuine B2 flew on February 15, 1969; others have followed, and 50 sets of Beta plans have been sold to amateur constructors. Betas race regularly against aircraft of US design in British Formula One contests.

Rollason /Druine D.31 Turbulent /UK

Span: 21ft 7in (6.58m).
Length: 17ft 6in (5.33m).
Gross weight: 620lb (281kg).
Cruising speed: 87–100mph (141–161km/h).
Max range: 250 miles (400km).

This ultra-light single-seater and its 2-seat counterpart, the Turbi, were designed by the brilliant young Frenchman, Roger Druine, who was only 37 years old when he died. Plans of both are available to amateur constructors and many have been built throughout the world. The Turbulent was also factory-built by Rollason, in England, and the data above apply to this company's basic D.31 model, with 45hp Ardem 4CO 2 Mk 4 (converted Volkswagen) engine, of which 30 had been completed by 1973. Rollason have also built three D.31As with Ardem Mk X engine, improved main spar and weight of 700lb (316kg); these have a full C of A instead of the usual Permit to Fly. Construction is of wood, with fabric-covered wings and plywood-covered fuselage. Some Turbulents have enclosed cockpits and wheel spats.

Rollason /Druine D.62 Condor /UK

Photo: D.62B Condor.
Data: D.62C Condor.

Span: 27ft 6in (8.38m).
Length: 22ft 6in (6.86m).
Gross weight: 1,475lb (670kg).
Cruising speed: 107–115mph (172–185km/h).
Max range: 328 miles (528km).

Roger Druine intended this more refined side-by-side 2-seater primarily for factory production. After building a prototype D.62, with 90hp Continental C90 engine, in 1961, Rollason Aircraft in England built two D.62As with the 100hp Rolls-Royce/Continental O-200-A engine. They retained this power plant in the further-improved D.62B, which became their main production type. Thirty-nine had been completed by the Spring of 1973, plus nine D.62Cs with 130hp Rolls-Royce/Continental O-240 engine, larger wheels and raised canopy, for glider towing. Construction is of wood, with fabric-covered wings and plywood-covered fuselage.

RRAFAGA J-1 Martin
Fierro /Argentina

Span: 42ft 7¾in (13.00m).
Length: 22ft 11¾in (7.00m).
Gross weight: 4,409lb (2,000kg).
Range: 305 miles (490km) at 131mph
(211km/h).

First flown on December 18, 1975, this single-seat agricultural duster/sprayer was designed and built in the Argentine by a team headed by Ing Norberto Cobelo. Power plant of the J-1 is a 300hp Lycoming IO-540-K1JG, driving a Hartzell variable-pitch propeller. Hopper capacity is 1,874lb (850kg) of solids or 187 Imp gallons (850 litres) of liquid chemicals. Five more J-1s are being built initially by Ronchetti, Razzetti Aviacion of Funes, Santa Fe Province, including one for structural testing.

Saab-91 Safir /Sweden

Photo: Saab-91C.
Data: Saab-91D.

Span: 34ft 9in (10.59m).
Length: 26ft 4in (8.03m).
Gross weight: 2,660lb (1,206kg).
Cruising speed: 136–146mph (219–235km/h).
Max range: 660 miles (1,062km).

The prototype Safir flew on November 20, 1945, with a 130hp Gipsy Major 1C engine. Subsequently, four production versions were built. The Saab-91A (145hp Gipsy Major 10) and Saab-91B (190hp Lycoming O-435-A) are 3-seaters; the Saab-91C (O-435A) and Saab-91D (180hp Lycoming O-360-A1A) are 4-seaters. Most of the 320 or so Safirs produced went to air forces as basic trainers, but numbers of Bs and Ds have been utilised by airlines and civil authorities for pilot training.

Saab Safari /Sweden

Span: 29ft 0½in (8.85m).
Length: 22ft 11¼in (7.00m).
Gross weight: 2,645lb (1,200kg).
Cruising speed: 129mph (208km/h).
Max endurance: 5hr 10min.

This two/three-seat basic training and utility aircraft was evolved from the MFI-9/Bölkow 208 by Malmo Flygindustri before Malmo was absorbed into Saab. It was known at that stage as the MFI-15, and had a military counterpart in the MFI-17, now produced as the Saab Supporter. The Safari is powered by a 200hp Lycoming IO-360-A1B6 engine, and can carry underwing loads for airborne relief, rescue and firefighting operations. A stretcher can be carried internally. More than 140 Safaris and Supporters had been sold by 1977.

S.A.I. KZ VII Laerke (and KZ III) /Denmark

Photo and data: KZ VII Laerke.

Span: 31ft 6in (9.60m).
Length: 21ft 3in (6.48m).
Gross weight: 1,910lb (866kg).
Range: 450 miles (725km) at 109mph (175km/h).

The prototype of this 4-seat light aircraft flew for the first time on November 11, 1946, and was followed by 55 production models. Standard power plant was a 125hp Continental C125-2, but seven Laerkes were supplied to Switzerland with 145hp Continental C145-2 engine. Several examples of each version remain airworthy, together with numbers of similar KZ IIIs, which are 2-seaters with a 100hp Cirrus Minor II engine. Both types have wooden wings and steel-tube fuselage, with fabric covering.

Scheibe SF-25 Falke Vickers-Slingsby T. 61 / Germany /UK

Photo and data: SF-25C Falke '76.

Span: 50ft 0¼in (15.25m).
Length: 24ft 9½in (7.55m).
Gross weight: 1,345lb (610kg).
Max range: 466 miles (750km) at 81mph (130km/h).

The original SF-25B version of this side-by-side two-seat powered sailplane, with a 45hp Stamo Volkswagen) engine, was built in quantity by both Scheibe in Germany and Slingsby in the UK, the latter as the T.61. The Scheibe SF-25C introduced a more powerful (65hp) Limbach SL 1700 (Volkswagen) engine; by March 1977 a total of 200 had been built by the parent company and 50 more by Sportavia. In addition, Scheibe had delivered 20 of the SF-25C-S version, with a Hoffmann feathering propeller for improved engine-off gliding. Current Scheibe versions, known as Falke '76s, can be identified by a more domed canopy and larger fin. Vickers-Slingsby is producing 15 special T.61E Venture T.Mk 2s for the Air Training Corps, with a Rollason-modified Volkswagen 1,600cc engine.

Schweizer Model TSC-1A Teal USA

Photo: TSC-1A1 Teal.
Data: TSC-1A2 Teal II.

Span: 31ft 11in (9.73m).
Length: 23ft 7in (7.19m).
Gross weight: 2,200lb (998kg).
Cruising speed: 110–116mph (177–187km/h).
Range: 472–748 miles (759–1,203km).

The Teal amphibian was designed by the former Thurston Aircraft Corporation, which set out to develop a simple, economical and easily-handled 2-seater for the general aviation market. The prototype flew in June 1968, and production was eventually taken over by Schweizer Aircraft Corporation. Construction is all-metal and the power plant a 150hp Lycoming O-320-A3B. The first 15 Teals were TSC-1A 2-seaters. Production then switched to the TSC-1A1, with an optional third seat in the baggage compartment, revised fuel tankage and other refinements. Final version was the TSC-1A2 Teal II, with slotted flaps.

Scottish Aviation
SA-3-200 Bullfinch /UK

Span: 33ft 9¼in (10.29m).
Length: 24ft 11in (7.59m).
Gross weight: 2,601lb (1,180kg).
Max cruising speed: 162mph
(261km/h).
Range: 622 miles (1,000km).

Following the success of its fixed-undercarriage Bulldog 100 and 120 series military trainers Scottish Aviation decided to develop the Bulldog Series 200 with retractable landing gear, up to four seats instead of three, and other refinements. A civil counterpart was offered, as the Bullfinch, and when the prototype flew for the first time on August 20, 1976, it carried the civil registration G-BDOG. Power plant was a 200hp Lycoming AEIO-360-A1B6, the fully-aerobatic version of the engine normally fitted in the Bulldog 100/120 series.

SIAI-Marchetti S.208
(and S.205 and Waco
S.220 Vela) Italy /USA

Photo and data: S.208.

Span: 35ft 7½in (10.86m).
Length: 26ft 3in (8.00m).
Gross weight: 3,307lb (1,500kg).
Max cruising speed: 187mph
(300km/h).
Max range: 1,250 miles (2,000km).

The S.205 is a 4-seat all-metal light aircraft which can have a retractable or fixed undercarriage. Versions built in 1964—72 were the S.205-18/F (=fixed undercarriage) and S.205-18/R (=retractable) with 180hp Lycoming O-360-A1A engine; the S.205-20/F and S.205-20/R with 200hp Lycoming IO-360-A1A engine; and the S.205-22/R with 220hp Franklin 6A-350-C1 engine. The 22/R was also built under licence in the USA for a time as the Waco S.220 Vela. A total of 475 S.205s were built, including 62 Velas. The S.208 is generally similar to the 20/R, but has a 260hp Lycoming O-540-E4A5 engine and 5 seats. About 80 were delivered, including 44 for the Italian Air Force. Still available are the S.205AC with 200hp IO-360-A1B6D engine, of which 140 are being built for the Aero Club d'Italia, and S.208A which is generally similar to the S.208.

SIAI-Marchetti SF.260 /
Italy

Photo and data: SF.260C

Span: 27ft 4¾in (8.35m).
Length: 23ft 3½in (7.10m).
Gross weight: 2,430lb (1,102kg)
Max cruising speed: 214mph
(345km/h).
Max range: 1,275 miles (2,050km).

The prototype of this all-metal aerobatic light aircraft was the F.250 with 250hp Lycoming engine. Designed by Ing Stelio Frati and built by Aviamilano, it flew for the first time on July 15, 1964. SIAI-Marchetti acquired production rights and built 100 of the developed three-seat SF.260As and SF.260Bs with a 260hp Lycoming O-540-E4A5 engine to meet orders from Air France, Sabena and other customers. Current civil version is the SF.260C, which is generally similar to the SF.260M/W/SW military variants in worldwide service.

151

SIPA S.903 /France

Photo and data: S.903.

Span: 28ft 8in (8.75m).
Length: 18ft 10½in (5.75m).
Gross weight: 1,390lb (630kg).
Range: 280 miles (450km) at 96mph (155km/h).

The prototype SIPA S.90, with 75hp Mathis 4G-60 engine, was designed by Yves Gardan to take part in a 1946 competition for a new 2-seat light aircraft for use by French flying clubs. A total of 100 production models were built subsequently, with a variety of engines. The only version still flying in any numbers is the S.903, with 90hp Continental C90-8F.

Socata (Gardan) GY-80 Horizon /France

Photo and data: 160hp version.

Span: 31ft 10in (9.70m).
Length: 21ft 9½in (6.64m).
Gross weight: 2,425lb (1,100kg).
Max cruising speed: 145mph (233km/h).
Max range: 590 miles (950km).

Designed as a private venture by Yves Gardan, this 4-seat all-metal lightplane was produced under licence by Socata, a subsidiary of Sud-Aviation. The first 75, delivered by March 1965, had alternative 150hp or 160hp Lycoming O-320 engines. A version with 180hp O-360 engine was also produced subsequently, and a total of 260 Horizons of all types were built.

Socata (Aérospatiale) M.S.880/890 Rallye Series /France

Data: Rallye 180GT.

Span: 31ft 6½in (9.61m).
Length: 23ft 9in (7.24m).
Gross weight: 2,315lb (1,050kg).
Max cruising speed: 139mph (224km/h).
Max range: 650 miles (1,050km).

The prototype Morane-Saulnier M.S.880A Rallye-Club, with 90hp Continental engine, flew on June 10, 1959. It went into production, with the M.S.880B (100hp Continental O-200-A) and the M.S.885 Super Rallye (145hp Continental O-300-C); all were 3/4 seaters. Many other versions have followed, with various engines. Those in current production by Socata (a subsidiary of Aérospatiale) are the basic 3/4-seat Rallye 100T (tourer) with 100hp Rolls-Royce Continental O-200-A engine; Rallye 100S (sport) 2-seater; Rallye 125 with 125hp Lycoming O-235-F2A engine and 4 seats; Rallye 150GT 4-seater with 150hp Lycoming O-320-E2A engine; the 4-seat Rallye 180GT for touring, agricultural and glider-towing duties, with 180hp Lycoming O-360-A2A engine; and Rallye 220GT with 220hp Franklin 6A-350-C1 and 4 seats. Well over 3,000 Rallyes of all types have been built.

Socata Rallye Agricole / France

Span: 31ft 11in (9.74m).
Length: 23ft 9in (7.25m).
Gross weight: 2,870lb (1,300kg).
Performance: no details available.

Spraygear to convert the standard versions of the Rallye into agricultural aircraft has been available for some years. On May 16, 1977, Socata flew the prototype of the Rallye Agricole, intended specifically for this role. Based on the most powerful current version of the aircraft, with a 235hp Lycoming O-540-B4B5 engine, the Agricole has tailwheel landing gear instead of the normal tricycle type, thicker wing skins and a completely revised cockpit area. Aft of the two side-by-side seats the rear of the cabin is faired in to accommodate a 110 Imp gallon (500 litre) chemical tank. A further tank of 17.5 Imp gallons (80 litres) capacity can replace the passenger seat. Dispersal is via four Micronair units above the wing trailing-edges, underwing spraybars or a dust spreader.

Socata ST 10 Diplomate / France

Span: 31ft 10in (9.70m).
Length: 23ft 9¾in (7.26m).
Gross weight: 2,690lb (1,220kg).
Max cruising speed: 165mph (265km/h).
Max range: 860 miles (1,385km) with full payload.

First flown on November 7, 1967, the prototype Diplomate (known initially as the Provence) was evolved by lengthening the fuselage of the GY-80 Horizon and redesigning the cabin. With further changes to the tail unit and a 200hp Lycoming IO-360-C1B engine, the Diplomate was certificated in 1969 and 56 had been delivered by the beginning of 1974. The basic version is a 4-seater, but the twelve bought by Varig of Brazil are used as airline pilot trainers.

Socata TB 10 /France

Span: 32ft 0¼in (9.76m).
Length: 25ft 0¾in (7.64m).
Gross weight: 2,425lb (1,100kg).
Max cruising speed: 143mph (230km/h).

The five-seat TB 10 is intended as the first in a new series of touring aircraft to supplement, rather than replace, the Rallye family of utility/trainers. As a result it lacks the wing leading-edge slats and certain other features that suit the Rallye for its roles. The prototype TB 10 flew for the first time on February 23, 1977, powered by a 160hp Lycoming O-320 engine. Later variants are expected to have engines of up to 250hp, and some will have retractable landing gear instead of the fixed undercarriage fitted at present to the TB 10. Production is expected to be centred initially on a version with a 180hp Lycoming O-360-A3A engine, and the second prototype is being completed to this standard.

Sportavia Avion-Planeur Series /Germany

Photo: RF5B Sperber.
Data: Sportavia RF5.

Span: 45ft 1in (13.74m).
Length: 25ft 7½in (7.80m).
Gross weight: 1,455lb (660kg).
Cruising speed: 75–118mph (120–190km/h).
Max range: 472 miles (760km).

Designed by Rene Fournier, the Avion-Planeur is fully aerobatic, with a performance that enables it to double as a sporting lightplane and training sailplane. Following production of 95 RF3s by Alpavia in France, production was transferred to Sportavia in Germany, where 160 of the improved RF4D single-seaters, with 40hp Rectimo-converted VW engine, were built in 1966–71. Sportavia continues to manufacture the tandem 2-seat Avion-Planeur RF5 (120 built by early 1973) with 68hp Sportavia-Limbach SL 1700E Comet engine; the RF5B Sperber, a high-performance development of the RF5 with 55ft 10in (17.02m) span; the RF55, differing from the Sperber in having a 60hp Franklin engine; and the SFS 31 Milan, which combines the RF4D fuselage, tail unit and power plant with the 15-m wings of the Scheibe SF-27M sailplane.

Sportavia Fournier RF6-180 Sportsman / Germany

Span: 34ft 5½in (10.50m).
Length: 23ft 5½in (7.15m).
Gross weight: 2,425lb (1,100kg).
Range: 938 miles (1,510km) at 142mph (228km/h).

Unlike earlier designs by Rene Fournier that were put into production in Germany by Sportavia-Pützer GmbH, the RF6 Sportsman is a fairly orthodox four-seat lightweight sporting monoplane of all-wooden construction. The original prototype, which flew on March 1, 1973, had a 125hp Lycoming O-235-F2A engine. It was followed by a second prototype, representative of the RF6-180 production version, on April 28, 1976. As well as having a 180hp Lycoming O-360-A1F6D engine, this introduced a more spacious cabin and an outer skin of glassfibre-reinforced plastics over the plywood covering on the fuselage, wing upper surface and fixed tail surfaces. By early 1977, production had built up to four RF-6Bs each month, and 25 had been delivered. The generally similar but smaller RF-6B Club two-seater was produced in France by Avions Fournier.

Stampe S.V.4 /Belgium / France

Photo: S.V.4B.
Data: S.V.4C.

Span: 27ft 6in (8.38m).
Length: 22ft 10in (6.96m).
Gross weight: 1,716lb (778kg).
Max cruising speed: 109mph (175km/h).

The original S.V.4B production version or this 2-seat primary trainer was built in Belgium with a 130hp Gipsy Major engine and enclosed cockpits. The open-cockpit S.V.4C was built by Nord, with a 140hp Renault 4 Pei engine, and large numbers of these continue in service with flying clubs in France and elsewhere. They are highly prized as specialised aerobatic aircraft, and many appear on the British Civil Register.

Stearman 75 (Boeing Kaydet) /USA

Span: 32ft 2in (9.80m).
Length: 24ft 9in (7.54m).
Gross weight: 2,635lb (1,195kg).
Range: 505 miles (812km) at 106mph (171km/h).

This tandem 2-seat primary trainer first flew in 1934 and subsequently became standard equipment in the USAAF and US Navy. When declared surplus to military requirements, more than 4,000 were converted for agricultural duties, of which many are still flying, mainly in the USA. Some have been improved by fitting special fabric-covered metal high-lift wings, with endplates, produced by the American Airmotive Corp. The standard Stearman 75 has a 220hp Continental R-670 engine. Various other engines are fitted, including the 225hp Jacobs R-755.

Stinson 10 Voyager (and 105 Voyager) /USA

**Photo: Model 108 Station Wagon.
Data: Model 10 Voyager.**

Span: 34ft 6in (10.52m).
Length: 22ft 3in (6.78m).
Gross weight: 1,625lb (737kg).
Range: 400 miles (643km) at 110mph (177km/h).

When the 3-seat Stinson Model 105 Voyager went into production in 1939, it was notable in being fitted with slots and flaps as standard equipment. Power plant was a 75hp Continental A75. In 1940, it was superseded by the Model 10 Voyager (80hp Continental) and its variants, the 10A (90hp Franklin 4AC-199) and 10B (75hp Lycoming). Many examples of both the Model 105 and Model 10 are still flying. Also to be seen are scaled-up Stinson 108 Voyagers and utility Station Wagons, built in 1946–50. Most have a 165hp Franklin 6A4 engine, length of 25ft 2in (7.67m), gross weight of 2,400lb (1,088kg) and a range of 554 miles (890km) at 130mph (209km/h).

Stinson (Vultee) V-76 Sentinel /USA

Photo: SSVV L-5 Super Stinson.

Span: 34ft 0in (10.36m).
Length: 24ft 1in (7.34m).
Gross weight: 2,050lb (930kg).
Range: 420 miles (676km) at 112mph (180km/h).

First flown in 1941, the Sentinel was a 2-seat liaison and observation aircraft developed from the Model 105 Voyager (*above*). A total of 3,283 were built for the US Army, with L-5 designations, and many of these passed into private ownership, usually with a 185hp Lycoming O-435-1 engine. Since 1972, the SSVV gliding centre in Milan, Italy, has been modifying L-5s into 'Super Stinson' glider tugs, able to tow, fully loaded, a 2,205lb (1,000kg) glider to a height of 3,280ft (1,000m). With a 235hp Lycoming O-540-B1A5 engine, the modified aircraft has a gross weight of 2,250lb (1,020kg) and maximum speed of 130mph (209km/h).

Taylorcraft Plus D (and F-19 Sportsman) /UK /USA

Photo: F-19 Sportsman.
Data: Plus D.

Span: 36ft 0in (10.97m).
Length: 22ft 10in (6.96m).
Gross weight: 1,450lb (657kg).
Range: 325 miles (523km) at 102mph (164km/h).

The prototype Plus D was the 25th aircraft built by Taylorcraft Aeroplanes (England) Ltd before the second World War, under licence from the American Taylorcraft company. After delivering eight more, they had to turn their attention to a contract for 100 similar aircraft required for AOP duties with the RAF. The military models were named Auster 1 and from them evolved the long line of Auster high-wing monoplanes described earlier in this book. After the War, 58 ex-RAF machines were sold as civilian Taylorcraft Plus Ds, supplementing a few survivors of the original eight. Several still fly in the UK and others on the continent. They are 2-seaters, with 90hp Cirrus Minor 1 engine. In current production by Taylorcraft Aviation Corporation of Alliance, Ohio, is the similar Model F-19 Sportsman 100, with 100hp Continental O-200-A engine, gross weight of 1,500lb (680kg) and range of 400 miles (643km) at 115mph (185km/h).

Temco D-16 Riley Twin and Camair Twin Navion / USA

Photo: Camair Twin Navion.
Data: Twin Navion D.

Span: 34ft 8in (10.57m).
Length: 28ft 0in (8.53m).
Gross weight: 4,500lb (2,041kg).
Max cruising speed: 200mph.

In April 1952, Jack Riley of Riley Aeronautics completed a twin-engined conversion of the Navion, substituting two 140hp Lycoming O-290-D2A engines for the original single 205hp Continental. It proved so successful that Temco set up a production line of Riley Twin conversions, stepping up the power to, successively, 150hp Lycoming O-320s and 170hp Lycoming O-340-A1As. Many are still flying, together with Camair Twin Navions. The latter are more powerful aircraft, the Twin Navion B having 240hp Continentals and the Twin Navion C having 260hp Continental IO470-Ds. Some Bs and Cs have been converted to Twin Navion D standard, with 300hp Continental IO-520 engines.

Tipsy Trainer and Belfair /Belgium

Photo: Tipsy Trainer.
Data: Tipsy Belfair.

Span: 31ft 2in (9.50m).
Length: 21ft 8in (6.60m).
Gross weight: 1,073lb (485kg).
Range: 300 miles (483km) at 100mph (161km/h).

Designed pre-war by Ernest Tips, then Managing Director of Avions Fairey in Belgium, the 2-seat Tipsy B and the externally-similar Tipsy Trainer have a 62hp Walter Mikron II engine. They were built in both Belgium and the UK and normally have an open cockpit. The Belfair (described above) is similar, with an enclosed cockpit as standard. A few aircraft of these types remain in service in Britain. Others are registered on the continent.

Transavia PL-12 and T-320 Airtruk /Australia

Photo and data: PL-12

Span: 39ft 3½in (11.98m).
Length: 20ft 10in (6.35m).
Gross weight: 4,090lb (1,855kg).
Max cruising speed: 109mph (175km/h).
Range: 531 miles (330km).

This strange-looking aircraft was designed by Luigi Pellarini specifically for agricultural duties. The tail unit is made up of two completely independent assemblies, each carried on its own slim tail-boom; this enables the chemical loader to drive between the booms, right up to the hopper, aft of the single-seat cockpit. The hopper space can be fitted with two seats. Power plant is a 300hp Continental IO-520-D engine. The prototype Airtruk flew on April 22, 1965, and 77 standard PL-12s had been delivered to customers in Australia, Denmark, India, Malaysia, New Zealand, Thailand and East and South Africa by January 1977, together with PL-12-U multi-purpose cargo, passenger, ambulance, survey versions, with seats for one person aft of the pilot and four more in a lower-deck cabin. Latest version, certificated in January 1976, is the T-320 with a 325hp Continental Tiara 6-320-2B engine. All variants are assembled also in New Zealand by Flight Engineers Ltd.

Trident TR-1 Trigull 320 (and Republic Seabee) / Canada /USA

Data and photo: Trigull-320.

Span: 41ft 9in (12.73m).
Length: 28ft 6in (8.69m).
Gross weight: 3,800lb (1,723kg).
Range: 848 miles (1,364km) at 148mph (239km/h).

Both the Trigull-320 and the Seabee owe their basic concept to veteran US designer P.H. Spencer, who made his first solo flight in a powered aircraft in May 1914. After being responsible for the design of a series of amphibians, he was granted a patent for his Air Car configuration in January 1950. In addition to forming the basis of the Trigull-320 and Seabee, the Air Car itself is being built by many amateur constructors from plans supplied by Mr Spencer. A considerable number of the 1,060 RC-3 Seabees built by Republic remain in service, mainly in North and South America; all are four-seaters with a 215hp Franklin engine. Although similar in configuration, the Trigull-320 is larger, with six seats and a 285hp Continental Tiara engine. Orders for 80 had been received by 1977, with deliveries scheduled to begin in late 1978.

UTVA-60 and UTVA-66 / Yugoslavia

Photo: UTVA-66.
Data: UTVA-66.

Span: 37ft 5in (11.40m).
Length: 27ft 6in (8.38m).
Gross weight: 4,000lb (1,814kg).
Max cruising speed: 143mph (230km/h).
Normal range: 466 miles (750km).

These aircraft had their origin in the UTVA-56 4-seat utility monoplane which flew for the first time on April 22, 1959. By replacing the 56's 260hp engine with a 270hp Lycoming GO-480-B1A6, and making other improvements, its designers evolved the production UTVA-60. Variants are the U-60-AT1 basic 4-seat utility aircraft, dual-control U-60-AT2, U60-AG agricultural sprayer /duster, U-60-AM ambulance for two stretcher patients, and U-60H floatplane with 296hp GO-480-G1H6 engine. The UTVA-66, with 270hp GSO-480-B1J6 engine and fixed slots, was added to the range in the mid-sixties, in utility, ambulance and floatplane versions.

157

UTVA-65 Privrednik /
Yugoslavia

Photo: Super Privrednik-350.
Data: Privrednik-GO.

Span: 40ft 1in (12.22m).
Length: 27ft 9in (8.46m).
Gross weight: 4,078lb (1,850kg).
Max speed: 128mph (206km/h).

The prototype of this single-seat agricultural aircraft, completed in the Spring of 1965, embodied the basic wings, tail unit and undercarriage of the UTVA-60. It was powered by a 270hp Lycoming engine; but this was replaced by a 295hp Lycoming GO-480-G1A6 on the Privrednik-GO initial production version, which carries a 1,323lb (600kg) payload. In 1967, work began on the Privrednik-IO, with Lycoming IO-540-K1A5 engine, softer landing gear and other changes to make it more attractive in the Western market. Both types were later superseded by the Super Privrednik-350, with a 350hp IGO-540-A1C engine and 1,455lb (660kg) payload.

Varga Kachina Model 2150-A /USA

Span: 30ft 0in (9.14m).
Length: 21ft 3in (6.48m).
Gross weight: 1,817lb (824kg).
Max cruising speed: 135mph (217km/h).
Max range: 525 miles (845km).

This design originated in 1957 as the all-wood Nifty tandem two-seat trainer/sporting aircraft, built by former Douglas Aircraft chief test pilot William J. Morrisey. He formed Morrisey Aviation, which built ten similar, but all-metal Model 2150s, with a 150hp Lycoming O-320 engine. Production of a slightly modified version, the Model 2150-A, was then taken over by Shinn Engineering, and the current Varga Kachina is generally similar, with an O-320-A2C engine. Deliveries totalled 26 by May 1977.

Wassmer WA-40A Super 4 Sancy (and WA 4/21 and WA-41 Baladou) /
France

Photo: WA-41 Baladou.
Data: WA 4/21.

Span: 32ft 9½in (10.00m).
Length: 25ft 7in (7.80m).
Gross weight: 3,108lb (1,410kg).
Max cruising speed: 193mph (310km/h).
Max range: 1,735 miles (2,790km).

The prototype WA-40 flew on June 8, 1959, and was followed by a production series of 52 similar aircraft. The 53rd machine, designated WA-40A, introduced a swept fin and other refinements which became standard on later aircraft. A total of 180 WA-40s were built; all were 4/5-seaters with a 180hp Lycoming O-360-A1A engine. The WA 4/21 is similar but has a 250hp Lycoming IO-540 engine. Also similar is the WA-41 Baladou, except for having a 180hp Lycoming O-360-A2A engine, fixed undercarriage and simplified systems. All of these types have wooden wings and tail unit, and a fabric-covered steel-tube fuselage. They were superseded by the all-plastics WA-51/54 series and the all-metal CERVA CE.43 Guépard.

Wassmer WA-51 Pacific, WA-52 Europa and WA-54 Atlantic /France

Photo: WA-54 Atlantic.
Data: WA-54.

Span: 30ft 10in (9.40m).
Length: 23ft 11½in (7.30m).
Gross weight: 2,447lb (1,110kg).
Normal cruising speed: 161mph (260km/h).
Max range: 870 miles (1,400km).

In 1962 Wassmer began development of an all-plastics 4-seat light aircraft, with the assistance of the Société du Verre Textile. Major airframe components were moulded in thin layers of glass-fibre, reinforced either by stringers or by double corrugated skin. The resulting prototype WA-50 flew for the first time on March 22, 1966, proving so successful that Wassmer decided to put into production the further refined WA-51 Pacific. This is a 4-seater of generally similar design, with a 150hp Lycoming O-320-E2A engine. First flight of the WA-51 took place on May 17, 1969, and deliveries of production aircraft began in the following year. The WA-52 Europa is similar, but has a 160hp engine and more fuel. The further-refined WA-54 Atlantic, with 180hp Lycoming O-360 engine, entered production in June 1973. The 100th aircraft of the series was delivered in December 1973.

Wassmer WA-80/81 Piranha /France

Data: WA-80/81.
Photo: WA-80.

Span: 30ft 10in (9.40m).
Length: 24ft 7½in (7.50m).
Gross weight: 1,763lb (800kg).
Range: 435 miles (700km) at 118mph (190km/h).

The prototype of the Piranha, which flew for the first time in November 1975, was a two-seater designated WA-80. It was followed in mid-1977 by the WA-81, with a third seat to the rear of the cabin. In most other respects the two versions are identical. Construction is all-plastics, and the fact that the fuselage is generally similar to that of the WA-51/54 series means that the cabin is unusually spacious for a two/three-seater. Both models are powered by a 100hp Rolls-Royce Continental O-200-A engine, with identical dimensions, weights and performance.

Yakovlev Yak-18 /USSR

Photo: Yak-18PS.
Data: Yak-18PM.

Span: 34ft 9¼in (10.60m).
Length: 27ft 4¾in (8.35m).
Gross weight: 2,425lb (1,100kg).
Cruising speed: 175mph (282km/h).
Max range: 250 miles (400km).

The Yak-18 was the standard primary trainer of the Soviet Air Force and its allies and friends for more than 20 years. It is still standard equipment of Soviet and East European flying clubs. The original Yak-18 was a tandem 2-seater, with retractable tailwheel undercarriage and a 160hp M-11FR engine. A switch to tricycle undercarriage was made on the Yak-18U. The Yak-18A is a cleaned-up development of the 18U with a 260hp AI-14R and, later, 300hp AI-14RF engine. The Yak-18P is a single-seat version of the 18A for advanced training, including aerobatics. The Yak-18PM is similar, with AI-14RF engine, reduced dihedral and the cockpit further aft. The Yak-18PS differs from the -18PM only in having a tailwheel undercarriage.

Yakovlev Yak-18T /USSR

Span: 36ft 7½in (11.16m).
Length: 27ft 4¾in (8.35m).
Gross weight: 3,637lb (1,650kg).
Max speed: 186mph (300km/h).
Range: 560 miles (900km).

The arrival of an unregistered example of this extensively-redesigned cabin version of the Yak-18 was one of the less spectacular surprises of the 1967 Paris Air Show. For several years afterwards there was no further news of the type. Then, in 1974, it was learned that 17 Yak-18Ts were being used to train the complete new intake of 100 pupil pilots at Sasovo Flying School in the Soviet Union. In the meantime, the original 300hp Ivchenko AI-14RF engine had been replaced by a 360hp Vedeneev M-14P, and cabin layout had been improved. During Aeroflot training, the Yak-18T carries a pilot/instructor and up to three pupils, but only an instructor and one pupil on aerobatic flights. As an ambulance the cabin is equipped to carry a stretcher patient and attendant. The passenger seats can be removed for freight carrying.

Yakovlev Yak-50 /USSR

Span: 31ft 2in (9.50m).
Length: 24ft 5¾in (7.46m).
Gross weight: 1,930lb (875kg).
Max speed: 199mph (320km/h).

The quality of this latest development of the 30-year-old Yak-18 design was demonstrated at the 1976 World Aerobatic Championships. Six Yak-50s were entered. They gained first, second, fifth, seventh and ninth places in the men's championships, the team prize, and first five places in the women's championships. The wings dispense with the Yak-18's centre-section and have no dihedral, but retain an asymmetrical section. Construction is all-metal, with a semi-monocoque rear fuselage. A blister canopy ensures an all-round field of view from the single-seat cockpit. The landing gear is retractable. A 360hp Vedeneev M-14P radial engine ensures the desired high power:weight ratio despite the large dimensions of the aircraft.

Zlin Trener Series /
Czechoslovakia

Photo and data: Z.226T Trener-6.

Span: 33ft 9in (10.29m).
Length: 25ft 7in (7.80km).
Gross weight: 1,808lb (820kg).
Range: 300 miles (483km) at 121mph (195km/h).

After the war, a new 2-seat primary trainer was needed urgently by the Czechoslovakian air force and flying schools. After evaluation against the Praga E-112, the all-wood Zlin Z.26 Trener was put into quantity production, with a 105hp Walter Minor 4-III engine. It was superseded by the all-metal, but otherwise similar, Z.126 Trener-2 in 1953, and then by the Z.226, with 160hp Minor 6-III engine, which was built in three versions: Z.226B Bohatyr glider tug, Z.226T Trener-6 trainer and Z.226A Akrobat single-seater for specialised aerobatics.

Zlin Trener-Master Series /Czechoslovakia

Photo: Z.526 AFS.
Data: Z.726.

Span: 32ft 4¾in (9.875m).
Length: 26ft 2in (7.975m).
Gross weight: 2,204lb (1,000kg).
Max cruising speed: 134mph (215km/h).
Max range: 273–490 miles (440–790km) (without/with tip-tanks).

First flown in 1957, the Z.326 Trener-Master introduced a retractable undercarriage and other refinements, including a slight increase in span. The Z.526 differed in having a constant-speed propeller and the main pilot's seat at the rear instead of in the front of the tandem cockpit. The Z.326A Akrobat and Z.526A Akrobat were single-seat aerobatic versions. Later production models were the Z.526F with 180hp Avia M 137A engine in place of the former Minor 6-III; the Z.526 AFS Akrobat with only one seat, double ailerons instead of flaps, shorter fuselage and span of only 29ft (8.84m); and the Z.526L with 200hp Lycoming AIO-360-BIB engine but otherwise similar to the Z.526F. Only versions still in production in 1977 were the Z.726 and Z.726K, with 180hp M 137 AZ and supercharged 210hp M 337 AK engine respectively. Both are two-seaters, differing from the Z.526F in having a shorter span than the latter's 34ft 9in (10.60m). More than 1,400 aircraft of the Trener/Trener-Master Series have been delivered.

Zlin 42 and 43 / Czechoslovakia

Photo and data: Zlin 43.

Span: 32ft 0¼in (9.76m).
Length: 25ft 5in (7.75m).
Gross weight: 2,976lb (1,350kg).
Cruising speed: 130mph (210km/h).
Max range: 375–714 miles (610–1,150km) (without/with tip-tanks).

These attractive sporting and touring lightplanes are manufactured by the Zlin Aircraft Moravan National Corporation at Otrokovice. The prototype of the two-seat Zlin 42 flew on October 17, 1967, and more than 120 production aircraft had been completed by early 1977. The current 42 M differs from the original 42 in having a constant-speed propeller and tail fin identical to that of the four-seat Zlin 43. Power plant is a 180hp Avia M 137 AZ. About 80 per cent of the components of the Zlin 43 are identical with those of the 42 M, the basic differences being an enlarged cabin, greater span and use of a 210hp Avia M 337 A engine. Eighty had been delivered by early 1977, including some for military service.

Zlin Z 50 L /Czechoslovakia

Span: 28ft 1¾in (8.58m).
Length: 21ft 8¾in (6.62m).
Gross weight: 1,587lb (720kg).
Range: 397 miles (640km) at 149mph (240km/h).

The Z 50 L is typical of the current generation of single-seat aerobatic monoplanes in having a fairly powerful engine and symmetrical wing, with negligible dihedral, so that it handles and performs in much the same way whether it is straight and level or inverted. Except for the fabric covered tail control surfaces, construction is all-metal, and the Z 50 L has a 260hp Lycoming AEIO-540-D4B5 engine. The prototype flew for the first time on July 18, 1975. Two more prototypes and seven production models had been completed by March 1976; five of the latter took part in the 1976 World Aerobatic Championships, gaining second place in the team event and third place in the men's individual championship. Ten Z 50 Ls were to be built in 1977.

Aérospatiale SA 318C
Alouette II /France

Part Four

Photo: SA 315B Lama.
Data: SA 318C Alouette II.

Rotor diameter: 33ft 5½in (10.2m).
Fuselage length: 31ft 11¾in (9.75m).
Gross weight: 3,630lb (1,650kg).
Cruising speed: 112mph (180km/h).
Range: 186–447 miles (300–720km).

The Alouette II (originally as the SE 3130 and then the SE 313B) with an Artouste engine was the first production variant of the well-known Alouette range originated by Sud-Est company. It was succeeded by the SA 318C version with a 530shp Turboméca Astazou IIA. Production of the SE 313B totalled 923 and over 350 of the SA 318Cs have been built. The SA 315B Lama is similar but has dynamic components of the Alouette III, with an Artouste IIIB. This is also built by HAL in India as the Cheetah. French production totalled 189 by mid-1976.

Aérospatiale SA 316B
Alouette III /France

Rotor diameter: 36ft 1¾in (11.02m).
Fuselage length: 32ft 10¾in (10.03m).
Gross weight: 4,850lb (2,200kg).
Cruising speed: 115mph (185km/h).
Range: 298–335 miles (480–540km).

Alouette III is an enlarged and improved version of the Alouette II, the prototype having first flown on February 28, 1959. In its SA 316B version (data quoted) the Alouette III is powered by an Artouste IIIB derated to 570shp; a further development is the SA 319 which has an 870shp Astazou XIV engine derated to 600shp. The Alouette III is produced under licence in India (as the Chetak), Romania and Switzerland, and over 1,325 have been built in France.

Aerospatiale / Westland
SA 330 Puma /France /UK

Rotor diameter: 49ft 2½in (15.00m).
Fuselage length: 46ft 1½in (14.06m).
Gross weight: 14,770lb (6,700kg).
Cruising speed: 162mph (261km/h).
Range: 385 miles (620km).

The Puma was developed as a medium-lift helicopter for military duties, and is in service in this guise with the French Army, RAF, SAAF and several other air forces. Three civil versions have also been certificated—the passenger SA 330F with 1,435shp Turbomeca Turmo IVA engines, the cargo SA 330G with 1,580shp Turmo IVCs, and the SA330J with composite main rotor blades and 16,315lb (7,400kg) gross weight.

Aérospatiale/Westland SA 341 Gazelle /France/ UK

Rotor diameter: 34ft 5$\frac{1}{2}$in (10.50m).
Fuselage length: 39ft 3$\frac{1}{4}$in (11.97m).
Gross weight: 3,970lb (1,800kg).
Cruising speed: 164mph (264km/h).
Range: 223–416 miles (360–670km).

One of the three helicopters in the Anglo-French joint production programme launched in 1967, the Gazelle is of wholly-French origin, and is in production in both military and civil guise. The principal civil version is identified as the SA341G with a 590shp Turbomeca Astazou IIIA engine. The civil SA 342J has an 870shp Astazou XIVH and 4,190lb (1,900kg) gross weight.

Aérospatiale AS 350 Ecureuil /France

Rotor diameter: 35ft 0$\frac{3}{4}$in (10.69m).
Fuselage length: 35ft 9$\frac{1}{4}$in (10.91m).
Gross weight: 4,190lb (1,900kg).
Cruising speed: 136mph (220km/h).
Range: 570 miles (920km).

The prototype 4/6-seat Ecureuil (Squirrel) flew on June 27, 1974, powered by a 592shp Avco Lycoming LTS 101 turboshaft and, after some refinement, entered production as the AS 350C AStar, with first deliveries in the North American market early in 1977. Outside North America, the AS 350B has a 641shp Turbomeca Arriel; a prototype of this version flew for the first time on February 14, 1975.

Aérospatiale SA 360 Dauphin /France

Rotor diameter: 37ft 8$\frac{3}{4}$in (11.50m).
Fuselage length: 36ft 0in (10.98m).
Gross weight: 6,613lb (3,000kg).
Cruising speed: 152–172mph (245–278km/h).
Range: 405 miles (650km).

Designed as a replacement for the Alouette III, the SA 360 first flew on June 2, 1970, with a 980shp Astazou XVI engine, and a second example flew on January 29, 1973, with definitive 1,050shp Astazou XVIIIA. Certification of the 10/13-seat Dauphin was obtained at the end of 1975 and deliveries began in 1976. A twin-engined version has also been developed as the SA 365, with 650shp Turbomeca Arriel turboshafts.

Agusta A 109A /Italy

Rotor diameter: 36ft 1in (11.00m).
Fuselage length: 35ft 1¾in (10.71m).
Gross weight: 5,400lb (2,450kg).
Cruising speed: 143—165mph (231—266km/h).
Range: 351 miles (565km).

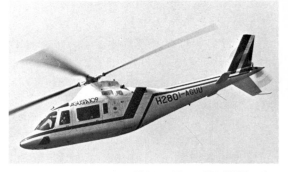

The Agusta company—the main activity of which is the production under licence in Italy of Bell (and Sikorsky) helicopters—launched development of this light twin-engined helicopter in the mid-sixties and the prototype flew on August 4, 1971. Powered by two 420shp Allison 250-C20B turboshafts, the A 109A seats up to eight. Deliveries for civil and military use began in 1976 following certification on June 1, 1975.

Bell (and Agusta-Bell) Model 47 /USA /Italy

Photo: Model 47G.
Data: Model 47G-3B-2A.

Rotor diameter: 37ft 1½in (11.32m).
Fuselage length: 31ft 7in (9.63m).
Gross weight: 2,950lb (1,338kg).
Cruising speed: 84mph (135km/h).
Range: 250 miles (400km).

Originally certificated by Bell on March 8, 1946, the Model 47 remained in continuous production at the parent company until 1974, final production models being the 47G-3B-2A with 280hp Lycoming TVO-435-F1A engine and the 47G-5A with a 265hp VO-435-B1A. Many hundreds are still used world-wide, supplemented by those built under licence by Agusta in Italy. In Japan, Kawasaki built 211 examples of a four-seat version known as the KH-4.

Bell (and Agusta-Bell) Model 204 and 205 /USA / Italy

Photo and Data: Model 205A.

Rotor diameter: 48ft 0in (14.63m).
Fuselage length: 41ft 6in (12.65m).
Gross weight: 9,500lb (4,310kg).
Cruising speed: 127mph (204km/h).
Range: 311—344 miles (500—553km).

Although the greater proportion of all Model 204s and 205s built by Bell, by Agusta in Italy, by Fuji in Japan and by the Chinese Nationalist state factory in Taiwan have been military models, substantial numbers are used commercially. The smaller Model 204 was succeeded by the 15-seat Model 205A-1 with 1,400shp Lycoming T5313A engine. The basic design has been evolved into the Bell 212 and 214, described separately.

Bell (and Agusta-Bell) Model 206B JetRanger / USA /Italy

Photo: Model 206B.
Data: Model 206B JetRanger.

Rotor diameter: 33ft 4in (10.16m).
Fuselage length: 31ft 2in (9.50m).
Gross weight: 3,200lb (1,451kg).
Cruising speed: 138mph (222km /h).
Range: 345–388 miles (555–624km).

Like most other Bell helicoptors, the JetRanger originated to military requirements, and the commercial model is the counterpart of the OH-58A used by the US Army. Powered by a 317shp Allison 250-C18A, the 206A has been succeeded by the 206B with a 400shp Allison 250-C20 and other improvements. The 206L LongRanger has a 2ft 1in (0.64m) fuselage stretch and seats up to seven, and like the new JetRanger III is powered by the 420shp Allison 250-C20B engine. The JetRanger is also built in Italy by Agusta.

Bell (and Agusta-Bell) Model 212 /USA /Italy

Rotor diameter: 48ft 2¦in (14.69m).
Fuselage length: 42ft 4¾in (12.92m).
Gross weight: 11,200lb (5,080kg).
Max speed: 126mph (203km /h).
Range: 273 miles (439km).

Model 212 is a development of the Model 205 (above), from which it differs primarily in having the 1,800shp Pratt & Whitney PT6T-3 Twin-Pac coupled turboshaft engine. A civil variant of the initial military model was certificated in 1970 as the Twin Two-Twelve, and this is now in commercial service in many parts of the world, over 250 having been delivered.

Bell Model 214 /USA

Rotor diameter: 50ft 0in (15.24m).
Fuselage length: 45ft 2in (13.77m).
Gross weight: 16,000lb (7,257kg).
Cruising speed: 150mph (241km /h).
Range: 250 miles (400km) at 3,000ft (915m).

Named the BigLifter, the Bell 214B is a commercial version of the Model 214A, originally developed for military duty in Iran from a single Bell 214 Huey Plus prototype. Use of a 2,930shp Lycoming T5508D turboshaft and an uprated transmission, plus other changes, gives the BigLifter major performance advantages over the earlier Bell 204 /205 variants. It can accommodate 14 passengers or lift 7,000lb (3,175kg) externally.

Bell Model 222 /USA

Rotor diameter: 38ft 11$\frac{3}{8}$in (11.87m).
Fuselage length: 39ft 9in (12.12m).
Gross weight: 6,700lb (3,039kg).
Cruising speed: 150mph (240km/h).
Range: 425 miles (685km).

The 6/10-seat Bell 222 was launched in 1974 as the first commercial light twin-engined helicopter to be built in the USA. Initially known as the project D 306, the Model 222 is powered by two 600shp Avco Lycoming LTS 101-650C turboshafts and the first prototype flew on August 13, 1976. Production deliveries were scheduled to begin in 1978.

Boeing Vertol (and Kawasaki) 107 /USA / Japan

Rotor diameter (each): 50ft 0in (15.24m).
Fuselage length: 44ft 7in (13.59m).
Gross weight: 19,000lb (8,618kg).
Cruising speed: 157mph (253km/h).
Range: 222–682 miles (357–1,097km).

This distinctive helicopter originated as a Piasecki design before the company was acquired by Boeing. Most production was for military use but a few entered airline service in the USA and others are operated commercially in Japan and Thailand. Since 1965, Kawasaki in Japan has had exclusive marketing rights for the design, which it produces under licence as the KV-107/II and /IIA, with two 1,400shp General Electric CT58-140-1 engines.

Brantly B2 and 305 /USA

Photo: Model 305.
Data for B-2E.

Rotor diameter: 23ft 9in (7.24m).
Fuselage length: 21ft 9in (6.62m).
Gross weight: 1,670lb (757kg).
Cruising speed: 90mph (145km/h).
Range: 250 miles (400km).

The original B-2 was designed by N. O. Brantly, one of the early post-war pioneers of rotary-wing aircraft in the USA, and was produced by his company prior to its acquisition by Gates Learjet. Manufacturing rights subsequently passed to Brantly Hynes Helicopter Inc, which resumed production of the two-seat B-2B in 1976, with 180hp Lycoming IVO-360-A1A engine. Also in production is the similar five-seat Model 305 with 305hp Lycoming engine.

Enstrom F-28 and 280 Shark /USA

Photo and data: F-28A.

Rotor diameter: 32ft 0in (9.75m).
Fuselage length: 29ft 6in (8.99m).
Gross weight: 2,150lb (975kg).
Cruising speed: 100mph (161km/h).
Range: 237 miles (381km).

The first Enstrom helicopter flew in 1960, being followed in 1962 by the prototype F-28. A small production batch was built, and more than 330 F-28As had also been produced by 1976, the latter being three-seat versions with 205hp Lycoming HIO-360-C1I engine. A version with increased fuel is the Model 280 Shark; the F-28C and Model 280C have turbo-charged HIO-360-E1AD engine. An F-28A derivative with 420shp Allison 250C-20B is marketed by Spitfire Helicopter Co as the Spitfire Mk I.

Hughes Model 300 /USA

Photo: Model 300C (269C).
Data for 300C.

Rotor diameter: 26ft 10in (8.18m).
Fuselage length: 30ft 11in (9.42m).
Gross weight: 1,900lb (861kg).
Cruising speed: 100mph (161km/h).
Range: 232 miles (373km).

The three-seat Hughes Model 300 (originally certificated as the 269B) is a developed version of the two-seat Model 269 light helicopter. The basic 300 has a 180hp Lycoming HIO-360-A1A, while the later 300C (or 269C) has a 190hp HIO-360-D1A and a bigger rotor diameter, plus other small changes. Several hundred Model 300s have been built. The Model 300CQ has special features that reduce noise emissions by 25 per cent. A version of the Model 300 is built by BredaNardi in Italy.

Hughes Model 500 /USA

Photo and data for Model 500D.

Rotor diameter: 26ft 5in (8.05m).
Length overall: 30ft 6in (9.30m).
Gross weight: 3,000lb (1,360kg).
Normal cruising speed: 150mph (241km/h).
Max range: 335 miles (539km).

The Model 500 is the commercial counterpart of the military OH-6A Cayuse, of which more than 1,400 were delivered to the US Army. Its 317shp Allison 250-C18A turboshaft engine is derated only to 278shp, compared with the military version's 252.5shp. Payload is normally a pilot and four passengers or equivalent freight, but up to seven persons can be carried. The Model 500C differs in having a 400shp Allison 250-C20 engine for hot day/high-altitude operations. The Model 500D, with 420shp 250-C20B engine, was certificated late in 1976 and has numerous detail improvements. Model 500 versions are built by BredaNardi in Italy and Kawasaki in Japan.

167

Kamov Ka-26 /USSR

Rotor diameter: 42ft 8in (13.00m).
Fuselage length: 25ft 5in (7.75m).
Gross weight: 7,165lb (3,250kg).
Cruising speed: 56–93mph (90–150km/h).
Max range: 745 miles (1,200km) with auxiliary tanks.

First flown in 1965, the Ka-26 is a standard general-purpose helicopter in the Soviet Union and other East European countries. By podding the two 325hp Vedeneev M-14V-26 radial engines and mounting them on short stub-wings, it has been possible to make the entire rear fuselage detachable, aft of the two-seat flight deck. Standard fuselage pods accommodate six passengers or equivalent freight. Minus pod, the aircraft can be operated as a flying crane; or the space under the rotor can be occupied by a hopper for a ton of agricultural chemicals or a platform for the same weight of cargo. Survey versions are available, with cameras installed in the cabin pod, or with an encircling hoop antenna and towed receiver "bird" for mineral prospecting. Other potential applications of the Ka-26 include fish-spotting, forest protection, firefighting and ambulance duties.

MBB BO 105 /Germany

Photo and data: BO 105

Rotor diameter: 32ft 2¼in (9.82m).
Length: 28ft 0½in (8.55m).
Gross weight: 5,070lb (2,300kg).
Max cruising speed: 144mph (232km/h).
Max range: 658 miles (1,060km) with auxiliary tanks.

The BO 105 flew originally with two Allison 250-C18 turboshaft engines and a conventional rotor. The second and third prototypes followed in 1967, with Allison and MANTurbo 6022 engines respectively, driving a specially-developed rigid, unarticulated rotor, with feathering hinges only and with folding glassfibre blades. Production BO 105Cs can have either 317shp Allison 250-C18 or 400shp 250-C20 engines and seat up to five. The BO 105D has special features for the UK market and BO 105S is lengthened to seat seven. A total of more than 300 had been built by early 1977. The BO 106, first flown on September 25, 1973, has a wider cabin to seat up to seven and is powered by 420shp 250-C20B engines. Boeing Vertol market the BO 105 in the USA as the Executaire.

Mil Mi-4 /USSR

Rotor diameter: 68ft 11in (21.00m).
Length: 55ft 1in (16.80m).
Gross weight: 17,200lb (7,800kg).
Economical cruising speed: 99mph (160km/h).
Range: 250 miles (400km) with 8 passengers.

Second Soviet helicopter produced in quantity, the Mi-4 is Mil's counterpart to the Sikorsky S-55/S-58 generation. Several thousand were produced for military and civil use, all powered by a 1,700hp Shvetsov ASh-82V piston-engine. Standard Aeroflot version is the 8/11-passenger Mi-4P, which can also carry eight stretchers and an attendant on ambulance duties. The Mi-4S agricultural version has a hopper capable of holding a ton of chemicals in its cabin. The freight-carrying Mi-4 has clamshell rear loading doors. All versions were exported widely.

Mil Mi-6 /USSR

Rotor diameter: 114ft 10in (35.00m).
Length: 108ft 10½in (33.18m).
Gross weight: 93,700lb (42,500kg).
Max cruising speed: 155mph (250km/h).
Typical range: 404 miles (650km) with 13,228lb (6,000kg) payload.

Largest helicopter in the world when it was first revealed in 1957, the Mi-6 was the first turbine-powered helicopter to enter production in Russia. It is powered by two 5,500shp Soloviev D-25V turboshafts and is equipped normally as a rear-loading freighter, with small wings to offload the rotor in flight. These wings are usually removed when the Mi-6 is operated as a flying crane. The standard freighter has tip-up seats along the cabin walls. These can be supplemented by centre-cabin seats to carry a total of 65 passengers, with baggage. Forty-one stretchers and two attendants form the max payload of the ambulance version. Firefighting conversions have been built, including a water-bomber able to dump several tons of water on forest fires.

Mil Mi-8 /USSR

Rotor diameter: 69ft 10½in (21.29m).
Fuselage length: 60ft 0¾in (18.31m).
Gross weight: 26,455lb (12,000kg).
Max cruising speed: 112–140mph (180–225km/h).
Range: 264–298 miles (425–480km) with reserves.

The original prototype of this 28/32-passenger helicopter had a single 2,700shp Soloviev turboshaft engine. The second Mi-8 switched to two 1,500shp Isotov TV2-117As, with which it flew for the first time on September 17, 1962, and this power plant is standard on production versions. Variants include a VIP version known as the Mi-8 Salon with an eight-place couch, three armchairs and tables; an ambulance for 12 stretchers; and the Mi-8T freighter with 24 tip-up seats along the cabin walls and an optional external cargo sling. Standard Mi-8s are used for ice patrol and reconnaissance, rescue operations and transport in support of Russia's Vostok Station in the Antarctic, near the South Pole.

Mil Mi-10 and Mi-10K / USSR

Photo and data: Mi-10K.

Rotor diameter: 114ft 10in (35.00m).
Length: 107ft 9¾in (32.86m).
Gross weight: 83,776lb (38,000kg).
Max cruising speed: 125–155mph (202–250km/h).
Ferry range: 494 miles (795km) with auxiliary fuel.

First displayed at Tushino in 1961, the original Mi-10 flying crane was almost identical with the Mi-6 above the line of the cabin windows; but the depth of the cabin was reduced considerably and the tailboom deepened to give a continuous flat under-surface. With a stalky four-wheel undercarriage fitted, loads as big as a prefabricated building or motor coach could be carried on an open cargo platform between the legs, plus 28 passengers or freight in the cabin. The Mi-10K (described and illustrated) is generally similar except for its shorter undercarriage and provision of an undernose gondola from which a second pilot, facing rearward, can control the aircraft in hovering flight and supervise loading. Max slung cargo payload, with the present D-25V engines, is 24,250lb (11,000kg); 6,500shp D-25VFs may be used in later models, increasing the payload.

Sikorsky S-58 and S-58T and Westland Wessex / USA/UK

Photo and data: S-58T Mk II.

Rotor diameter: 56ft 0in (17.07m).
Fuselage length: 47ft 3in (14.40m).
Gross weight: 13,000lb (5,896kg).
Normal cruising speed: 127mph (204km/h).
Range: 278 miles (447km) with reserves.

Sikorsky built a total of 1,821 helicopters of basic S-58 design between 1954 and January 1970. Most were for military customers, but 16/18 -passenger commercial S-58s were also used on scheduled services by operators in the USA and elsewhere, each powered by a 1,525hp Wright R-1820-84 piston-engine. In the UK, Westland produced both single-engined and twin-engined turbine-powered versions under the name Wessex.

Some of these also continue in service with commercial operators, notably Bristow, whose Wessex 60s are each powered by two Rolls-Royce Gnome turboshafts, totalling 1,550shp. Sikorsky is currently producing kits for a similar conversion, known as the S-58T (data above), with an 1,800shp Pratt & Whitney (Canada) PT6T-6 Twin Pac power plant and 10/16 seats. Over 100 S-58Ts have been delivered.

Sikorsky S-61 /USA

Photo and data: S-61N Mark II.

Rotor diameter: 62ft 0in (18.90m).
Length: 59ft 4in (18.08m).
Gross weight: 19,000lb (8,620kg).
Normal cruising speed: 138mph (222km/h).
Max range: 518 miles (833km) with reserves.

The S-61N is a 30-passenger commercial development of the military Sea King, with a longer fuselage and other changes, but retaining amphibious capability. The S-61L differs in being suitable for land operation only. Both were powered originally by two 1,350shp General Electric CT58-110 turboshaft engines, but 1,500shp CT58-140-2s are standard in the current Mark II models. The

first S-61L flew on December 6, 1960, and went into service with Los Angeles Airways, which eventually bought seven. Other operators of the S-61L include New York Airways. S-61Ns have been bought by All Nippon Airways, Ansett-ANA, British Airways Helicopters, Bristow, Elivie, Greenlandair, JAL, KLM and Nitto Airways. Nearly 100 S-61Ls and S-61Ns have been built.

Sikorsky S-64 Skycrane / USA

Rotor diameter: 72ft 0in (21.95m).
Length: 70ft 3in (21.41m).
Gross weight: 42,000lb (19,050kg).
Max cruising speed: 105mph (169km/h)
Max range: 230 miles (370km) with reserves.

The S-64 pioneered the concept of a large, turbine-powered flying crane when it flew for the first time on May 9, 1962. Production models served with distinction in Vietnam, under the US Army designation CH-54A. Commercial S-64Es have been supplied to operators such as Rowan Drilling Company, Erickson Air-Crane Company, Tri-Eagle Company and Evergreen Helicopters, for heavy-lift support of oil exploration, logging, power-line, shipping and general construction industries.

Powered by two 4,500shp Pratt & Whitney JFTD12-4A turboshaft engines, the S-64E can lift loads of up to $12\frac{1}{2}$ short tons, suspended from strong points under its slim "backbone" structure, or in quickly interchangeable containers or pods. A rearwardfacing compartment in the crew cab enables one of the pilots to control the aircraft from this position during loading and unloading. The projected S-64F has 4,800shp JFTD12-5A engines.

Sikorsky S-76 /USA

Rotor diameter: 44ft 0in (13.41m).
Fuselage length: 44ft 1in (13.44m).
Gross weight: 9,700lb (4,399kg).
Cruising speed: 144–178mph (232–286km/h).
Range: 460 miles (742km).

Sikorsky launched the 8/12-seat S-76 in January 1975, adopting the S-76 designation out of sequence to mark the USA Bicentennial year. Aimed particularly at the off-shore oil support market, the S-76 is powered by two 700shp Allison 250–C30 turboshafts and the first of four prototypes began ground-rig running early in 1977. By that time, over 80 S-76s had been ordered, for deliveries starting in 1978.

Silvercraft SH-4 /Italy

Rotor diameter: 29ft 7½in (9.03m).
Length: 25ft 1¼in (7.65m).
Gross weight: 1,900lb (862kg).
Cruising speed: 73–81mph (117–130km/h).
Max range: 200 miles (320km).

Silvercraft SpA flew its original Model XY prototype light multi-purpose helicopter in October 1963. With the help of SIAI-Marchetti, this was evolved into the three-seat SH-4, which flew for the first time in March 1965 and was followed by five pre-production examples by the end of 1967. To widen the market, Silvercraft then designed an ambulance version, with provision for mounting an enclosed stretcher pannier externally on the port side of the cabin. A demonstration model of the SH-4A agricultural version followed, with 32ft 9½in (10m) spray-bars and tanks for 441lb (200kg) of chemicals. Over 50 SH-4s had been built up to the end of 1976, with 235hp (derated to 170hp) Franklin 6A-350-D1B engines, and a 205hp (170hp) Lycoming LHIO-360-C1A was offered as an alternative in 1976.

WSK-Swidnik Mi-2 / Poland

Data: Mi-2M.

Rotor diameter: 47ft 6¾in (14.50m).
Length: 37ft 4¾in (11.40m).
Gross weight: 8,157lb (3,700kg).
Cruising speed: 118–124mph (190–200km/h).
Range: 242 miles (390km) with max fuel and reserves.

The Mi-2 was designed in the Soviet Union by Mikhail Mil's bureau, as a turbine-engined replacement for the Mi-1, with the same overall dimensions. By switching to the lightweight power of two Isotov GTD-350 turboshaft engines, mounted above the cabin, it was possible to provide accommodation for up to eight passengers and their baggage, or 1,543lb (700kg) of freight, in the basic versions. Other versions were designed to carry four stretchers and an attendant in an ambulance role, and for agricultural, search and rescue, pilot training and flying-crane duties with an underslung cargo load. Development and production were taken over by the WSK-Swidnik organisation in Poland, to follow its earlier manufacture of the Mi-1/SM-1. Many hundreds have been delivered, for both military and civil use, with 400shp and later 450shp GTD-350P engines. The Mi-2M, first flown on July 1, 1974, has a wider, 10-seat cabin and retractable nosewheel.

Index

172